TV on Strike

Television and Popular Culture

Robert J. Thompson, *Series Editor*

Other titles from Television and Popular Culture

Athena's Daughters: Television's New Women Warriors
Frances Early and Kathleen Kennedy, eds.

Critiquing the Sitcom: A Reader
Joanne Morreale, ed.

Inside the TV Writer's Room: Practical Advice for Succeeding in Television
Lawrence Meyers, ed.

Screwball Television: Critical Perspectives on "Gilmore Girls"
David Scott Diffrient, ed., with David Lavery

"Something on My Own": Gertrude Berg and American Broadcasting, 1929–1956
Glenn D. Smith Jr.

Starting Your Television Writing Career: The Warner Bros. Television Writers Workshop Guide
Abby Finer and Deborah Pearlman

TV Creators: Conversations with America's Top Producers of Television Drama, vol. 1
James L. Longworth Jr.

TV Creators: Conversations with America's Top Producers of Television Drama, vol. 2
James L. Longworth Jr.

Watching TV: Six Decades of American Television, expanded 2nd ed.
Harry Castleman and Walter J. Podrazik

"The West Wing": The American Presidency as Television Drama
Peter C. Rollins and John E. O'Connor, eds.

TV on Strike

Why Hollywood Went to War over the Internet

Cynthia Littleton

New Lenox
Public Library District
120 Veterans Parkway
New Lenox, Illinois 60451

SYRACUSE UNIVERSITY PRESS

For Scott and Mary Ann Littleton,
with deepest love and appreciation

Cynthia Littleton is a journalist and author who has covered the television industry for the past two decades. She is the coauthor with Susanne Daniels of *Season Finale: The Unexpected Rise and Fall of the WB and UPN*, published by HarperCollins in 2007. Littleton has served as deputy editor of *Variety* since 2007 and has also worked as a reporter and editor for the *Hollywood Reporter, Broadcasting and Cable,* and United Press International. A graduate of Occidental College, Littleton lives in Los Angeles with her husband and daughter.

Contents

ACKNOWLEDGMENTS | *ix*

INTRODUCTION | *xi*

1. Fear of the Unknown | *1*

2. Path to the Picket Line | *22*

3. Sowing the Seeds | *40*

4. Brinksmanship Across the Table | *63*

5. United Showrunners | *88*

6. Angst in the Executive Suite | *113*

7. Rallies, Retrenchment, and Late-Night
   Returns | *137*

8. Cue the Directors | *165*

9. Deal or No Deal? | *190*

10. The Finish Line | *212*

11. The Bloodletting | *231*

   Epilogue | *256*

NOTES | *269*

INDEX | *281*

Acknowledgments

The idea for *TV on Strike* came to me about a month after the Writers Guild of America (WGA) strike ended in 2008. I was thumbing through my notebooks full of reporting from picket lines, rallies, and other strike-related events, and it hit me in one big brainstorm rush that the strike was the perfect prism for examining all of the changes that are roiling the prime-time television business. Writing about the future of television is a hard subject to wrangle, but the strike provided the framework of a dramatic story with a beginning, middle, and end, and no shortage of colorful characters. Most important, the strike was waged over the central issues that are upending television's traditional business models, namely, the influence of digital technologies and the rise of unruly alternative distribution platforms for Hollywood's wares—authorized and otherwise.

Fundamentally, I felt the first industry-debilitating strike to hit Hollywood in nearly twenty years was a historic moment that needed to be documented. The WGA's labor action stirred great passion, commitment, and sacrifices by guild members of all social and economic strata. WGA leaders, for all the just criticism of their tactics, displayed extraordinary fortitude in the face of the superior force presented by the handful of media giants that dominate film and television production. And after the war began, key industry figures made valiant efforts to use backroom diplomacy to bring about a truce.

The heroes of this story are the picket-line foot soldiers, the men and women who left the comfort of their writers rooms on the night of November 4, 2007, to walk in circles outside studio gates for three months. The men and women I spoke with during those weeks gave me invaluable perspective on how the digital revolution is affecting the creative community.

There were many others who contributed significantly to the writing of this book—some who are identified in these pages by name, while others preferred to stay behind the camera. I am grateful to all who gave their time and energy to help me put it all in perspective. Special thanks are due Lesley Goldberg for her careful guidance on the early drafts; Bob Broder and Gil Schwartz went above and beyond to help me get to the finish line.

I am also indebted to the work of fellow journalists who covered the strike, notably Claudia Eller, Richard Verrier, Carl DiOrio, Nellie Andreeva, Josef Adalian, and Michael Schneider. But there is no one who works harder at reporting every aspect of Hollywood's labor scene than my *Variety* colleague Dave McNary. He tackled the challenge of manning a 24/7 strike beat with tireless dedication, even when he faced personal attacks from partisan forces. McNary's work is reflected throughout *TV on Strike*, and he provided extremely valuable insights and assistance in many other ways.

Finally, this book would not have been possible without the support and unending patience of my husband, Tom Troccoli, and daughter, Daisy. They give me the inspiration to aim high, and the time to pursue my ambition. For that, I love them dearly.

Introduction

Avenue of the Stars is a majestic, six-lane concourse that runs through the most affluent business district in Los Angeles. It cuts north-south through the heart of Century City, the West LA enclave so named because of its historical affiliation with the 20th Century Fox studio, which once called the 176-acre area its back lot. After the studio sold off most of the land in 1961, Century City evolved into a clutch of hotels and skyscrapers that today house most of Los Angeles's top law firms.

Avenue of the Stars borders the eastern edge of the 75 remaining acres of the 20th Century Fox lot, and the street's mile-long span is bookended by major thoroughfares, Pico Boulevard to the south and Santa Monica Boulevard to the north. Avenue of the Stars' high-rises are home to a slew of entertainment industry offices, including the distinctive Fox Plaza tower and the block-long steel-frame edifice that contains Hollywood's largest talent agency, Creative Artists Agency (CAA).

Most weekdays, Avenue of the Stars is abuzz with the sound of high-performance auto engines revving and tires squealing as Mercedes and BMWs zoom up to valet parking stands and zip inside multilevel underground parking garages. Despite the density of office buildings and hotels, the street rarely sees much pedestrian traffic outside of the lunchtime rush. Most of the glass-box buildings are well equipped with restaurants, gyms, banks, retailers, and other amenities.

As such, a jarring sight greeted Avenue of the Stars regulars on the morning of Friday, November 9, 2007. It was day five of the Writers Guild of America strike against film and television production entities, notably those controlled by Hollywood's heavyweights: Walt Disney Company,

News Corporation, Time Warner, NBC Universal, Viacom, Sony Corporation, and CBS Corporation. Nearly two years of rhetoric and posturing by leaders of the guild and the major entertainment conglomerates had devolved into a bare-knuckles street fight. It was the first industry-wide walkout to hobble Hollywood in nearly twenty years, since the WGA went out for five months in 1988.

The catalyst this time had been the pervasive growth of new media and the transformative effect digital technology is having on the businesses of the traditional media conglomerates that employ the vast majority of the WGA's twelve thousand members. The divide between labor and management on how television and film writers should be compensated in a fast-changing media landscape sent thousands of writers to picket lines at more than a dozen sites in Los Angeles and New York starting on Monday, November 5.

The strike ensued on the heels of a marathon day of eleventh-hour contract talks. Negotiators for the conglomerates broke off the talks after the WGA refused to suspend its plan to go on strike at midnight, four days after the expiration of its previous master contract.

By eight o'clock on November 9, the street and sidewalks on Avenue of the Stars were swelling with striking writers and their supporters. Stem to stern, Avenue of the Stars was closed to traffic that morning, reinforced by Los Angeles Police Department (LAPD) patrol cars parked kitty-corner at either end of the street. Many people who worked in Century City wound up with an unexpected day off, once building owners were alerted the day before by police of the WGA's plans for a demonstration outside the Fox Plaza building.[1]

The thirty-four-story Fox Plaza, where hundreds of employees of Fox and its News Corporation parent company work, had been a prime picket site for the previous four days, but that Friday morning was different. Guild leaders decided to close out the first week with a mass rally at a single location, complete with rabble-rousing speeches, protest music, and a permit from the LAPD to shut down the street from ten until noon.

The rally was envisioned as both a morale booster for guild members and a visceral demonstration of the WGA's strength in numbers to management and to the media. Patric Verrone, the tough-talking, hard-nosed president of the WGA West, which represented most Hollywood writers, served as master of ceremonies. The gathering would prove to be a defining moment of the strike. "We're shutting down production . . . ," Verrone defiantly told the crowd in his opening remarks, "and we're kicking corporate ass."

Verrone proudly hailed the Fox rally as the largest mobilization of members in the Writers Guild's seventy-four-year history. More than four thousand writers and supporters gathered outside the Fox Plaza, known for its geometric setbacks and granite-and-steel color pattern. It is recognizable to the general public for having served as the setting for 20th Century Fox's 1988 blockbuster *Die Hard*.

For many writers, the rally was an electrifying demonstration of solidarity and unanimity. For the industry executives who warily monitored the goings-on from afar, it was the full flowering of the thing they feared most—a militant spirit among the rank and file, stoked by Verrone and the architect of the strike effort, WGA West executive director David Young.

Even after four days of impressive turnouts at fourteen picket sites in Los Angeles and environs, many in the crowd were awestruck on that warm Friday morning by the numbers that turned out. Writers with seven- and eight-figure annual incomes joined the cause. There was a heady sense of members rising to the moral challenge of linking arms in pursuit of the common good.

At times the gathering took on a jovial, college-reunion vibe. Writers who had worked together on TV shows canceled long ago ran into one another for the first time in years. One participant remarked on how unsettling it was to see "so many people who beat me out for jobs" in one place. Others marveled at how hard it was to get this many writers to agree on anything, let alone show up before ten o'clock for a protest rally.

The dress code for the morning was the new picket-line chic: jeans, crimson WGA T-shirts, sneakers, and baseball caps. Some wore T-shirts specially made for the occasion with messages decrying corporate greed, studio bosses, and, in a few cases, the Bush administration. One man had a *Los Angeles Times* headline declaring "Viacom Profits Up 80%" enlarged and reproduced on his shirt. Many people brought children and dogs, who toddled around with makeshift signs on their backs declaring "Residuals feed me" or "Learn to share." In the case of one mutt, the message was "Residuals keep me in kibble."

The strike's first mass rally was held outside Fox in part because of reports that Peter Chernin, the CEO of Fox Entertainment Group and president and chief operating officer of News Corporation, was one of the hard-liners among the top executives who dictated the negotiation strategy for the studios' collective bargaining unit, the Alliance of Motion Picture and Television Producers. The AMPTP's long-serving president, J. Nicholas Counter, had become a reviled figure on the picket lines. One guild member at the Fox rally toted a homemade picket sign with block letters declaring, ominously: "Nick Counter Sleeps with the Fishes $$$."

It was no secret in the industry that Fox was well positioned to withstand a long work stoppage. The new season of the network's most potent weapon, the top-rated *American Idol,* was fortuitously timed to premiere in January. With a show capable of drawing twenty-five to thirty million viewers a night, Fox could withstand a lot.

The WGA figured the Fox Plaza was a perfect backdrop for a show of force—to the studios and to the membership that needed to be fired up for the long haul. The emotional current in the crowd and the visuals brought to mind images of antiwar and civil rights demonstrations of an earlier era. But there were a few only-in-Hollywood touches.

The nearby Creative Artists Agency dispatched assistants in dark suits to walk through the crowd carrying silver serving trays piled high with churros, a doughnutlike Mexican dessert. Not to be outdone, the William Morris Agency set up a stand at the southern edge of Avenue of the Stars, where interns and assistants handed out bagels with cream cheese and bottled water. Other enterprising businesses took advantage of the captive and highly desirable audience. A startup bottled water company dispensed free samples in the shape of liquor flasks. A local vendor of blended juice drinks handed out hundreds of free samples. The heavy concentration of so many well-paid Hollywood insiders made it an irresistible marketing opportunity for some entrepreneurs.

Judd Apatow could not have been hotter at that moment as a screenwriter, director, and producer. He had landed a one-two punch at the box office in the summer of 2007 with raunchy comedies *Knocked Up,* which he wrote and directed, and *Superbad,* which he produced. As the crowd on Avenue of the Stars waited for the rally to begin, a cluster of friends and fans formed around Apatow. He offered his thoughts in a characteristically unassuming way on the issues at stake in the strike: "Whatever we get is going to be way worse than what we deserve," Apatow observed as he leaned on his picket sign and exchanged handshakes, hellos, and "how-are-yas" with a stream of well-wishers. "We have to fight this hard, and we'll still not reach that 1 percent" of revenue generated worldwide by film and TV productions, he said incredulously.

With his success and hard-won reputation as an auteur not afraid to fight for his creative vision, Apatow's presence carried weight with guild members, particularly younger writers. He drew on his personal experience to illustrate what he saw as the inequity in the traditional compensation formulas for Hollywood writers. He noted that he stood to make more money as the cowriter of a song in another 2007 feature that bore his name, mockumentary *Walk Hard: The Dewey Cox Story,* than he would from DVD sales of *Knocked Up* under the WGA's existing contract.

Also ubiquitous in the crowd that morning were prominent writers espousing the idea that it was crucial for WGA members to take a strong stand on new media now to protect the rights of future generations. "I'm a guy who won the lottery," said *Everybody Loves Raymond* creator Phil Rosenthal, who has earned millions of dollars from the success of his long-running CBS sitcom. "But I only have what I have because somebody struck for it before me. I feel like it's an honor and a privilege to be here on behalf of the next generation of writers."

As the rally program began, the crowd packed in shoulder to shoulder and sidewalk to sidewalk around the platform erected in front of Fox Plaza. Speakers ranged from legendary writer-producer and entrepreneur Norman Lear to Seth MacFarlane, the wunderkind behind Fox's animated hit *Family Guy,* and the Reverend Jesse Jackson. Jackson's presence conferred a national importance and civil rights imperative to the writers' cause.

First up to the microphone was activist rocker Tom Morello of Rage Against the Machine, toting an acoustic guitar and a Dylanesque harmonica brace fastened around his neck. He led the crowd in a fist-pumping sing-along: "Union men and women / standing up and standing strong." He was then joined by Rage Against the Machine singer Zack de la Rocha for a performance of the band's signature anthem, "Bulls on Parade," with lyrics tailored for the occasion: "We rally with the writers / for their fair share of the wealth."

Patric Verrone followed Morello and de la Rocha. He got an enthusiastic response from his stock opening line: "My name is Patric Verrone . . . and I am a writer." By the time Verrone spoke, the last of the morning clouds had lifted; the sky above Avenue of the Stars was a flawless turquoise.

Verrone's steely gaze eased into a satisfied smile for a few moments as he paused to take in the crowd's roar. A few dozen guild officials and assorted VIPs had piled onto the steps of the Fox Plaza entryway behind the platform, and they too cheered him. Those who knew him could see the fatigue on Verrone's face, the dark circles around his eyes, and the sallow complexion of his skin. He was by nature intense and contrarian; the extraordinary strain of the strike only magnified those qualities.

But to the vast majority of his audience, Verrone was a hero, a fearless leader—the little guy who was not afraid to speak truth to power and fight for writers. Verrone was the face of the strike that had so far defied the naysayers for its smooth organization and strong turnout among guild members. The recognition and trust placed in him by members were the fuel that kept Verrone going. He chose his words carefully and delivered them with fervor. "All we're asking for is fair play and a square deal," he told the crowd. "Fair play and a square deal."

Later, Verrone assured his receptive audience that the strike was evidence that the WGA, under his leadership, would not knuckle under to the studio's hardball tactics. "We won't get fooled again," Verrone insisted. "We won't get boned again."

Jesse Jackson followed Verrone. Always savvy about courting media attention, Jackson had lent his moral authority to the writers' cause by touring numerous picket sites with Verrone the previous day.

Jackson did not expand much from his trademark "Keep hope alive" stump speech. He didn't need to. His rhythmic oratory struck a chord with many in the crowd, elevating the strike into the loftier realm of a David-versus-Goliath fight for civil rights and social justice.

The strike was "part of the larger struggle in America today," Jackson asserted. "Too few control too much." "Save the workers." "Save the families." Jackson punctuated each statement with a pause. The crowd took its cue and applauded and cheered. "Share the wealth." "Share the wealth."

John Bowman, an experienced television writer-producer who played a crucial role in the WGA's contract drama as chair of the guild's negotiating committee, lightened the tone considerably as he followed Jackson onstage. The alumnus of *Saturday Night Live* and sitcoms played to his comic strengths. Bowman mocked the studios' refusal to negotiate by offering an over-the-top "apology" to the AMPTP's Nick Counter: "This whole thing has been 100 percent my fault," Bowman said, with arms outstretched in mock sincerity. "When I called your rollbacks draconian, that was the liquor talking, not me. So come back to the table, baby, we can work this out. We made the lawyers rich. Let's put our differences aside and make each other rich."

Despite his sarcasm, Bowman would earn high marks from many on both sides of the battle for being a pragmatist and a diplomat under extraordinarily trying circumstances.

One of the morning's most affecting speakers was Norman Lear, the famed writer-producer behind *All in the Family, Maude, The Jeffersons, Sanford and Son,* and other hits. Lear was not part of the guild's advance planning for speakers, but he was quickly recruited after WGA staffers saw him turn up on Avenue of the Stars.

Lear beamed as he surveyed the size of the crowd and soaked up their admiration. "This is fabulous," he said, with awe in his voice. "*This* is my nuclear family."

Lear's words about the importance of the guild and solidarity had great impact on his listeners because of what he represents—the ideal of the wildly successful writer-producer, the savvy innovator who parlayed his talent as a writer into his own mini studio. After an impressive run in the 1970s and early '80s, Lear sold his Embassy Communications to the Coca-Cola Company, then owner of Columbia Pictures, in 1985 for $465 million.

The level of wealth and power that Lear achieved as an independent producer in his heyday is virtually unattainable for contemporary writers.

Macroeconomic shifts in Hollywood and the consolidation of media ownership during the past twenty years have made it next to impossible for independent producers, let alone individual writer-producers, to maintain absolute ownership of their product. That shift in the balance of power residing with a handful of network-studio conglomerates makes Lear a revered figure in Hollywood's creative community.

But more important to WGA leaders was the fiery message of support delivered by Screen Actors Guild (SAG) president Alan Rosenberg. At high decibels, Rosenberg's declaration of "actors and writers united, never to be divided" meant the WGA could count on the muscle that actors flex in Hollywood and in the court of public opinion. Through the bitter end of the WGA strike, SAG was a pillar of support for writers.

Rosenberg unleashed his rhetorical rage against the consolidation in the industry, the studios' intransigence on increasing payments for home video sales, and the economic hardship put on the "working actors" who command far less than twenty million dollars per picture. He echoed the sentiments of other speakers that Hollywood creative laborers were paying for the greed, missteps, and largesse showered on the executive ranks.

Building on Rosenberg's populist rant was the rousing speech delivered by the WGA West's David Young. From the day he was promoted into the job as executive director of the WGA West, Young was eyed with extreme caution by executives at the major studios. His background as an organizer for unions representing plumbers and textile workers raised immediate red flags and fears that he would bring blue-collar agitation and negotiation tactics to the fore in representing the decidedly white-collar workers in the WGA West.

The fact that Young did not appear to spend much time in his first months on the job doing the glad-handing and charm offensives that are de rigueur for Hollywood executives set off still more alarm bells. Young's public statements and media interviews in his first two years as WGA West executive director were parsed and scrutinized by labor executives at the studios and networks, whose job it is to know what is going on with the unions and alert their bosses to potential problems long before they erupt.

By the time the WGA organized a handful of producers to go on strike in 2006 against the reality show *America's Next Top Model*, demanding a WGA contract and asserting that they functioned as writers for the show, executives were aware that David Young was unlike any leader in the modern history of Hollywood's creative guilds. He was seen as a threat to the peace that the studios had enjoyed for nearly twenty years with the three major talent guilds, the WGA, SAG, and Directors Guild of America (DGA).

By the time Young left the stage, he had given a performance that convinced the CEOs he was a neo-Marxist and master propagandist who was bent on furthering a social agenda, not reaching a compromise at the bargaining table. Leaders of the major media conglomerates took Young's words as a call to arms, a declaration that the guild would not be satisfied with anything less than a massive redistribution of wealth. The CEOs worried about the influence his rhetoric would have on impressionable guild members, particularly the lowest-earning members who had the least at stake in going on strike.

The crowd did not leave Century City that day ready to renounce capitalism and engage in class struggle, but Young's fire and brimstone was important in pumping up the rank and file at a key moment in the walkout.

Those participants who had not experienced the 1988 strike heard the warnings from their elders that it was likely be a months-long slog this time around too. The ones who did have firsthand memories of the '88 strike stood in awe of the level of unity and organization guild leaders had mustered. And they had never heard such conviction, such defiance, coming from guild officers as they did that day.

Young, low-key by nature, was obviously energized by the crowd as he followed Bowman on the speaker rotation. He surprised his colleagues at the guild by how big his personality seemed to become in the spotlight. He opened with a roaring burst of call and response. "Oh YEAAH," he bellowed, cuing his startled audience to join in. " . . . Ooo-hhh YEEEAAAHHH!"

After pausing to let the roar die down, Young reeled off a list of thank-yous and commendations to guild staffers and others for the smooth operation of the strike so far. He led the crowd in a brief chant of "Thank you, SAG."

Then his expression turned somber. "Brothers and sisters . . ." The folksy salutation sounded odd to Hollywood-jaded ears. But Young had their attention as he launched into the speech that would define him in the eyes of the CEOs.

"Brothers and sisters, we are involved in a huge struggle, and all of you are making a huge sacrifice for the Writers Guild, for the labor movement, and for Hollywood. This is a watershed moment in our history. We had a good relationship at one time perhaps with our employers. We are in the process of being left behind. Is that okay with you?"

"No!" the crowd responded.

"Every time a new market develops, every time a new genre comes around, every time there's a new technology, it's un-*fathom*-able for them. They don't know what the *business* model is. Was there a business model for VCR and DVD?"

"No!"

"Was there a business model for reality television?"

"No!"

"Was there a business model for basic cable?"

"No!"

"Is there a business model for the Internet?"

"No!"

"Brothers and sisters, we cannot screw this up. We're going to get it right this time," Young assured, with absolute conviction.

The crowd's response grew louder and more defiant. The substance of his remarks was startling to many, invigorating to some.

We are part of a broader struggle—part of a struggle for justice in Hollywood. We are part of a broader struggle that has been going on between the American middle class and power concentration. Everywhere in America families are dropping out of the middle class. Without pensions, without health insurance, without overtime pay, without decent benefits, without a fair share of the wealth so they can take care of their families. It's time to put a stop to that. As power has been concentrated in six corporations that control everything that we read and see and hear, and everything that you produce, writers and talent are being strangled not just economically but creatively.

Wild applause forced a pause, which Young needed to catch his breath. "Brothers and sisters it's time for us to take a stand! I'm here to tell you, on day five, we are winning this strike! Let me hear you!"

Fists shot into the air, and picket signs waved side to side and up and down amid the cacophony of shouts, whistles, howls, and hands clapping.

"But our goal is to negotiate," Young resumed at the first lull in the din. "It will be our goal every day. That's where our focus will be until we bring you back a fair contract . . ."

The noise from the crowd again drowned him out. After a beat, Young closed abruptly with a tacit acknowledgment that the strike would not be over any time soon.

"Here's my message to you," Young instructed. "Suck it up. Stick it out. We shall prevail."

More than anything else, it was the language Young used that alarmed the CEOs: "We shall prevail," "Brothers and sisters," "broader struggle," and "power concentration." As news and blog coverage of the rally began to surface on Friday afternoon, industry executives went into a quiet panic.

The most vocal among the CEOs warned their counterparts that Young was the embodiment of their worst nightmare—an ideologue with power and influence. As they got firsthand reports from their employees and others who attended the rally, the CEOs became convinced that they would not be able to do business with Young. His motivations and commitment to writers were disparaged. Young was viewed as an opportunistic interloper who was using the clout of his position to further his own social-engineering goals. The CEOs, most of whom were liberal Democrats at heart, never for a moment believed he would succeed in turning Hollywood writers into socialists, but they knew that powerful propaganda could prolong the pain of the strike.

Young's oratory put the studios on the defensive, and it encouraged them to dig in their heels. By the time they learned of Verrone's closing remarks at the rally, the CEOs shared a collective disgust at what they viewed as a gross oversimplification of the financial issues at stake. They resented being exploited and targeted as "greedy executives" by Young and Verrone, whom they regarded as a backbencher in the pecking order of the creative community.

As the rally unfolded, television production was paralyzed by the work stoppage—an unplanned hiatus that could inflict long-term damage on the prime-time business, executives feared. While thousands gathered outside the Fox Plaza to hear speeches and protest tunes, just down the street the 20th Century Fox lot was half empty because of the sudden shutdown of television production.

As the noontime sun bounced off the skyscrapers that line Avenue of the Stars, Verrone closed the two-hour rally by reciting a variation of the World War II–era poem "First They Came . . ."

"With apologies to Martin Niemöller," Verrone began, referring to the German pastor and pacifist credited with writing the verse.

> First they came for the animation writers and I did not speak out
>> because I wrote live-action.
> And then they came for the reality, game show, and nonfiction writers,
>> and I did not speak out because I worked in scripted fare.
> Then they came for the variety, longform, sitcom, dramatic TV, and
>> screenwriters, and I did not speak out because I had an overall deal.
> And then they came for me, and there was no one left to speak for me.

Verrone had no trace of sarcasm in his voice as he spoke, only conviction. He finished not with a smirk but with a steely look of resolve.

When the word spread in the executive suites that Verrone had made the comparison between the guild's fight and groups persecuted by the Nazis, the CEOs wrote him off as delusional and in love with the spotlight and the sound of his own voice.

As with Young, studio brass saw in Verrone a lethal combination of inexperience with the give-and-take of labor negotiations and an abiding arrogance that led him to believe he could lead his troops to victory no matter what the cost.

It was an overreaction to Verrone's overdramatization, to be sure. But all of the ill will stirred up by the rally—the protest-march symbolism and antistudio sentiment on display—helped deepen the divide between WGA leaders and studio executives during the standoff and fitful negotiations that would play out during the months ahead. The nature of the fight between writers and their employers was far more intense by the early afternoon of November 9 than it was when the sun rose over the Fox Plaza that morning.

TV on Strike

1

Fear of the Unknown

If the prime-time television business were a third world country, it would find itself at the mercy of the World Bank and the International Monetary Fund. The reins of power would have been turned over to a team of economists and bankers tasked with implementing draconian reforms and a five-year plan for rehabilitating the national economy.

The economic crisis in broadcast television is part and parcel of the digital upheaval that is challenging every aspect of the business of traditional media and entertainment companies. The spread of digital technologies and distribution platforms, broadband access, and radical behavioral shifts among younger consumers are reshaping—some say irrevocably undermining—the business foundation of network television. The digital revolution promises to be a far greater transformative force for the pillars of the national television business—ABC, CBS, NBC, and Fox—than even the competitive threat from the rise of cable programming in the 1980s and '90s. Nor are cable- and satellite-delivered channels immune to the disruptions caused by the exponential growth of video distribution options.

In the new media paradigm, television programming that was once exclusive to a single licensor is slowly but surely becoming a commodity—a high-end item, for sure, but still something that can be obtained through any number of outlets, authorized and illegal.

Want to watch an episode of Fox's *Family Guy*? Set your digital video recorder (DVR) to nab the latest airing. Or go to iTunes for a $1.99 download—or maybe you'll buy an entire season for $45. And there are any number of illegal file-sharing services that will offer an unauthorized download of the show for free. Or you can log on to the Web to watch

1

a free video stream, with commercials, of a recent episode at Fox.com or Hulu or Netflix or Amazon Prime. Reruns of the show are also carried daily by cable channel TBS and by local TV stations. And there's always the option of buying a home video box set.

The vast expansion of the availability of programming since 2005 has produced an upheaval unlike anything the US television industry has experienced in its previous six decades. It is a shakeup that is rewriting the show-business playbook for how networks and studios make money— except that nobody is quite sure where the new playing field is, let alone the best strategic advance moves.

The pervasive uncertainty about television's future was both the spark and the fuel for the one-hundred-day strike by the Writers Guild of America. The WGA's 2007 master-contract negotiations marked the first time a Hollywood guild had negotiated with the industry's major players since legal downloads and Web streaming of full-length television programs became readily accessible to consumers.

Hollywood's largest unions traditionally negotiate master contracts that run for three-year terms. It was a quirk of contract-expiration timing that the WGA was the first up at the bargaining table after a burst of new media innovations in 2005 and 2006.

The corporate leaders of the seven media conglomerates that rule the prime-time television business—Time Warner, the Walt Disney Company, News Corporation, Viacom, NBC Universal, Sony Pictures Entertainment, and CBS Corporation—were united by their shared fears of dwindling profits, splintering market share, and worries that the first generation raised with the Internet as a household appliance was turning away from traditional Hollywood fare. The conglomerates' collective bargaining unit, the Alliance of Motion Picture and Television Producers, knew the WGA would come into the negotiations looking to secure new forms of compensation for these new distribution mechanisms.

But the CEOs also knew well the hard facts behind the glamour of new media. The profits generated by paid downloads and advertising-supported Web streaming are minute compared to the money networks make from traditional commercials, even with the Big Four's steadily declining market share, and compared to the money studios make from sales of TV shows and movies in syndication and through international licensing. To make matters worse, the increased exposure of programming via new media platforms is undercutting the prices that networks and studios can command for thirty-second spots and sales of rerun packages. As the new breed of network-studio conglomerates like News Corporation and Disney grappled with this central quandary of old-versus-new media, executives were in no mood to concede to what they viewed as unrealistically high expectations from the WGA based on the guild's inflated revenue projections.

WGA members were just as unnerved about the future, and they were still smarting over past fights with the studios over compensation terms. The battle between the WGA and the studios in the mid-1980s over how writers would be paid for home video sales resonated loudly when it came to new media. Back in 1985, the studios argued that they needed to pay writers a significantly reduced rate on home video sales because they needed to better understand the developing market, and they needed to cover a new category of manufacturing and distribution costs. But over the years, even as home video sales grew to outstrip annual theatrical box-office receipts, the studios steadfastly refused to significantly sweeten the terms of their profit-sharing agreements with writers, actors, and directors.

Two decades later, WGA leaders saw it as just another attempt at Hollywood accounting when the studios' labor negotiators asserted that new media would not be a significant source of profits for some time. Much of the strike was fought in the gray area of the gulf between the guild's demands and the studios' insistence that there was no profit windfall from the Internet, yet.

Writers' pent-up anger and frustration overflowed on the morning of November 5, 2007. Studio execs scoffed at the sight of multimillionaire screenwriters and showrunners walking in picket lines and chanting about "a fair deal." But by then, the CEOs were paying for having committed cardinal Hollywood sins: they had misread the mood of their audience and overplayed their hand.

The only thing Hollywood's major players agreed on when the guild's contract talks began in the summer of 2007 was that the Internet was a game changer for the entertainment industry. "Working writers in television and film . . . know the Internet is the distribution channel of the future," John Bowman wrote when the guild formally issued its pattern of demands for the 2007 contract talks. Bowman, an experienced TV writer-producer, served as chairman of the WGA's seventeen-member negotiating committee, which was carefully selected by guild leaders to feature prominent film and TV writers with a lot at stake in the outcome of the 2007 contract negotiations.[1]

Writers feared that the Internet would eventually supplant traditional broadcast and cable distribution of television programming and that the conglomerates would balk at extending the WGA's traditional residual payment system for writers into the broadband realm. "The companies are seeking to take advantage of new technology to drastically reduce the residual income that sustains middle class writers and keeps them in the business," WGA West president Patric Verrone said at a news conference a few days before the strike began. "Their proposals would destroy the very pool of creative talent that is the basis of their immense revenues and profits."[2]

But Hollywood's business leaders had far more questions than answers about the long-term impact of new media on their traditional businesses at the time the WGA contract talks formally began in July 2007. Carol Lombardini, the veteran labor negotiator and longtime second in command to AMPTP president Nick Counter, raised the litany of unknowns about television's future in her response to the WGA's opening salvo on the second day of negotiations. "How long will it be before piracy overtakes the legitimate purveyors of our product?" Lombardini said. "How long will television continue to be an ad-supported medium? . . . How will we deliver our product to people who don't want to watch it on a given channel at a given time on a television screen? And how much can we expect them to pay to see it? Anything? How much longer can we expect to generate sizeable revenues from the hit shows that began on the network that are later released in syndication or on basic cable?" Lombardini said. "There are signs that that business model is obsolete."[3]

The WGA dismissed these concerns as illegitimate excuses for inaction, but Lombardini's cautionary remarks reflected the worries of every

Hollywood CEO. And that anxiety influenced the decision making on both sides of the picket lines, according to Barry Meyer, chairman and CEO of Time Warner's Warner Bros. studio. "Purely it was the fear of the unknown" that drove management and labor to the strike point, said Meyer, a forty-year veteran of the studio. "From the studios' vantage point we saw old traditional (business) models changing, reforming, some of them crumbling. All of the ways that we have known to monetize content are changing and audiences are fractionalizing. Media companies were afraid of all of these changes to a model that generated significant revenue that was disseminated out through the industry. It was able to pay for high salaries, high production costs, long production schedules and ambitious programming," he said. "There was a real fear with new businesses that were Internet-based, if we started saddling them with the old (guild) rules—rules that were put in place when the audiences were much bigger—we would kill the new industry."[4]

Since the early 1960s, the principle of residual and royalty payments has been an integral part of the master-contract agreements that govern employment terms for members of the WGA, Screen Actors Guild, and Directors Guild of America. Whenever a production is reused beyond its premiere market—for example, a repeat of a television program, a TV telecast of a feature film, or a home video release—writers, actors, and directors are due additional compensation. The guild contracts set floor prices, or "minimums," for initial compensation for various types of work, but in many cases those minimums can be greatly increased by creatives with the clout to negotiate higher prices. The schedule of residual fees in various job categories, on the other hand, is uniform for all guild members.

Residuals are usually calculated as a small percentage of the minimum initial compensation fee for a given job category, or as a small percentage of the revenue generated by the reuse of the production. For all but the top tier of WGA, SAG, and DGA members, these additional dollars, often involving ongoing payments over many years, are a vital source of income for workers in an industry where most are employed on a freelance basis and jobs can be spotty, even for experienced creatives.

Of the guilds, the WGA has the most complex contract, termed the Minimum Basic Agreement (MBA), in part because writers have expanded rights and payments due them as creators of intellectual properties. The acronym is fitting, because it takes a person with a master's degree in business administration or a law degree to decipher the contract. The guild's 2004 MBA, the contract that preceded the strike, ran some 624 pages.

As the film and television business began to embrace digital distribution in late 2005 and 2006, the absence of a specific residual compensation formula for new media was an effective rallying cry for WGA leaders in the buildup to and during the strike. To make the case even stronger, as the WGA sounded the alarm about the future, it summoned a bogeyman from the past. "Don't let them screw us on the Internet like they did on home video" was the message WGA leaders sent to members through an unprecedented outreach and education campaign that started more than a year before the 2007 contract negotiations began. Patric Verrone and David Young wanted members to understand the urgency of the threat posed by the Internet to the cherished principle of residual compensation.

Many writers were paying attention. It was impossible to ignore the changes rocking the industry in the two years leading up to the strike. The Walt Disney Company led the charge in October 2005 with its groundbreaking licensing agreement with Apple's iTunes online retailer, making ABC hits including *Desperate Housewives* and *Lost* available for legal downloading to a home computer or iPod portable video player within hours of each episode's network debut. Disney's ABC was also the leader in embracing advertising-supported Web streaming of programming via the ABC.com website, starting with a trial run of a handful of Disney-produced shows in the spring of 2006. The response from viewers was so overwhelming that in the 2006–7 season, most of ABC's prime-time programming was made available for streaming through the websites of the network and its affiliate stations. Within a year, Disney rivals News Corporation and NBC Universal would team to develop the Web-streaming service that became Hulu.

Hollywood's business leaders are petrified by the pace of change among consumer habits, particularly digitally savvy younger consumers. From

TiVo to the iPod to YouTube, the innovations of the first ten years of the twenty-first century transformed the way people watch television and movies. And it has come at a time when those traditional mediums face an onslaught of competition from the growing popularity of video games, online multiplayer games and virtual worlds, social networking services, and other made-for-Internet content.

These new entertainment options have been made possible by the exponential growth of broadband, or high-speed Internet access, in the United States, particularly among young people. In 2008 55 percent of adults had access to a broadband connection in their home, up from 10 percent in 2002. Among adults in the eighteen-to-twenty-nine demographic, the penetration rate was 70 percent, according to surveys conducted by the Pew Internet and American Life Project. By May 2010, broadband penetration in the home had climbed to 66 percent of adults, including 80 percent of those in the age range of eighteen to twenty-nine, the generation of movie ticket buyers and TV viewers that Hollywood is most eager to reach.[5]

But vigorous competition from online entertainment sources is only one aspect of myriad competitive issues vexing television's traditional titans. Digital video recorders have upended the rules of the game even when viewers do seek out broadcast and cable network programming. TiVo and other DVRs give viewers the option of watching programs on their own timetables, and even skipping past the commercial spots with the touch of a button.

In just a few years, the on-demand programming revolution has been eagerly embraced by viewers, who are watching more TV than ever before. But the new ways that they are able to watch are posing a threat to the traditional business model that drives major broadcast and basic cable networks.

From the days of *Texaco Star Theater* and *Your Show of Shows*, the prime-time business has hinged on the national networks' ability to draw mass audiences to programs on a predetermined night and time. Viewers were trained to tune in to NBC on Thursday at 8:00 p.m. to catch *Friends*, or Sunday at 7:00 p.m. for CBS's *60 Minutes* or Tuesday at 9:00 p.m. for ABC's *Home Improvement*.

The larger the audience, the more the network can charge for commercial spots in the show. The networks' pitch to Madison Avenue was simple: buy our thirty-second spots, and your advertising message will reach a broad, demographically desirable swath of America in one fell swoop. To draw those large crowds, networks were largely dependent on Hollywood studios and a handful of independent production entities to supply high-end programs. Networks paid sizable six- and seven-figure license fees (eight figures in the case of a handful of blockbusters) and relied on collecting advertising revenue from not only the initial telecast of each episode, but at least one repeat telecast to help amortize license-fee expenditures.

Since the late 1970s, video cassette recorders offered viewers the ability to record programs for playback at a later time, but not with the same ease of use and storage capability that DVRs have brought to America's living rooms. TiVo, the most recognized DVR brand, also gives viewers the ability to skip through commercials. This function was so alarming to broadcasters and to the advertising industry that it dominated the industry debate about DVRs for years after the machines were introduced in the late 1990s. The rampant concern about ad skipping undermining, if not destroying, advertisers' incentive to spend big bucks on national TV spots hastened the industry's embrace of product placement and branded integration in programming.

In the rush to develop "TiVo-proof" marketing campaigns, brand names and product plugs have popped up in prime time on a scale not seen since commercial television's first decade, when most entertainment programs were financed and controlled entirely by a single sponsor in exchange for name-above-the-title placement or other plugging privileges. (Think Ozzie, Harriet, Ricky, and David drinking Coca-Cola at every opportunity on *The Adventures of Ozzie and Harriet.*)

Beyond the ad-skipping issue, another significant disruption to traditional network operations wrought by DVRs and other on-demand options is the ability to direct the focus of millions of viewers on a nightly basis. Broadcast and cable networks bank on their most successful series to serve as "launchpads" for other programs. That audience-funneling function only increases the value of a hit show to its network. If viewers are watching more shows on their own schedules via DVR playback, networks have to work harder to entice viewers to check out new programs. They cannot rely nearly as much on a new show's proximity to an established success to generate initial sampling.

As DVRs have taken root (by 2012 Nielsen Media Research estimated that 43 percent of the nation's 114.7 million television households had DVRs), research has shown that viewers in homes with DVRs tend to watch more prime-time television overall than viewers in non-DVR homes.[6]

Yet another challenge for the networks presented by DVRs is how to factor time-shifted viewing into a program's ratings. Ratings generated by the independent audience measurement firm Nielsen Media Research are the currency of television. Ratings points, measured down to a tenth of a decimal, are the basis for determining the advertising rates that networks charge—and are obligated to deliver—in a given program.

In January 2006, Nielsen Media Research incorporated DVR viewing into its national audience sample for the first time. Nielsen reports ratings based on a "Live Plus Same Day" standard, which means the rating includes DVR playback viewing done on the same day of a program's premiere telecast, and "Live Plus Seven Day," which incorporates viewing done within a week of the premiere telecast.

The measurement issue is of special concern to broadcast networks, which have been fighting the erosion of their market share for more than twenty years. Nevertheless, ABC, CBS, NBC, and Fox still represent TV's big leagues, the only outlets that can regularly draw mass audiences of ten million viewers or more, with the right program. Because of their historical competitive advantage, broadcast network TV commands the highest rates of pay for Hollywood union members—often substantially higher than for the same work done for basic- or pay-cable outlets.

The increase in DVR usage since 2006 has had a clear impact on the live ratings of contemporary hits, including ABC's *Lost* and *Desperate Housewives*, NBC's *Heroes* and *The Office*, and Fox's *24*. As much as 20 to 30 percent of a successful series' total audience can come from DVR playback viewing. Advertisers initially resisted network efforts to use cumulative ratings, or combining the viewership of the premiere telecast plus later DVR playback, as a basis for setting the price for commercial spots.

But in 2007, the networks and the advertising industry reached a compromise to include three days of DVR playback viewing in a cumulative rating. In exchange, the networks agreed to use the ratings for the commercial breaks within a program, rather than ratings for the program itself, as the basis for commercial pricing, a shift that had long been sought by advertisers.[7]

As Hollywood's angst over DVRs was growing, the television business was jolted by the introduction in October 2005 of another digital innovation, Apple's video iPod.

The device's debut came in tandem with Apple's announcement of an unprecedented program-licensing pact with the Walt Disney Company. Alone among the Hollywood studios, Disney took the plunge into download-on-demand distribution with its deal to sell episodes of ABC and Disney Channel shows for $1.99 apiece through Apple's iTunes online retailer.

Disney had numerous motives for wanting to help Apple's chief executive, Steve Jobs, add more sizzle to the unveiling of the video iPod. Chief among them was Disney's keen interest in maintaining a movie-production partnership with Jobs's Pixar Animation Studios, the acclaimed production company behind such Disney-distributed blockbusters as *Toy Story* and *Finding Nemo*.[8]

But as much as Pixar was a catalyst for the deal, so were the mounting concerns among Disney executives about the growth in the number of unauthorized sites offering downloads of TV shows and movies. Anne Sweeney, Disney's top television executive and cochair of its Media Networks division, was wrapping up a meeting with members of her staff in May 2005 when one of the executives asked if they would stick around in the conference room for a moment to watch something. It was the morning after the first-season finale of *Desperate Housewives*, the instant hit that helped pull ABC out of a long ratings slump. Viewership of the finale was spectacular, adding an exclamation point to what had been an incredible turnaround for the network in the 2004–5 season.

Vince Roberts, Disney–ABC Television Group's head of worldwide technology and operations, congratulated Sweeney on a job well done with

Housewives as he cued up a DVD on the player in the conference room. Up came the opening scene of the *Housewives* finale. "Fifteen minutes after the show ended last night, I downloaded this from BitTorrent.com," Roberts informed Sweeney. Sweeney was stunned. The quality of the video was pretty good, and the commercials had even been stripped out.

Roberts's demonstration of the *Housewives* finale was the eye-opening example that made Sweeney and other Disney executives realize piracy was no longer a matter of someone sneaking a camcorder into a movie theater. It was about digitally enabled copyright infringement on a world-wide scale, distributed at no cost by file-sharing networks and websites that were often housed far outside of US borders. "That was the moment when we knew we had to do something, but we didn't have many options," Sweeney said in 2006. "We started talking about piracy in a new way, which was piracy as a true competitor for our viewers."[9]

Disney executives and their counterparts at other studios were eager to protect the film and television business from the digital devasta-tion suffered by the music industry at the hands of Napster and its ilk. Music was the first form of content widely traded through illegal online sources because audio files were relatively small, compared to the band-width and storage space required for video content. But as Internet video quality improved and more homes became wired for broadband, Holly-wood knew from the music industry's example that digital piracy would become rampant. The major music labels had tried to hold back the tide of digital distribution of music with copyright-infringement litigation against the operators of illegal download sites and even individual users, but it did little to quash the consumer demand for music in easily acces-sible digital formats.

Steve Jobs filled the void in the spring of 2003 by convincing the major record labels to license a wide range of music for legal downloading at ninety-nine cents a song through the online retailer that Apple dubbed the iTunes Music Store. After rewiring the music industry's business model, Apple's charismatic CEO set his sights on television and movies.

A few weeks after the *Desperate Housewives* demonstration, Sweeney got a call from her boss, Disney president and CEO Robert Iger, asking her to give Jobs a call. Jobs had reached out to Disney regarding an iTunes licensing deal for television programming, to dovetail with the launch of the video iPod. It was an offer that Disney, with its nervousness over the profit-eroding threat of digital piracy, could not refuse.

Sweeney's conversation with Jobs in the summer of 2005 got the ball rolling toward Apple's launch announcement on October 12 at San Jose's opulent California Theater. Iger, who had taken the CEO reins of Disney from Michael Eisner two weeks before, was also invited to share the stage briefly that day with Jobs to herald the historic meeting of the minds between Hollywood and Silicon Valley.

The Disney licensing pact made the video iPod immediately relevant to the creative community, not to mention the general public. The iPod was not just a cool device with promise for the future; it was a new way of watching television today.

Disney's ABC, Disney Channel, and ESPN were the only prominent TV content partners Apple had in hand on the day of the announcement, but that was enough to grab the public's attention. There was little doubt among Hollywood veterans that if one studio found a way to help thwart piracy and get paid per download—with virtually no additional distribution or manufacturing costs—Disney's rivals would soon follow suit.

Nonetheless, making the deal with Apple required an enormous leap of faith on Disney's part. The iTunes deal had the potential to generate new sources of profits for the company, as it would receive 70 percent of the revenue generated by each sale. But it also came with many risks, including the potential to hurt ABC's first-run ratings, as well as DVD box set sales and, most important, the long-term value of programs in traditional syndication. It might also anger ABC's 175 affiliate stations and the cable operators that Disney depended on to carry its cable networks throughout the country.

Among the many decisions Disney executives made in setting up the iTunes deal was how it would compensate actors, writers, and directors now that their work would be distributed in a wholly new media format. There was no question that the members of the WGA, SAG, and DGA would be owed something for this new form of reuse. The issue for Disney, amid the frenzy of hammering out the iTunes agreement in secret, was how that compensation would be calculated under existing guild contracts.

Disney settled on defining the iTunes downloads as a form of home video. Compensation for creatives would therefore be determined by the existing residual formula governing home video sales. Disney executives had no illusions about how this decision would be received by the guilds. They knew the creative community had long nursed a grudge over what many view as a woefully inadequate and antiquated formula.

In 1985, when the home video formula was firmed up in guild contracts, the sector was still young and not yet the profit center it was destined to become. The studios took the position that in order to allow this new market to develop, and to help cover manufacturing and marketing costs, residual payments should be based on only a portion of revenue generated by home video sales and rentals.

Despite the sector's growth and reinvigoration with the transition from the VHS to DVD format in the late 1990s, the studios have resolutely refused to adjust what is known as the "80/20" formula. It is so named because the studios, which are by far the largest producers of home video releases, take 80 percent of the revenue off the top, leaving a much smaller pool of 20 percent of the revenue from which the percentage-based residuals are derived. Writers receive a residual payment of 1.5 percent of that 20 percent of revenues (rising to 1.8 percent if sales gross more than one million dollars). The 20 percent revenue formula is known as the much-reviled "producer's gross" calculation.

The WGA mounted a brief strike in 1985 over the home video formula, but the pressure from external and internal forces was too great for the guild to withstand. But the anger only grew, as the studios refused to budge on producer's gross, and it was expertly channeled by WGA leaders to rally the troops leading up to the 2007 contract talks. "We were fighting the residual hangover of the 1985 strike on videocassettes," said Carol Lombardini. "In every other negotiation since, that has been an emotional sore point. I think we were fighting that (in 2007), and we were fighting what it represented."[10]

Although there was no doubt the guilds would be unhappy with Disney's decision to designate paid downloads as home video transactions, it did not help matters that guild leaders learned about the decision from media reports on the Apple-Disney deal. In the effort to keep the news under wraps until Jobs could make a splashy announcement, there was no advance notice given to the guilds by Disney executives.

The iTunes agreement was not Disney's only attempt to experiment with the marriage of new and old media. On April 10, 2006, ABC took another giant step with the news that it would conduct a two-month test of offering full-length episodes of selected shows for on-demand viewing via its ABC.com website, the day after their premiere telecast on the network.

The episodes would be offered as streaming video, with advertising spots embedded at various intervals, much like a regular television broadcast. The video could be accessed only via the ABC.com site, but could not be downloaded, and the commercials could not be skipped. The guinea-pig shows were ABC's red-hot hits *Desperate Housewives* and *Lost* and its cult-fave drama *Alias* and first-year (and soon to be canceled) series *Commander in Chief.* In an effort to avoid undercutting the shows' regularly scheduled telecasts, the programs were made available on the website about twelve hours after each episode premiered on the network. This decision was an important consideration for ABC's affiliate station managers, who were not happy about losing their exclusive hold on ABC network programs.

ABC's test went so well that its servers were frequently overwhelmed by the demand for Web streams. It was an entirely new approach to delivering television programming, and once again ABC's Big Four rivals would soon follow Disney's cue.

ABC's Web-streaming initiative was technologically ambitious and trailblazing. It was also a "promotional" activity, in the eyes of the network. That was no doubt true, given that the easy on-demand access to the programs would let viewers watch whenever they wanted, and possibly encouraging them to check out new shows at their convenience. But calling it "promotional" was also a business decision with implications for WGA, SAG, and DGA members. Promotional activities on behalf of a production are broadly defined in guild contracts as generally being free of obligation for additional compensation.

The guilds, on the other hand, saw the advertising in the Web streaming of full-length episodes as something that went beyond promotion. It was profit making for ABC, and therefore creatives deserved compensation along the lines of the residuals that writers, actors, and directors would receive for a traditional broadcast TV rerun. Calling Web streaming promotional was viewed as a greedy maneuver on the part of the networks, and it stoked the sparks from the iTunes decision into a raging wildfire.

When CBS announced a plan to make some of its programs available on numerous websites for ad-supported streaming in August 2006, the move prompted a rare joint policy statement from the WGA East and West, SAG, and DGA. "As new methods of content distribution are rolled out, the three guilds remain united in our assertion that members must be compensated for the reuse of their work as guild contracts require," the statement said. "The ad-sponsored Internet streaming of prime-time CBS shows is only the latest in a series of new ventures that could ultimately benefit both the entertainment industry and the actors, directors and writers who create the content that will allow these Internet sites to flourish. We will continue working to ensure that our guild members receive their contractual fair share."[11]

The words were tempered, but the message was clear. New media compensation would be the prime focus for the guilds in the next round of contract negotiations in 2007 and 2008.

Another burning economic issue for creatives that would come into sharper focus in the months leading up to the strike was how the spread of on-demand access to programming was cutting into the number of regular on-air reruns that networks carry. For an hourlong drama series, the first repeat telecast of an episode after its premiere airing would generate a residual payment of about $20,000 for a writer or director and more for a top-billed actor.[12]

Despite these fees, repeats have been a pivotal means of amortizing programming costs for networks. License fees for broadcast network series on average run between $650,000 on the low end for a half-hour series to $3 million or more for hourlong shows. (Megahits can fetch significantly more; *ER* in its heyday commanded $13 million per episode from NBC.) The right to one or two rerun telecasts of a show is built into those license fees, giving the network another opportunity to generate advertising revenue from the show.

But in recent years, ratings for most repeat telecasts have plummeted. It is easy to understand why. Not only do viewers have more programming options overall in the three-hundred-channel era, but they also have many more options for keeping up with favorite shows.

With negligible ratings, repeats are far less cost-effective for networks because of the guild residuals, music rights fees, and other costs they incur. Networks found they could do better by slotting in lower-cost unscripted programs during the summer months and other times of the year that were once laden with reruns. This shift in viewer behavior has made high-end scripted programming a more costly proposition for broadcast networks, which in turn has fueled the development of even more unscripted programming.

Television writers in particular could be forgiven for feeling as though they were under attack from the digital onslaught. Their works were being exploited to launch new viewing platforms and businesses for network-studio conglomerates, at the direct expense of their traditional compensation for repeats.

Beyond the network concerns, the instant access to program repeats also has ominous implications for studios on the production side of the equation. For decades, the financial model for series production revolved around the production entity absorbing significant losses in a show's first few seasons, as network license fees rarely cover a show's total production cost. For shows that lasted more than three seasons, those losses would be recouped with profit to spare when the rerun rights to a package of eighty to one hundred episodes were sold in syndication to local TV stations and cable networks.

Studios and other sizable production entities could afford to absorb the losses from short-lived shows, as well as the six- and seven-figure budget deficits on ongoing series, because one solid success in the syndication market every few years would produce huge long-term profits. The 1990s amounted to a bull market for syndication, with big hits including

Seinfeld, Home Improvement, Friends, ER, and *Law and Order* generating as much as five hundred million to one billion dollars.

But bull markets do not last forever. The prices paid for so-called off-network series began to drop even before the on-demand boom took off. Now that programs have such broad rerun exposure early on through new media and DVD sales, there are grave doubts among buyers and sellers about what the market will bear for off-network programs in the coming decade.

DVD sales can be a significant source of profit for a top-selling title, such as HBO's *The Sopranos* or Fox's *The Simpsons,* but paid downloads and Web streaming of even the most popular network shows to date bring in only a fraction of the revenue once generated by syndication sales.

The largest studios are more dependent than ever on the revenue generated by foreign sales of TV series, and this focus has had an impact on the types of programs that studios are willing to invest in. Action and fantasy fare is an easier sell overseas than talky, cerebral dramas or period pieces.

The need to balance ever-rising production costs with shrinking profit margins has forced many writers and producers to accept product placement on their sets and, increasingly, the integration of brand names into their story lines.

The changing business landscape of the 2000s stands in sharp contrast to the professional prospects for TV writers in the 1980s and '90s. A wave of hit series—from *The Cosby Show, Cheers,* and *Family Ties* to *Friends, Seinfeld, Home Improvement,* and *Everybody Loves Raymond,* plus dramas like *Law and Order, The X-Files,* and *NYPD Blue*—primed the syndication marketplace. In flush times, networks and studios were willing to invest in rich contracts with writers in the hopes of generating the next billion-dollar franchise.

Writers, particularly young writers, were courted by studios to sign exclusive multiyear contracts to develop series ideas and pilot scripts. Writers with only a few years of experience working on comedy or drama series were regularly offered so-called overall development deals that paid them as much as one million dollars a year or more to brainstorm ideas that the studio could shop as pilots to network program buyers.

The spending spree on writers coincided with the dawn of a new regulatory era for Hollywood that culminated with the passage of the 1996 Telecommunications Act. After years of intense lobbying and legal challenges brought by ABC, CBS, and NBC, the Federal Communications Commission (FCC) repealed a twenty-five-year-old rule, known as the financial interest and syndication rule, that effectively prevented ABC, CBS, and NBC from owning most of the entertainment programming they carried, nor could they share in syndication profits from those shows.

The so-called fin-syn rule had been adopted by the FCC in 1970 as a check against the oligopoly power the Big Three networks exerted over the national television marketplace. It was designed to ensure that the networks would not dominate television production as well, and in so doing it guaranteed that ABC, CBS, and NBC would rely on Hollywood studios and other major production entities to supply each network's most successful programming. By the early 1990s, with Fox taking root as the fourth network and cable penetration growing rapidly, the Big Three argued long and hard that there was no longer any macroeconomic justification for tying their hands in the production-syndication area.

Fin-syn had also effectively prevented the merger of a Hollywood studio with one of the Big Three networks. But all that changed by mid-1995, when it became clear that fin-syn would be done away with for good by Congress as part of the long-gestating overhaul of telecommunications policy. Rupert Murdoch's 20th Century Fox studio and Fox network had already paved the way for the new breed of network-studio conglomerate. It was no accident that the Walt Disney Company made its stealth move to acquire Capital Cities/ABC, Inc., in July 1995. CBS, Inc., cut a deal to merge with Viacom, parent company of Paramount Pictures and MTV Networks, in 1999. (CBS would be spun off again as a separate entity in January 2006, a move that would have implications for the WGA strike.) NBC's parent company, General Electric, was famously reticent about Hollywood's unpredictable economics. But the consolidation trend eventually prodded GE to expand NBC's size and scope with its 2003 agreement to buy 80 percent of Universal Studios from French conglomerate Vivendi.

The mandate of fin-syn created a well-defined ecosystem for those working in scripted television. Writers, actors, directors, and other creative talent worked for the studio or production entity that bankrolled the series. Networks licensed programs for two or three airings per episode but otherwise had no ongoing rights in a program. Network executives exerted influence in the creative development of programs, particularly in the early stages of pilot development. But it was the production company's responsibility to serve as the program's staunchest advocate. The studio had every incentive to make sure it surveyed the marketplace and found the optimum network buyer for its show. In success, the studio also had every incentive to extract as much money as the market would bear for a program.

These checks and balances went awry with the end of the fin-syn era. With Hollywood's consolidation into a half-dozen vertically integrated network and studio conglomerates, networks increasingly found themselves doing business with sibling production units owned by the corporate parent. At times, broader corporate agendas took precedence over those intracompany relationships. Program license fees might be kept artificially low, compared to what a hit show might command on the open market, or a show might be kept on the air at the behest of senior management to help bolster a production unit's bottom line. The steady stream of what became known in industry shorthand as "self-dealing"—or transactions between sibling units of the same conglomerate—spurred a wave of lawsuits in the late 1990s and early 2000s from profit participants claiming breach of fiduciary duty.[13]

For many television writers, the effect of consolidation was felt most acutely in the changes it spurred in the program development and production process. Seasoned TV writers complain that the process of pitching and securing green lights to write a script, to shoot a pilot, and, ultimately, to get a program on the air has grown increasingly bureaucratic. More executives from multiple units of a conglomerate weigh in on the merits of series concepts and pilots.

Writers who sign exclusive development deals with studios that have sibling networks are generally funneled into developing projects for that network; they can no longer count on a studio to vigorously shop his or her idea to multiple networks. If a network wants a project that is being developed by its sibling studio, it is difficult, if not impossible, for a rival network to snare the project away by offering more money or other guarantees.

These changes descended on writers in the years leading up to the 2005–6 period when new media distribution became a big factor for television programming. Writers whose experience was based on Hollywood's fast-fading boom times were understandably on edge about the future of their profession. Patric Verrone and David Young felt this nervousness acutely among WGA members. From the day he was elected WGA West president in 2005, Verrone pointed to the 2007 contract talks with the conglomerates as a watershed moment for the guild.

All of this upheaval roiling the creative community explains why thousands of writers—most of them well paid, some extremely wealthy— took to the streets with picket signs on November 5, 2007.

Perhaps the most unsettling aspect of the strike's legacy is that it is not over, not by a long shot. The walkout of 2007–8 is likely to be the first act in a high-tension drama that will play out at least through the next several rounds of WGA contract talks. "It happens about every 20 years. There is a new development that requires a new way of looking at the business," said Tony Segall, general counsel for the Writers Guild of America West and a key player behind the scenes with Verrone and Young. "Those are tough negotiations."[14] The prospect of hostilities flaring anew is but one big question weighing heavily on the minds of Hollywood professionals, particularly longtime writer-producers who have enjoyed great success.

The ramifications of the WGA strike have been felt far and wide in the creative community. Contracts were canceled, development and production budgets were slashed, and the networks looked for more unscripted reality shows for their prime-time schedules. All of which added up to a tightening of the job market for TV writers in the immediate aftermath of the strike.

Some see the strike as the bookend on a golden age for television writers in Hollywood that began in the three-network era but could not survive the new media explosion. "It's over," says one of Hollywood's most successful television writer-producers. "The television business as we knew it is essentially over. The strike accelerated what was already happening in the business by three to five years. It was the watershed moment that essentially marks the beginning of the end of the business. There is no longer a way to make money in series television."[15]

2

Path to the Picket Line

"The East is on *strike?*" Nick Counter asked incredulously. Counter, the longtime chief labor negotiator for Hollywood's major studios, looked stunned as the news sunk in. It was shortly after nine o'clock on Sunday, November 4, 2007.[1]

Counter, who had spent twenty-seven years as the chief labor negotiator for Hollywood studios, was worn out from a marathon day of negotiations with representatives from the Writers Guild of America, the union representing twelve thousand film and TV writers. Counter and his staff had been meeting with WGA officials in a conference room at the Sofitel hotel in West Hollywood since before ten that morning. The sides were making an eleventh-hour run at averting the strike that was scheduled to begin one minute after midnight if the guild and Alliance of Motion Picture and Television Producers could not come to terms on major elements of a new three-year contract.

The WGA's previous contract had expired three days before. Representatives from the WGA West and WGA East, a separate entity that represents film and TV writers who live east of the Mississippi River, had been sparring with their AMPTP counterparts on and off since July. The sides were at loggerheads on a host of issues, none more intractable than new media.

The sessions on that Sunday had been somewhat productive—to the surprise of the two dozen or so executives, WGA members, and support staffers who were holed up for the day at "an undisclosed location," as the media were informed. There was a galvanizing sense of urgency in the meeting rooms on the hotel's second floor where WGA and AMPTP representatives gathered, in large and small groups, for discussions that were more substantive than any others during the previous four months. Participants on both sides of the bargaining table even went so far as to send positive signals to interested outside parties that a strike was likely to be averted. "On Nov. 4, we were still enormously far apart," said Carol Lombardini. "But that was probably the day we had the first real spontaneous conversation in the negotiations, and it was on the streaming issue."[2]

But after months of public fighting over competing contract proposals, there was also a deep reservoir of frustration and suspicion among the key players around the table that day. A career labor negotiator, Counter was outraged at what he viewed as underhanded tactics used by WGA leaders to distort the facts about the negotiations. He was aghast at some of the unrealistic proposals the WGA kept pushing and the hard-line rhetoric the guild had been disseminating to members about what it would take to get a "fair deal." In Counter's view, those demands only made it harder to zero in on the nitty-gritty of what it would take to make a deal.

Patric Verrone, a comedy writer who got his start writing jokes for *The Tonight Show Starring Johnny Carson*, had been elected president of the WGA West two years earlier by a wide margin after campaigning on a platform of toughening the guild's stance in its dealings with the studios. Verrone also pledged to vastly increase the resources the guild devoted to organizing, not only among prospective new recruits but also in education and outreach to members.

Organizing was the forte of David Young, the firebrand former textile-union executive who ascended to the top paid position at the WGA West shortly after Verrone was elected in September 2005. Young's predecessor, industry veteran John McLean, was fired by the board days after the election for being too cozy with management in past negotiations, in the view of Verrone and WGA West board members who were elected along with him. The incredibly high-stakes battle over new media marked Young's first effort to negotiate a master film and TV contract for the guild.

Also representing the WGA was John Bowman, the chair of the negotiating committee that the WGA West and East had assembled to represent a cross-section of guild members at the bargaining table. Bowman was part of the single most important constituency in the 2007 contract talks, namely, top television writer-producers, known in industry parlance by their literal job description as "showrunners."

Through their public and private statements, Verrone and Young left no doubt about what it would take to make a deal. Although the WGA West and WGA East had been at odds in the past, there was no such division on these contract talks. Verrone's counterpart, WGA East president Michael Winship, was unwavering in his willingness to go out on strike for the cause of new media. The WGA East's executive director, Mona Mangan, was well known for embracing hardball tactics that often prolonged WGA East contract negotiations.

With the clock ticking, there was some forward momentum in the talks. After stalling for months, the AMPTP in the early afternoon put forth the broad strokes of an offer for compensation on Web streaming. It was not much in the way of dollars and cents, but it was something. And the sides had a discussion about the best way to measure viewership in this emerging platform.

Presently, the WGA made a big move of its own. The guild formally withdrew item number 9 on its original list of twenty-six contract negotiating points—the push for a 20 percent to 40 percent increase in the residual for home video sales and rentals. In truth, the quixotic bid for such a large increase in an area that had long been off-limits for the studios was included in the WGA's initial pattern of demands only so that it could be taken off the table at a key point in the talks. No one on the WGA negotiating team thought there was actually any hope of moving the needle on home video, not with so many other contentious issues in the mix.

Politically, however, the WGA had to include it in the initial proposal to the studios to help screenwriters feel that their concerns were being addressed, as home video transactions remain largely a film-driven business. And it also gave the WGA the chance to make a grand gesture of sacrifice in the hopes of gaining concessions in other areas. AMPTP negotiators understood the realpolitik of the situation for guild negotiators, even as they scoffed at the wildly unrealistic request.

To the WGA's dismay, Counter's team responded to the guild's gesture by initiating a discussion about an extremely peripheral issue involving compensation terms for writers of made-for-TV movies. The WGA representatives in the room did not hide their frustration. They were expecting a meaningful proposal on Web streaming, or the removal of items from the AMPTP's negotiating platform that the WGA deemed onerous. The made-for-TV movie provision was not even on the WGA's radar.

As the anxiety grew, the sides decided to take a dinner break. Some lower-profile participants in the marathon sessions took a walk through the Beverly Center shopping center across the street from the hotel, just for the chance to stretch their legs. The core WGA group stayed mostly together in their private meeting room. They shared the ominous feeling that the AMPTP was deliberately stalling.

As the sides began to regroup at the hotel, Bowman saw Harry Isaacs, the longtime head of labor relations for CBS, in the hallway. "You guys have got to make a move," Bowman implored.

Isaacs wanted to know if the WGA was dead set on going on strike at midnight. "You guys going?"

Bowman's tight-lipped nod left no room for interpretation. Bowman had made a point of enlisting a key emissary a day earlier to get the word to the CEOs. The guild's machine was well oiled and ready to roll. In the absence of major movement in the talks on Sunday, the WGA would hit the streets on Monday.

Isaacs went back into the AMPTP's meeting room. He noticed the time and noted that it was about ten minutes past midnight on the East Coast. He went over to his laptop computer and pulled up the WGA East's website. Isaacs was taken aback by what he saw, though he should not have been. "Writers Guild on Strike," the home page declared. "All Guild-Covered Work under the MBA Ceased at 12:01 a.m. EST on Monday, November 5, 2007."

Counter's patience had been stretched thin during the previous four months of unproductive discussions. He believed that the WGA's leaders were reckless and inexperienced in the give-and-take of contract negotiations. He, on the other hand, had some three hundred labor agreements under his belt. Counter had believed for some time that the WGA was bound and determined to go on strike, no matter what the studios put on the table.

Counter and Lombardini had twice asked Verrone and Young earlier in the day if they would be willing to "stop the clock" on the promised 12:01 a.m. start of the strike as long as they were still meeting. Both times, the reply was a firm no.

"We felt an agreement was near, which is why we removed DVDs from the table," Bowman says. "We expected a night of back and forth negotiations which would result, finally, in a deal. When the AMPTP responded to the removal by addressing an area of importance to neither side, we got the impression that they weren't serious about striking a deal that night."[3]

When Counter saw that the WGA East had declared itself on strike even as the meeting stretched late into the night, he was in no mood to be diplomatic. He walked into the hallway, where he saw Young, Verrone, and the WGA East's Mona Mangan. "Are you guys willing to stop the clock," a red-faced Counter asked Young, and hold off on the strike while the sides continued to meet?[4]

Young's response was blunt: "No." The WGA was ready to continue talking but would not call off its strike plans, Young informed Counter.

"Oh yes, we're on strike," Mangan reinforced. Counter gruffly declared the meeting over and walked back to the AMPTP's room.

Within minutes, most of the AMPTP and studio executives who had been hunkered down in the hotel had dispersed. The labor executives who had been phoning in mostly positive updates to their CEOs throughout the day now had to report the breakdown of the talks and the onset of the work stoppage. The WGA group stayed at the hotel and began to activate their carefully crafted strike plan, alerting the guild's many recruits that it was time to head for the trenches.

"There came a point where the AMPTP had just decided they were going to let it happen," said WGA East president Michael Winship. "It was sort of like George W. Bush and the weapons of mass destruction (in Iraq). The inspectors are saying 'We don't see anything. Let us keep inspecting' and Bush saying 'No, forget it; I'm going in.' There was such intractability about it, so that when midnight hit (in New York), that's when all hell broke loose."[5]

By ten that night, media coverage of the negotiations meltdown was widespread. The one-hundred-day war that would shut down Hollywood and torpedo the 2007–8 television season had begun.

The strike that crippled film and television production was a watershed, divisive moment for Hollywood with repercussions that have extended long after the walkout formally ended on February 12, 2008. The labor action would be hailed by many in Hollywood's creative community as a long-overdue response to more than a decade of change and corporate takeovers. It was labeled "the first significant 21st century strike" by prominent voices in the broader US labor movement, eager to demonstrate that unions retain some relevance in a white-collar industry like screenwriting.[6] It was decried by Hollywood's captains of industry as shortsighted and ideologically driven, the by-product of a masterful campaign waged by union leaders with broader social agendas and no grasp of the monumental challenges facing the television and film industries. What no one disputes is that the one-hundred-day work stoppage will stand as a seminal event in the evolution of digital media as a distribution channel for commercial entertainment.

The flash points of the WGA strike were a crystallization of myriad issues that continue to challenge the traditional entertainment industry, television in particular. Compensation for new media was the crux of the dispute. But for many who manned the picket lines, the fight became a David-versus-Goliath struggle against the tide of vertical integration and consolidation of media ownership during the previous fifteen years. The strike was the safety valve that finally blew after years of mounting frustration.

As much as the strike was a symptom of broader upheaval, its course was steered by a handful of strong-willed personalities, WGA's Verrone and Young, the AMPTP's Counter, and four supremely powerful CEOs who largely set the agenda behind the scenes: News Corporation's Peter Chernin, the Walt Disney Company's Robert Iger, CBS Corporation's Leslie Moonves, and Warner Bros.' Barry Meyer. The breakdown in communication early on between Young and Counter seemed to doom the formal bargaining process from the start. Both sides were determined to play hardball.

The AMPTP handed Verrone and Young all the ammunition the guild needed to keep their idled members fired up through aggressive proposals made at the start of the WGA contract talks in July 2007. The studios put on the table a radical proposal to revamp all residual formulas to allow the studios to recoup certain costs before any fees were paid to writers. WGA leaders cried "rollbacks," and the battle was on.

But while the writers marshaled an impressive army to wage the fight with courage and devotion, there were other forces that had a profound influence on the outcome of Hollywood's civil war over the Internet. The Directors Guild of America and Screen Actors Guild were also girding for their separate master film and television contract renewal talks with the studios, and both unions grappled with the same issues as the WGA. The DGA and SAG were both facing a June 30, 2008, contract expiration date, and that eight-month lag behind the WGA's deal-making timetable would prove to be significant for the negotiating strategies of all three guilds.

From the beginning through the final hours of the writers' strike, SAG leaders and many of its members were important allies for the WGA. The DGA, on the other hand, has a history of conflicting with the WGA's agenda on industry issues. The tension between the WGA and DGA mirrors the age-old professional tensions between writers and directors.

The DGA took a very different approach than the WGA in preparing to tackle new media in its contract negotiations with the studios. The WGA focused its efforts on raising awareness among members of the importance of the issues and the need to establish the infrastructure for mounting an effective, well-organized strike. Guild leaders dismissed the AMPTP's assertions that there were no profits yet flowing from new media licensing. The WGA pointed to the flurry of groundbreaking deals made by the major conglomerates and the rosy predictions to Wall Street of the skyrocketing growth potential for their film and TV assets in an array of digital formats.

The DGA also made extensive preparations for wrangling over new media long before it was due to meet the AMPTP at the bargaining table. The guild spent more than one million dollars to commission two in-depth studies from separate research outfits to gauge the scope and near-term profit potential of the new media marketplace as it related to the work of guild members. The DGA's research jibed with the AMPTP's assertion that the conglomerates were not yet realizing significant profits from new media endeavors, nor were they likely to during the next three-year contract term.

The fact that the directors were waiting in the wings behind the WGA was a tactical advantage skillfully used by the AMPTP to hold the writers at bay during a crucial phase of the strike. The DGA wound up calling most of the shots in the compensation formulas included in the final contracts agreed to by the three guilds. At the same time, the DGA had extremely heightened leverage because the writers were on strike and because the conglomerates needed to cut a deal that could serve as a template for a settlement with the WGA.

The clout wielded by Hollywood unions is notable in an era of declining unionization for the US labor force overall. The overwhelming majority of film and scripted television work is done by DGA, WGA, and SAG members, as well by the technical and craft workers represented by the International Alliance of Theatrical Stage Employees (IATSE). The use of guild-represented actors, writers, and directors remains the dividing line for professional and amateur productions.

SAG, WGA, and DGA have been able to maintain a firm grip on Hollywood because the vast majority of creatives have been so steadfast about guild representation. Guilds have historically been seen by actors, writers, and directors as a bulwark against the difficulty of making a living in film and television, where careers can go from hot to cold in a weekend. The studios are always looking out for the bottom line; the guilds are looking out for their members and the interests of the disciplines they serve. With virtually all employment in Hollywood done on a freelance basis, the guilds, not the studios, are the providers of health care insurance and pension plans for actors, writers, and directors. Guilds police the conglomerates to enforce their master contracts and ensure that members are paid all the residuals and royalties that they are owed under those contracts.

The enduring strength of the guilds also reflects the insular nature of working in Hollywood. Having a SAG, WGA, or DGA card means you are an insider, and you're recognized as a professional in a sea of wannabes. Even the most successful Hollywood players are members of the various guilds. It is in the DNA of the creative community.

The formation of SAG, WGA, and DGA in the 1930s is a big part of the legend of Hollywood's golden age as it persists in the minds of filmdom's contemporary workers. It is not forgotten that it took the courage of filmdom heavyweights—among them actors Ralph Morgan, James Cagney, and Eddie Cantor; directors King Vidor, John Ford, and Howard Hawks; and screenwriters John Howard Lawson, Robert Riskin, and Frances Marion—to galvanize their colleagues to organize against the threat of 50 percent pay cuts and worse that studio bosses sought to implement during the Great Depression.

It took years for SAG, WGA, and DGA to be recognized by employers as the collective bargaining agents for their respective members. The WGA and SAG were formed in 1933. SAG signed its first master contract in 1937, after thousands of members vowed to strike unless the guild was recognized by the studios. The DGA was established in 1936 (as the Screen Directors Guild) and signed its first studio deal in 1939. In a sign of how hard the power structure fought to keep writers from organizing, the WGA (then the Screen Writers Guild) did not secure its first contract until 1942, though the terms were backdated to 1940.[7]

Despite their common roots, the guilds have often sparred with one another, particularly the DGA and WGA, on issues ranging from creative rights to compensation demands made of the studios. The DGA has the reputation of being the "millionaire's union" because its most prominent members are so successful, overlooking the fact that the guild represents thousands of lower-level workers who serve as assistant directors, unit production managers, and stage managers, among other jobs. In its history, the DGA has gone on strike only once, in 1987, when the studios pushed for reductions on certain basic minimum pay rates. The walkout lasted all of three hours and five minutes in eastern time zones and only five minutes on the West Coast.

The WGA has long had the reputation of being aligned with left-wing causes and a propensity to strike. Two of the WGA's founders were among the "Hollywood 10" who refused to be grilled as part of the anticommunist witch hunt waged by the House Un-American Activities Committee in 1947 and were sentenced to a year in jail for contempt. In the blacklist era that followed, dozens of WGA members saw their careers destroyed because of their political beliefs and from guilt by association.

In the modern era, the WGA has been more volatile than the DGA or SAG in its relations with the studios. The WGA went on strike three times in the 1980s alone. In 1981 the WGA went out for three months; in 1985 writers struck over the home video residual rate for two weeks. The last of the 1980s work stoppages was the 1988 walkout, which ranks as the longest in Hollywood, at 160 days. By all accounts, it was a debacle for writers, who had nothing to show for their sacrifice in the end. Worse, the strike revealed the fissures in the guild that separated the interests of the most successful film and television writers and showrunners and the rank-and-file members. By the end of the twenty-two-week strike, dissidents had organized a group of more than six hundred prominent members who threatened to bolt from the WGA unless the strike was settled.

The memory of the 1988 action was so bitter that for two decades, the executive leadership of the guild assiduously worked to avoid taking the membership to the brink of a strike. The conventional wisdom held that the guild could not withstand another prolonged walkout and that the highest-earning members would make good on their 1988 threat and break away. During this period, a vocal minority of mostly older members did regularly advocate using the strike threat to push for gains in contract negotiations, but guild leadership effectively held them at bay. They were seen as wild-eyed idealists by many members with strong memories of how much was lost in 1988. Younger members were generally enjoying the prosperity of the 1990s boom years and had no motivation to lay down their pencils.

It took the election of Patric Verrone as WGA West president and the elevation of David Young to executive director in 2005 for strike talk to be taken seriously again by a broad swath of WGA members. And that came only after Verrone and his supporters laid a strong foundation of understanding with their methodical member-outreach and education campaign. Under Verrone and Young, with the emphasis on organizing and noisy public pressure campaigns on various issues, the WGA began to function more like a traditional trade union than it had since its inception on the heels of Franklin Delano Roosevelt's inauguration. That plus the magnitude of the issues at stake in the 2007 contract talks gave many members a level of confidence that the Verrone-Young regime would be able to wage an effective strike.

Early on the morning of November 5, 2007, more than three thousand writers fanned out across fourteen sites in and around Los Angeles and numerous spots in Manhattan to form picket lines in front of the gates of power in the entertainment business.[8] Word spread quickly among writers the night before about the angry end to the talks at the Sofitel. By that time, many guild members already knew what was expected of them.

WGA leaders had been preparing for this morning for two years, mounting an unprecedented outreach and organizational effort among members. The infrastructure for managing picketing and other strike activities had been laid down through recruiting members to serve as strike captains and in other leadership roles on the front lines.

Even with the best-laid plans, the guild exceeded its own high expectations with the strong turnout and the coordination with which picketing commenced. Writers arrived at each site to find an organized effort with a sign-in table and strike captains giving instructions and handing out coffee, breakfast foods, and red-and-black "Writers Guild of America on Strike" picket signs. The signs came complete with duct tape wrapped around the end of the thin plywood handle so as not to leave any splinters.

From day one, the WGA walkout was an impressively well-organized effort. Even David Young's most vehement detractors allowed him the credit for executing the work stoppage brilliantly. "A strike is like a military operation and we had the right people leading us," Bowman says. "We had a lot of people who had done this before—a lot of union people who knew what they were doing. That made it different from every other previous (WGA) strike."[9]

On a crisp but typically warm LA fall morning, the sight of demonstrators walking in circles and chanting outside of the iconic studio entrances was a shock to virtually everyone in the industry. The studios were not nearly as coordinated, as the contract battle shifted to open warfare. AMPTP president Nick Counter made it clear in his statements to the media that there would be no negotiations while the WGA pickets were in force outside studio lots. But people were still unprepared for the scenes that unfolded on that first day.

Writers had been urged to arrive as early as five in the morning to picket sites in an effort to discourage truck drivers for the studios, most of whom were members of the Teamsters Union, from leaving the gates with loads of gear and props needed for location shoots, among other delivery functions. In most instances, the strategy worked. At least one or two pickets were dispatched to every entrance and exit of the sprawling studio lots of Paramount Pictures and CBS Television City in Hollywood; Warner Bros., NBC, and Disney in Burbank; 20th Century Fox in West Los Angeles; and Sony Pictures Entertainment in Culver City, among other sites. "I will not cross any picket line whether it is sanctioned or not because I firmly believe that Teamsters do not cross picket lines," Leo Reed, head of Hollywood's Teamsters Local 399, wrote in a message sent to his members on October 29.[10] Local 399 represents about four thousand Hollywood drivers, location managers, and scouts.

On day one, and for the duration of the strike, most Teamsters drivers refused to drive through picket lines. This demonstration of support was uplifting to those on the line, and it reinforced a sense that writers were as much working stiffs for the studios as those laboring in blue-collar jobs. Throughout the strike, the WGA picket lines were enveloped in the din of honks and hoots of support from passing motorists and particularly from union-represented truck drivers.

Some of the studio drivers who made predawn runs on the first day of the strike parked their rigs on the street after they returned to find pickets ringing their usual entryways. Drivers gathered in small clusters outside Paramount and other studios to watch, with some amusement, their white-collar brethren pound the pavement and chant union slogans.

The call-and-response chants led by strike captains with bullhorns succinctly stated the reasons for the strike: "What part of it is it that you don't get? We want our share of the Internet." "Two, four, six, eight: If you want your scripts, negotiate." "Why are we standing outside this gate? 'Cause we got screwed in '88!"

Perhaps the most unexpected sight on that first morning was the high turnout among the industry's most successful showrunners and screenwriters—the WGA's top earners with the most to lose in a prolonged work stoppage. The sight of those notable names walking the picket lines energized other strikers. It reinforced a sense of collective purpose, and that even those members making millions of dollars each year were willing to join in the fight in principle.

Mike Scully, an experienced showrunner and longtime writer-producer on *The Simpsons,* exemplified the determination of WGA members as he made the picket rounds on crutches outside 20th Century Fox. He had broken his left foot just a few days before the strike began. Like many others who had been through the 1988 strike, Scully knew that the WGA was a very different entity this time around. "There was much more unity within the guild and an overall feeling that we were doing the right thing not only for ourselves, but for future generations of writers," Scully says. "There were far fewer leisure suits on the picket line, which was refreshing."[11]

Just like the efficiency with which the picketing operations were deployed, the response among the WGA's big shots came about because of the intense lobbying and educational outreach efforts by WGA brass. Patric Verrone knew he needed the support of the guild's most powerful members to wage an effective strike.

The influence of the guild's member outreach efforts during the previous eighteen months was immediately evident. Many on the picket line cited similar talking points about how the distribution of television programming was shifting to the Internet and how guild members had to take a stand now to protect the future generations of writers. "By the time a lot of us who are marching out here are out of the business, it's not going to matter," David Fury, executive producer and showrunner of Fox's *24,* said as he walked a loop outside 20th Century Fox's West LA lot with more than two hundred pickets on day one of the strike. "If we don't do it now, a lot of writers (in the future) are going to wonder why we let them down."

Across town at Paramount Pictures in Hollywood, screenwriter Lewis Colick echoed Fury's sentiment. "It's been a long time coming," Colick said. "Everybody's unified, and of one mind that this has to happen now—for future generations, not just us."

Tales of personal sacrifice spread quickly along the picket lines. Greg Daniels, the executive producer of the NBC comedy *The Office*, rallied his staff writers to shut down a location shoot for their own show by forming a picket line on the first day of the strike. They gathered at about five in the morning near the site to form strategically placed picket lines that Teamsters drivers would not cross, which meant the crew was unable to receive the heavy equipment required for the shoot. The moment was documented in a three-minute Internet video, dubbed *The Office Is Closed*, that circulated widely around the Web and distilled the issues behind the strike in an easily understandable way. "I encourage the companies to send the lawyers in to write our episodes," Daniels says in the video, "because their lawyers are very creative. Terming a full-length airing of an episode with paid-for commercials online a 'promo' is really a good example of creativity and imagination."[12]

Shonda Rhimes, the creator and executive producer of ABC's top-rated *Grey's Anatomy*, was also proactive in shutting down production of the fledging *Anatomy* spin-off *Private Practice* by mounting a picket line outside the site of a planned location shoot.

The demonstration of resolve and solidarity by Daniels, Rhimes, and dozens of other top showrunners inspired many other writers, particularly younger WGA members who had never been through a strike. *Office* star Steve Carell, who is a WGA member as well as an actor, became a hero on the picket lines when the story spread that he had informed NBC executives he would not report to work as scheduled because he was suffering from a case of "enlarged balls."

Rhimes's cast members were vociferous in their support for writers. A few days into the strike, *Grey's Anatomy* stars Patrick Dempsey, Ellen Pompeo, Katherine Heigl, and Sandra Oh walked out to the front of the production facility in the Silver Lake area of Los Angeles to hoist picket signs to make their case for the waiting news crews.

Ugly Betty star America Ferrera did the same thing during her breaks from filming across town at Raleigh Studios in Hollywood. So did actors on many other TV series. "A huge percentage of writers, actors and directors work from paycheck to paycheck. Studios don't have the product without the talent busting their butts," Ferrera told reporters on the first morning of the strike.

Actors had no choice but to keep working if they were under contract, but they could not be prevented from using their celebrity to gain attention for the writers' cause. Actors who made statements in support of the WGA were quick to note that their union, the Screen Actors Guild, would soon be battling the same issues, as SAG's contract covering film and TV work was due to expire in June 2008. "How greedy can they *get*," Oh exclaimed to reporters about the studios' position on new media residuals. "The networks are profiting from shows, from people downloading them on their computers for free, and they don't want to share the profits from that," Pompeo explained. Heigl, who had just seen her movie career ignite with the summer comedy hit *Knocked Up*, chimed in with an observation that neatly summed up the heart of the dispute: "I watch almost everything on the Internet now," Heigl declared.[13]

The shock of the writers actually walking out hit Hollywood like an earthquake, even though the studios and networks had been developing contingency plans for a walkout for nearly a year. In the month leading up to the expiration of the WGA contract, most actively employed film and TV writers worked around the clock, particularly those on TV series, to bank as many scripts as possible to allow their shows to keep shooting as long as possible after the strike ensued. Each of the major broadcast networks had a reserve of reality series ready to call up if production on scripted shows came to a halt. Every studio had run the numbers and conducted feasibility studies to determine how many employee suspension and layoff notices would be needed to allow them to weather a prolonged strike.

But when it happened, the strike still came as a belt in the gut to executives and staff at all levels. Network and studio lots stopped humming with production activity. Commissaries were half empty during the lunch rush period. Writers had been prepared by the guild's extensive education campaign for the jolt of upending their regular daily routines by going on strike. The employers had not.

The first entities to bear the brunt of the cessation of WGA-covered work were television's late-night talk shows and NBC mainstay *Saturday Night Live*. There was no banking of scripts for the nightly national programs that rely on topical humor and timely guests.

NBC's *The Tonight Show with Jay Leno, Late Night with Conan O'Brien*, and *Last Call with Carson Daly*; CBS's *The Late Show with David Letterman* and *The Late Late Show with Craig Ferguson*; ABC's *Jimmy Kimmel Live*; and Comedy Central's *The Daily Show with Jon Stewart* and *The Colbert Report* had no practical alternative but to go dark on November 5. With the exception of Carson Daly, the hosts of the late-night shows were also writers and WGA members.

Early on, they were inclined to support the WGA's cause by staying off the air, and the alternative of having to improvise entire shows for an undetermined period was a daunting task even for the quickest wits. Moreover, with the Screen Actors Guild staunchly supporting the WGA, it would be a challenge to book high-profile guests in a strike scenario where actors might have to cross picket lines to get to the show's studio (as several experienced later on in the strike). The networks were forced to cue up repeats, at a cost of tens of millions of dollars in lost advertising revenue per show.

Aside from news coverage of the strike, the fact that Jay Leno and David Letterman, *Saturday Night Live,* and the others were in repeats was the most visible sign of Hollywood's labor strife to the general public during the first half of the work stoppage. The majority of scripted prime-time series had enough scripts finished before the strike to stay in production for a few more weeks. The drought of fresh episodes of prime-time scripted series did not become readily apparent until mid-January. The networks usually run plenty of repeats and specials in December, because TV viewing levels overall typically drop during the holiday season.

The sudden halt to writing weighed heavily on the creative community, derailing plans and schedules for movie and TV productions that were carefully plotted months, if not years (in the case of feature films), earlier. But nowhere was the blow felt more acutely than in the production offices of the fall's fledgling new series. In all but the rare Cinderella story, there is nothing trickier than getting a new scripted television series through the production of its first thirteen episodes. Most new shows do not survive the creative Darwinism that goes on during the production of the first six to thirteen episodes after the pilot. This is the period when the cast members, writers, directors, and producers endure the exhausting process of finding what works and what does not work so well through on-air trial and error. The hope is that the show finds its footing, or at least impresses network executives enough to earn an order for additional episodes.

Startups are grueling even for the most seasoned creative professionals; it is an assignment to catch lightning in a bottle. And so it was an incredible blow to the momentum and confidence of those working on fall freshman shows to have that work shut down abruptly by an outside force. In most cases, new series were in the midst of producing episodes 7–10 when the strike began.

Beyond the jolt delivered to existing shows, the WGA walkout hit at another crucial point in the prime-time calendar: development season. November and December are the period when network executives hunker down on finding new projects for the following season. During the summer, just after the end of the season, broadcast network development executives typically order as many as 100 to 120 comedy and drama scripts for prospective pilots. Those scripts are usually turned in by Thanksgiving or shortly thereafter, and that is when executives winnow the list of hopefuls to the two dozen or so with enough promise to be shot as pilots. Pilots are generally turned in by late April. Executives evaluate them and often put them through market-research testing just before the networks make their fall-schedule presentations to major advertisers in New York in mid-May.

The November 5 start date of the strike ensured that the traditional timetable for prime-time development would be thrown out the window, which promised to extend the impact into the 2008–9 television season. Writers worked furiously to get first and second drafts of scripts in to networks before the November 5 "pencils down" deadline, but there was still no certainty about when writers would be free to resume the revising and polishing that are part and parcel of pilot development.

The threat of an extended disruption to not one but two television seasons was all part of the calculation made by WGA leaders in settling on the timing of the labor action. It was the first and loudest indication from the WGA that the walkout would be a "TV strike," or a fight that would turn on the issues that were most important to top television writer-producers. Those high-earning members in the past had wielded enough clout to subvert the guild's agenda, as proven during the 1988 strike with threats of a mass defection. But this time around, things were very different. "They were all once staff writers who were dependent upon residuals to help them through tough times," Bowman said. "Television writing is a collaboration between showrunners and their staffs. So to be unsupportive of your own writers' economic security would be both unethical and suicidal. Therefore, showrunners responded to the threat management's negotiating posture posed to residuals by leaving their shows. The issue was very clear here. Residuals were under threat. At long as the guild focused on this, showrunners stayed united."[14]

3

Sowing the Seeds

Patric Verrone was keenly aware of how significant the timing of the guild's walkout would be for the prime-time television business. After starting out as a lawyer, Verrone had been working as a television writer for more than twenty years.[1] By the time of the strike, Verrone had enjoyed a successful but not extraordinary career in television. He had made his mark writing for prime-time animated comedies, including Fox's *Futurama*, *The Simpsons*, and *The Critic*. He was known for having a far-out, sardonic sense of humor—one episode of *The Simpsons* he wrote involved the Simpson clan throwing a "chicken pox party."

Verrone was the definition of the "middle-class writer," the members who most relied on the gains the guild achieved in contract negotiations, which guild leaders emphasized in their public statements on the contract talks. Verrone and his wife, Maiya Williams, also a TV writer, novelist, and WGA member, were not in the top echelon of writers and showrunners. Residual income was an important source of support for their three children. As such, Verrone had a visceral understanding of how the prospect of seeing those residual fees dwindle in the digital era would threaten the well-being of most WGA members.

At first blush, Verrone seemed an unusual choice to lead the WGA West at such a momentous time for the industry. His detractors dismissed him as the Hollywood equivalent of a backbencher in Congress. As one CEO frequently lamented during the strike: "He's the third guy on 'Futurama,' for god's sake, and the writers are gonna follow *him*?"[2]

As a leader, however, Verrone was endowed with unshakable confidence and the courage of his convictions. His dedication and attention to detail are reflected in his hobby of crafting three-inch plastic figurines of American presidents, Supreme Court justices, and other historic personalities. The pastime has evolved into a side business for Verrone, who sells his figurines via the Internet, at www.verrone.com and on eBay, for twenty to thirty dollars apiece. As a kid he collected presidential figurines made by the Marx Toy Company, which stopped producing them by the early 1970s. In 2003, after *Futurama* was canceled, Verrone took it upon himself to bring his collection, which stopped at Richard Nixon, up to date. From there, he moved on to Supreme Court justices and other historic personalities ranging from Mark Twain to Martin Luther King Jr.[3]

A man of modest height and build, with a broad forehead and expressive face, Verrone has never fitted the stereotype of the Hollywood writer whose second skin is jeans and a T-shirt. Even at the depth of the strike, when WGA leaders had worked around the clock for weeks on end, in public Verrone was always impeccably groomed, usually with a coat and tie, and neatly trimmed dark hair. Verrone has the enunciation of a radio announcer and a standup comic's penchant for peppering his conversation with jokes and zingers. "Homogenization is good for milk, but bad for ideas. . . . To this we ask—got ideas?" Verrone quipped during testimony at a Federal Communications Commission hearing in October 2006 about the dangers of the concentration of media ownership among a handful of megaconglomerates.[4]

A native of Queens, New York, Verrone grew up in New York and Florida, where he went to high school. His father was an electrical engineer; his mother was a teacher and union member. He went to Harvard as an undergraduate, graduating magna cum laude with an AB in American history in 1981. He went on to earn a law degree from Boston College School of Law in 1984. After college, he moved to Fort Myers, Florida, to work for a firm handling real estate and estate-planning transactions. But he was not fulfilled.[5]

During Verrone's Harvard days, he had worked as an editor on the famed *Harvard Lampoon* humor magazine and befriended numerous classmates who went on to successful careers as film and TV writers, including his future wife, Maiya Williams. He was encouraged by Williams and others to come to Los Angeles to try his hand at comedy writing. He arranged to take a three-month sabbatical from the law firm that never ended.

Once in Los Angeles, he landed a job as a joke writer for Joan Rivers as she prepared for the late-night talk show that would mark the inauspicious launch of the fourth network, Fox Broadcasting Company. Verrone has said that he stood a few feet away from Rupert Murdoch on the night of the network's debut on October 9, 1986.[6]

From *The Joan Rivers Show*, Verrone moved on to writing jokes and monologues for *The Tonight Show Starring Johnny Carson*. He later worked on HBO's late-night satire *The Larry Sanders Show*. He was eventually recruited by Harvard classmates Al Jean and Mike Reiss, who had become top writer-producers on Fox's *The Simpsons*, to write for that show and another animated series they produced for the network, *The Critic*.

By this time, Verrone and Williams had married and were expecting their first child. Verrone had been a WGA member for seven years, but was dismayed to realize that he was in danger of losing his eligibility for health care benefits through the Writers Guild because *The Critic*, as an animated production, was not covered by a WGA contract. That tricky situation was a wake-up call to Verrone that spurred him to pay more attention to the WGA and what the guild did for its members.[7]

A few years later, when Verrone was hired to work on another Fox animated series, *Futurama*, he helped lead the successful effort to organize the writers of Fox's animated prime-time comedies to insist on WGA coverage for their shows, *The Simpsons*, *King of the Hill*, *Futurama*, and *Family Guy*. It was not an epic struggle. When informed by network executives in 1998 that writers on the highly profitable *Simpsons* wanted a WGA contract to ensure they would earn credits toward health insurance and other benefits, Peter Chernin, then head of 20th Century Fox's film and television operations, famously responded, "Well, *give* it to them."[8]

Verrone's involvement with the guild deepened after the animation organizing effort. In 2001 he ran for the post of secretary-treasurer, the number-three officer position at the WGA West. As a member of the board of directors, Verrone got a firsthand look at the guild's contract-negotiation strategies and its other priorities, and he was dismayed. Verrone came to feel that the union's executive leadership was too cozy with the industry and its top leaders, and too focused on maintaining labor peace in Hollywood, to aggressively represent writers' interests at the bargaining table.

Verrone served on the WGA West's negotiating committee during the contract negotiations in 2001 and again in 2004. In 2004 he and thirteen other members of the 2004 negotiating committee were so angered by how the WGA leadership handled the talks that they took out a full-page advertisement in the trade newspaper *Daily Variety* to voice their opposition. The ad ran on November 17, 2004, during the period when the WGA was holding its ratification vote among members. The ad marked the first public stirring of the Writers United caucus of WGA West members that would propel Verrone to the top of the guild.

By the time the contract reached in 2004 expired, on October 31, 2007, Verrone had twice been elected president of the WGA West by overwhelming majorities. Verrone and a slate of eight like-minded new board members first won their seats in September 2005 by waging a vociferous campaign that promised to get tough in contract talks, to seek better coordination with sister Hollywood unions, and to devote far more of the guild's resources to organizing and outreach. Verrone vowed to commit 30 percent of the guild's twenty-million-dollar annual budget to organizing efforts, compared to the 3 percent the WGA West had been spending. "All we lack is the will to make this a union that expands its jurisdiction with industrywide organizing campaigns to recapture market share and regenerate collective power," Verrone said while campaigning for the presidency in August 2005. "The conglomerates have themselves organized. So should we."[9] The election results that validated Verrone's approach were revealed on September 20, 2005, nine days before Verrone's forty-sixth birthday.

The first step taken by the Verrone-led board after the election was to remove executive director John McLean from the WGA West's highest paid position. McLean steered the 2001 and 2004 negotiations that had so riled Verrone and others. McLean had worked in labor relations at CBS for eighteen years before joining the WGA West in 1999. Verrone and others concluded that he was the wrong man to forcefully take on the new media residual fight and lead the guild into its future.

McLean was replaced on an interim basis by David Young, the guild's director of organizing. Young had joined the WGA West the year before, moving into the heart of Hollywood's creative community after several years as assistant director of organizing for the Laborers' California Organizing Fund, a construction-industry union.

Young, who grew up in Pasadena, California, came to the WGA West with a long résumé of union organizing in blue-collar and low-wage sectors. A tall man of medium build, Young's outwardly reserved personality is enhanced by a sharp intellect and the keen eye of a master campaign strategist. He spent time working as a plumber after graduating from San Diego State University with a BA in economics. He is a passionate trade unionist, unwavering in his belief in the ability of organized labor and collective bargaining to improve the lives of working people.[10]

Young's career included a stint as director of organizing for the Southern California–Nevada Regional Council of Carpenters. From 1991 to 1997, he worked for the Union of Needle Trades, Industrial, and Textile Employees (UNITE) during a period of strong growth for the garment-workers union. Young could point to many successes in his career before joining the WGA West, but one major defeat frequently cited by Young's detractors was a long campaign during his tenure at UNITE to organize low-wage employees of the apparel firm Guess, Inc., and its suppliers. Guess wound up moving thousands of jobs out of Southern California to Mexico.[11]

Young's move to the WGA in 2004 represented a 180-degree turn in the type of workers he was tasked with organizing, even with the grim conditions of reality TV's sweatshops. Once he became executive director of the WGA, Young became a polarizing figure in Hollywood labor circles. He was feared by some as a master propagandist who was using the WGA's contract negotiations to advance a broader social agenda far beyond the reasonable purview of movie and TV writers. But to many WGA members, he quickly became a heroic figure, an experienced fighter from outside the velvet rope who was not afraid to stand up to power. Young's resolve about labor's and management's roles did not lend itself to the Hollywood tradition of back-slapping and socializing as a way of getting business done.

Instead of courting industry rainmakers, Verrone and Young embarked on a member-outreach campaign that was unlike anything the guild had mounted since its formative years in the 1930s. WGA leaders and board members held countless meetings and informal get-togethers at the guild, in members' homes, in restaurants, and anyplace where Verrone and Young could get face time with writers. In 2007, as the start of the contract negotiations approached, the WGA West president traveled as far as Seattle, Portland, and San Francisco to meet with writers far outside the Hollywood hub. WGA leaders also stepped up their traditional workplace visits to the production offices of dozens of TV series to speak with writers and gauge general working conditions.[12]

Verrone wanted to hear from members. He wanted to let them know what the guild's priorities were and what he saw as the guild's obligations to members. He wanted to explain why the new regime was focused on expanding the WGA's clout by organizing in nontraditional sectors such as producers on reality TV shows. It was a stretch in the eyes of some writers, but Verrone had a persuasive argument that the people who edited hours and hours of vérité footage or shaped other content were in fact the "writers."

Most of all, Verrone wanted to put members on notice that the WGA needed to get serious—and get prepared to go on strike if need be—in its 2007 contract negotiations. Too much money had been left on the table for too long for the sake of avoiding a strike, Verrone argued. WGA members needed to understand the potency of a work stoppage as a leverage point for the guild in negotiations. Writers would need every bit of ammunition they had in fighting for their future livelihoods in a world dominated by the Internet. Writers needed to better understand how quickly and how significantly the entertainment marketplace, particularly in television, was changing in ways that promised to severely cut into writers' income.[13]

After two years of nonstop outreach, the WGA had accomplished its mission. The house parties and other gatherings opened the eyes of many members to the impact that new technologies promised to have on their rarefied world. Showrunners and writers who spent most of their days holed up in writers rooms generally did not have the time to think about much else beyond delivering next week's episode on time. And because so many screenwriters work in solitary conditions, Verrone's big-picture discussion of the industry, complete with Venn diagrams, was the first time many writers paused to consider the long-term impact of iTunes, YouTube, et al.

Through all of the face time and flesh pressing, the WGA West built a network of more than four hundred "contract captains," who volunteered to reach out to other members once the negotiations got started to build a communication tree. The contract captains pledged to spread the word about the issues and deliver updates as warranted to fifteen to twenty members. "I've volunteered to work as a captain to support these negotiations because we are right," TV writer Marjorie David wrote in the guild's September 2007 newsletter. "They are important to me because I want fair payment for my work, and I don't want to live in a country where one percent of the population rolls around in billions of dollars while everyone else sinks lower by the year. Anything I can do to stop that trend, I will do."[14]

Contract captains like David became strike captains as the WGA's talks with the AMPTP deteriorated. "That's how you move 8,000 people into action," Young said during the second week of the strike.[15]

The barnstorming by Verrone and Young came in sharp contrast to the guild's leadership style during the years immediately preceding Verrone's election. The WGA West looked like the Keystone Kops in early 2004 when president Victoria Riskin was forced to resign after she was found to be ineligible according to the guild's constitution to serve a second term as president. She was replaced on an interim basis by Charles Holland, the board's vice president, who was forced to resign barely two months later when questions surfaced about the veracity of claims he made about his background.[16]

Riskin's problem was that she had not earned enough income under WGA-governed writing contracts during the previous four years to be considered an active member, as was required when she ran for reelection as president in 2003. Riskin's eligibility was formally challenged on the heels of the September election by the campaign manager of her opponent. The controversy drew the attention of officials from the

Department of Labor, which prompted the WGA West board of directors to bring in an outside investigator, labor-law expert and Stanford University professor William B. Gould, to review the complaint. Eric Hughes, the member who challenged Riskin for the presidency, had long been a thorn in the side of WGA leaders.

Riskin fought hard to hold on to her post but ultimately resigned under pressure in January 2004.[17] Within weeks, Holland's hasty resignation added to the guild's embarrassment when he was forced to step down amid questions about statements he had made about having served in a US Army special-forces unit, among other claims.[18]

Gould's report recommended that Riskin resign and that the guild hold a new election in September 2004 that was supervised by the Department of Labor. In that rerun, Hughes was easily defeated by Daniel Petrie Jr., a respected former WGA West president and board member who had been tapped as the interim replacement for Holland.

The WGA West's internal problems handicapped the guild just as it was embarking on contract negotiations with the Alliance of Motion Picture and Television Producers. WGA West and WGA East members wound up working for nearly seven months beyond the May 2, 2004, expiration of the previous contract before the membership ratified the three-year deal that expired on October 31, 2007.

There was heated speculation at the time about the WGA going on strike, but it was nothing more than talk. The WGA West's public leadership scandals had greatly complicated the guild's tactical planning for the negotiations. There was no way the WGA, with the distraction of a federal probe and mandated election rerun, could have pulled off an effective work stoppage among members. The guild knew it, and the studios knew it.

To some WGA members, Riskin's ascent to the presidency was an example of the clubby nature of the management of the WGA West and the composition of its board of directors. Riskin, the daughter of famed screenwriter Robert Riskin and *King Kong* star Fay Wray, is married to David Rintels, a former WGA West president and longtime vocal force in the guild. Riskin and Rintels are among an older generation of writers who had long dominated the WGA board and officer positions. The election of John Wells, the producer of such high-end drama series as *ER* and *The West Wing*, as president of the WGA West from 1999 to 2001 was a rare example of an A-list producer leading the guild at the height of his or her professional game.

The emergence of Verrone as a candidate for the presidency in the guild's regularly scheduled 2005 election was not surprising. He had served as secretary-treasurer for two terms, and he had been a member of the 2001 and 2004 contract-negotiating committees, serving as cochair in 2004. Verrone mounted an unusually elaborate campaign for the unpaid position. He assembled a slate of like-minded candidates to run for the open board seats with him under the banner "Writers United."[19] The main tenet of the group's platform was that the guild needed to devote much more of its annual budget to organizing and recruiting new members working in such nontraditional sectors as reality TV and video games. "My theme is going to be all organizing, all the time," Verrone said in June 2005.[20]

The Writers United campaign echoed Verrone's disappointment with the 2004 contract; a number of the board candidates had served on the negotiating committee with Verrone. Led by Verrone, they sounded the alarm on the need for the guild to take a tougher stance in the 2007 contract talks.

In a move that predicted how Verrone would govern, Writers United coordinated dozens of small group meetings with members at private homes and restaurants and on TV-show sets. After the scandals of 2004, the Writers United campaign was a welcome sign to many that the WGA had a renewed energy that would be good for the guild. Verrone's slate easily defeated its primary competition, a group of candidates who dubbed themselves the "Common Sense" slate. That group opposed Writers United's plan for a vast expansion of organizing efforts. In the end, Writers United commanded nearly 68 percent of the vote in one of the highest turnouts for a presidential election in the guild's history.[21]

Writers United recruited a member, Roger Wolfson, with political experience to serve as a kind of unofficial campaign adviser. As explained by Wolfson, Writers United impressed members simply by articulating a vision for how the guild should be governed, in the wake of the

Riskin-Holland controversies, and a strategy for approaching the 2007 contract talks.

Writers United had turned out the vote by training a huge team of vote captains and honing a singular message of bringing the guild into the new era. The Writers United slate managed to focus the energy of the membership and gave voice to their concerns about the impending negotiations. Not only did this lead to victory, but it also demonstrated an organizational structure that would prove invaluable in the case of a strike.[22]

The new regime at the WGA West grabbed the industry's attention just days after the election with the abrupt dismissal of executive director John McLean and the appointment of Young as his interim replacement.[23] Labor executives at the networks and studios kept a close eye on Verrone's moves. Their wariness of the WGA West's new leadership increased, as there was no sign of Verrone tempering the stridency of his public statements about expanding the guild's leverage through organizing or the need to "empower" members for the 2007 contract talks.[24] Young, even in his interim status, quickly implemented a major shakeup of the WGA West staff, forcing out a number of senior executives, including chief spokeswoman Cheryl Rhoden, a nineteen-year employee, and deputy executive director Marshall Goldberg. Young would soon recruit a number of union executives with strong backgrounds in organizing and mounting labor actions but no experience in the entertainment industry.

Amid these shuffles, there was plenty of palace intrigue within the guild to keep WGA watchers engaged. But there were two battles with studios that the guild took on during Verrone's first year in office that set the tone for the newly assertive—some called it militant—approach taken by the WGA.

In one case, the guild was handed a victory by NBC when the network overreached in ordering additional work from writers on original Internet content without setting firm guidelines for compensation. The dispute bubbled up as NBC made a concerted effort to produce "webisodes" and other original Internet content tied to most of its prime-time series for the 2006–7 season. NBC's aggressive move to file an unfair labor-practice charge against the guild with the National Labor Relations Board

(NLRB) gave the WGA's new regime a perfectly timed chance to flex some muscle on behalf of influential showrunner members.

The other case saw the WGA's new regime trying to fulfill campaign promises of organizing producers in reality TV. But the WGA West stumbled badly in its attempt to secure a union contract for a dozen staffers on the hit reality program *America's Next Top Model*. Wooed by Young and his team of organizers, the *Top Model* producers asserted that they functioned as writers, or "storytellers," for the show and should be allowed to work under a WGA contract. After a seventy-one-day strike, the guild found itself outmaneuvered by the production company and a fellow entertainment-industry union. The outcome made the WGA look ineffectual in achieving its stated goal of expanding its reach in the fast-growing reality TV sector.

To Hollywood's CEOs, the *Top Model* situation reinforced their belief that the guild was fighting an uphill battle in its efforts to gain a toehold in reality. On the surface, it also cemented the conventional wisdom that the WGA West did not have its act together enough to pull off a prolonged work stoppage. In hindsight, however, the fight over the *Top Model* writers in 2006 was a warm-up for the industry-wide walkout that would hit the following year. Young said as much in an essay on the guild's reality organizing campaign written before the *Top Model* situation arose:

> I believe deeply in the power of the strike as an economic weapon. But I've also learned that our struggles have a David-and-Goliath element to them, and that winning campaigns against huge corporations requires us to utilize every weapon that we can develop and be prepared to attack every weakness that the other side may have. We have strength in numbers but we also have to be prepared to take smart risks to achieve our objective. In the coming months you can expect to see the guild engage in some out-of-the-box tactics that we have never used before. These tactics may lead industry executives to accuse us of breaking the "gentleman's agreement" that has existed between the talent and the studios. . . . We have taken some significant first steps in what could be a serious struggle. But I believe this fight will make us stronger and that it will inspire the network and studio heads to take very seriously

the needs of our membership in the next round of MBA negotiations in 2007 and beyond.[25]

The WGA West's skirmish with NBC over the production of webisodes for several NBC Universal–produced prime-time series was driven by the same fundamental disputes over new media that would divide the guild and the studios during the 2007 contract negotiations. It also reflected the television industry's fitful effort to use traditional media to harness the power of the Internet. NBC sought to extend the value of its TV properties with original webisodes. It was as much an effort to attract online advertising dollars as it was an exercise in trying to keep the NBC brand relevant to Internet-savvy viewers.

NBC was not the first network to commission original Internet content derived from its shows. But it intended to have the most expansive slate of original Internet content of any major network in the 2006–7 season. The "webisodes" were two- to four-minute shorts featuring characters and cast members from *The Office, Heroes,* and *Crossing Jordan,* among other shows.

The WGA and NBC could not even agree on how to characterize the webisodes as a business transaction. The guild scoffed at the network's contention that they were "promotional" material that did not require additional pay for writers. And the sides could not see eye to eye on what would amount to fair compensation for writing work done on these shorts.[26]

NBC's push on webisodes also touched a nerve for writers because it veered into the gray area known as "separated rights," or the stipulation that writers who create a film or TV program have certain rights when a spin-off, sequel, or other new product is derived from their existing work. They are also due additional compensation.

The battle of the webisodes did not start with show creators demanding additional payment for the webisodes. It started with an effort by Greg Daniels, showrunner of NBC's *The Office,* to get the young writer that he had chosen to pen the *Office* webisodes into the guild. Jason Kessler had been an assistant to the writing staff of *The Office*—a common entry-level route to a TV writing career. As it became apparent to Daniels in the spring of 2006 that the webisodes would require a dedicated writer of their own, he opted to give the job to the promising assistant, who was not yet a member of the guild. As a longtime guild member, Daniels instinctively sought to facilitate WGA membership for Kessler once he was tapped for the assignment.

NBC executives did not balk at Kessler's assignment or his entry into the WGA. But in preparing some paperwork for Kessler, NBC business-affairs executives determined that there was a provision in the WGA's master contract stipulating that the specific terms of the writers' compensation would be negotiated on a case-by-case basis. NBC Universal's TV production arm was obligated to make payments to the WGA's pension and health plan on Kessler's behalf (based on a percentage of his total earnings for the job), but NBC took the position that the pay rate for webisode work was not spelled out in the guild's Minimum Basic Agreement.

The WGA, of course, balked at NBC's plan for Kessler's employment, and Young immediately took steps to raise red flags about webisode production with Daniels and other NBC showrunners. The guild pressed NBC executives to negotiate a separate contract specifically to cover webisodes so that pay rates would be uniform for all writers working in the format. The WGA did not want a young writer with no clout to set a compensation precedent for a new medium. NBC did itself no favors with its showrunners by insisting in legalese in the paperwork it submitted to the guild on Kessler's behalf that it would reserve the right in other instances to deem webisodes promotional material that did not require any additional compensation to writers, actors, and directors.

Even before the *Office* webisodes scuffle ensued, Young had let labor executives at the studios and networks know that the WGA was increasingly concerned about the growing prevalence of made-for-Internet content and the lack of appropriate compensation for the work. Among those with whom Young had discussed the webisode problem were the same NBC executives who were working with Daniels to sort out Kessler's situation.

A few weeks before he was to drop the "interim" tag from his title as WGA West executive director, Young told NBC executives that the provision in the Minimum Basic Agreement that NBC cited as allowing for case-by-case negotiations of salary applied to wholly original works created for the Internet, not to material derived from existing TV shows. The clause in question was included in a side letter added to the guild's 2001 MBA, crafted when Internet video delivery was still herky-jerky and definitely not ready for prime time. Young insisted that NBC would have to negotiate a separate contract covering webisodes before WGA members would render their services.

WGA leaders moved quickly to inform members of the guild's position on webisodes. In late July, the WGA hosted a dinner at a popular Los Angeles restaurant, Pinot Bistro, for Daniels, *Heroes* creator and executive producer Tim Kring, and a few other showrunners. Young was earnest and direct in telling his guests that the WGA needed them to present a united front on the webisode issue. If the guild hoped to make any gains for writers in new media, it had to stand firm and demand that networks and studios negotiate detailed contract terms that would set the floor for all writers' compensation in the new realm. The webisode issue was also discussed at a more elaborate dinner and issues forum the WGA hosted the same month for about a hundred members at the Beverly Hilton hotel.

The guild's concerns were taken to heart by the showrunners. They stopped working on the webisodes and explained the guild's position to their writing staffs. Alarmed at the prospect of NBC's plans derailing, NBC Universal labor executives, led by senior vice president Keith Gorham, held two meetings with Young and other guild staffers in late July and early August.

The NBC executives seemed to realize that the webisode wrangle was a precursor to tough talks for the 2007 master contract negotiations. Gorham suggested that NBC would agree to retroactively pay the webisode writers according to whatever terms were negotiated for made-for-Internet content in the next master contract. Young rejected that idea. The WGA sent letters to NBC showrunners on August 2 and August 10 reiterating the guild's position and asking writers to be patient while the guild pressed the issue.

Around this time, the WGA and NBC filed grievances against each other with a private arbiter, in accordance with the guidelines for conflict resolution spelled out in the MBA. But NBC did the WGA one better. It filed an unfair labor-practice charge against the guild with the National

Labor Relations Board. NBC asserted that Young specifically had overstepped his bounds by encouraging the showrunners to breach their contractual responsibilities as producers—distinct from their WGA-covered writing responsibilities—in refusing to even oversee work done by others on the webisodes. NBC claimed the showrunners were threatened with disciplinary action by the union if they worked as producers on the webisodes. NBC also tried to rattle the cages of the showrunners by sending letters to their personal attorneys suggesting that they were in breach of their contracts by refusing to perform producing duties on the webisodes.

In testimony before an administrative law judge in Los Angeles in December 2006, Daniels, Kring, and others denied that they had ever been threatened with fines or other action by Young or other guild members. The showrunners maintained Young had only ever discussed their writing services, and they emphasized that they could not oversee another writer's work without using their own writing skills.

NBC's complaint was dismissed by administrative-law judge Gregory Z. Meyerson in February 2007. The decision was upheld on appeal to the NLRB board in Washington, DC, five months later. Perhaps inspired by his interaction with TV writers, Meyerson observed in a footnote to his decision, "In view of the paucity of evidence I am reminded of the words from an old television commercial, 'Where's the beef?'"

But the guild's real victory came long before the judge issued his decision. The WGA proved to be strong, forceful, and proactive in the eyes of some of its most prominent members, as the webisode dustup at NBC was closely watched by other showrunners. Perhaps most significantly, Verrone and Young demonstrated to management that the guild could summon the support of top members to take a hard line on compensation for new media.

The WGA's position was bolstered by the fact that two months before the guild began sparring with NBC, Disney's Touchstone Television production unit hammered out agreements with the WGA, SAG, and DGA to cover work done on a series of original shorts tied to the ABC hit *Lost*. The *Missing Pieces* shorts were designed for new media and distributed via Verizon's mobile phone network and later on ABC.com and iTunes.

The guild agreements were instigated at the insistence of *Lost* showrunners Carlton Cuse, who would serve the following year on the WGA's negotiating committee, and Damon Lindelof. The *Lost* guild agreements came about in part through the sway that Lindelof and Cuse had with ABC as the stewards of one of its most profitable TV properties. And the deal reached represented a rare example of cooperation among the WGA, DGA, and SAG. "This deal could not have been reached without the courage of our members who stood together and insisted that this work be guild-covered," Verrone said in announcing the *Lost* guild agreements in April 2006. "As a result of the solidarity of the WGA, SAG, and DGA, no guild was forced to take a lesser deal."[27]

But *Lost* was definitely a unique case. ABC's plans for made-for-Internet properties were not as expansive as NBC's, and ABC and Disney executives were quick to let it be known that the deal was not "precedential" as far as future projects were concerned. As a worldwide success for Disney, demand for *Lost* Web shorts and advertising connected to them was so strong that the studio was willing to commit to a residual formula similar to the existing pay scale for theatrical films telecast on cable outlets, plus a onetime $125 "reuse" fee if the shorts were made available for more than thirteen weeks.

A year after the NLRB's final decision on the NBC webisodes, NBC executives were still smarting from their run-in with the WGA. At an annual television-industry press event in July 2007, days before the WGA and AMPTP were to begin their contract talks, NBC Entertainment cochairman Marc Graboff and the AMPTP's Nick Counter blasted the guild's conduct in the webisode incidents. Counter emphasized that the NLRB's ruling reaffirmed that the WGA had no right to instruct its members to withhold producing services—an issue that would soon be relevant to more than just Internet shorts. Counter's choice of words, in a roomful of reporters, was telling. "We're going to have a down and dirty fight to get (the WGA) to live up to their agreement," Counter vowed.[28]

The *America's Next Top Model* tussle boiled over in the summer of 2006, right around the time David Young was chosen as the guild's permanent executive director. However, the WGA's interest in organizing selected producers and story editors in the reality TV realm predated Young's arrival at the guild. Patric Verrone's predecessor, Daniel Petrie Jr., had made it a high-profile priority of his tenure as president in 2004 and 2005.

At that time, Verrone was the guild's secretary-treasurer and head of its committee dedicated to organizing—a modest effort that would grow exponentially after Young was recruited as director of organizing in July 2004. With prodding from Verrone and others, the guild began to focus on recruiting in the reality sector because it feared that the major networks were grooming reality producers into a vast nonunion workforce that would blunt the WGA's leverage—even if it went on strike—in contract negotiations. By the guild's count, the boom in unscripted primetime programming, ignited in 1999 and 2000 by the overnight success of ABC's *Who Wants to Be a Millionaire* and CBS's *Survivor,* had cost Hollywood writers some one thousand jobs, as networks ordered fewer comedy and drama series.

A bid to expand the WGA's jurisdiction to encompass the new breed of unscripted prime-time shows (it already had jurisdiction over quiz shows and variety shows) had been part of the guild's contract proposals in 2004, but it was quickly tabled as a nonstarter for the AMPTP. As such, the guild turned its focus to organizing workers on a show-by-show basis, with the hopes of spurring a domino effect that would prod the conglomerates to agree to negotiate blanket terms with the WGA for reality workers, if only for the stake of stability.

To build support within the industry, Petrie took aim at the grueling working conditions, low pay, long hours, and lack of health care and pension benefits for the production staffers. Those producers who are tasked with assembling episodes from hours and hours of raw footage, and who are responsible for devising challenges and surprises for contestants, function as the writers for this fast-growing genre of television, the WGA argued. "Reality TV is a 21st-century telecommunications industry sweatshop," Petrie told reporters in June 2005. The guild sought to publicize the fact that through meetings and other outreach efforts, it had collected one thousand signatures from reality production workers who wanted to join the WGA West.[29]

As part of this outreach campaign, the guild assisted numerous employees of unscripted TV shows in filing complaints with the state of California against production companies for labor and wage violations, including the lack of overtime pay for marathon workdays. But for all of these efforts, the guild had no success in organizing a single show. One of the challenges in putting public pressure on the production companies was that most reality shows hailed from smaller independent companies. These outfits were less concerned about a burst of negative publicity than a larger company would be. And they were more inclined to resist anything that would result in even a small increase in their production costs. The WGA did not have the leverage of shaming a Hollywood institution like Warner Bros. or Paramount for putting staffers through eighteen-hour days for weeks without a break.

Another obstacle for the guild was the bias in the creative community against unscripted programs. As widespread and successful as reality programming has become, a pervasive feeling remains that such shows are second-class TV citizens compared to scripted series. And there is a deep vein of resentment for the shrinkage in the TV job market for writers, directors, and producers as unscripted programs fill time slots that otherwise would have gone to comedies and dramas.

Despite the lack of progress, the heavy emphasis on reality organizing did not hurt Verrone and the Writers United slate in the 2005 election. Verrone was eloquent in insisting the guild needed to ensure its ability to effectively represent the interests of writers was not diminished by the changing programming tide. Put another way: if you can't beat 'em, organize 'em.

The focus on reality organizing undoubtedly played a part in the hiring of Young as the WGA West's director of organizing in 2004. His background in the hardscrabble world of garment workers and carpenters made him well suited to the job of cracking a hard nut for the WGA. The reality TV sector, with its ample horror stories of harsh working conditions and paltry compensation, lent itself to a blue-collar activist approach to organizing. These were not sheltered, well-paid film and TV writers. These were mostly young people with little experience in TV who were tasked with monitoring around-the-clock shoots, editing, and postproduction sessions with no overtime or health benefits.

By the spring of 2006, it became apparent that the successful competition series *America's Next Top Model* would provide a unique opportunity for the WGA to kick-start its organizing campaign. *Top Model*, a modeling competition hosted by model-actress Tyra Banks, was the top-rated program on the UPN network. In January 2006, CBS Corporation and Warner Bros., the parent companies of UPN and its rival, the WB Network, surprised the industry by announcing that the two money-losing networks would combine into a single entity in September 2006.

Top Model was a prized asset of the newly minted CW network. The new network's leaders decided that the CW would debut with a two-hour edition of the show on September 20. The WGA calculated that *Top Model*'s independent production company and the network would be vulnerable to pressure from the WGA because of the show's importance to the CW's launch plans. Most important, the appropriate staffers on *Top Model*—six who were designated "show producers" and six who were "associate show producers"—were uniformly eager to secure a WGA contract. For sure, they had been heavily courted by WGA officials. According to one producer, Daniel Blau, who later became disenchanted with the WGA, guild representatives assured the *Top Model* 12 that their counterparts on a number of other reality programs were on the verge of going on strike if their production companies refused to recognize the WGA as their collective bargaining representative.[30]

After many meetings, the *Top Model* producers signed union cards, and guild officials began the process of trying to negotiate a contract with the show's production company, Anisa Productions, headed by *Top Model* executive producer Ken Mok. Not surprisingly, Mok balked at allowing WGA representation for producers on his show. CW executives were also unwilling because of the precedent it could set for the new network. The official line from Mok and CW was that the guild should follow the formal protocol of holding a secret-ballot election among the *Top Model* staffers through the auspices of the National Labor Relations Board. That amounted to a delay tactic, because the NLRB election process could take as long as a year to complete. The WGA countered that there was plenty of precedent for production companies negotiating a WGA contract without an election if staffers voluntarily agreed to sign union cards.

With the sides at an impasse, the *Top Model* fight went public. On Thursday, July 20, the twelve staffers staged a "stutter stop," in which they walked out of the production office for a few hours in the morning (they milled around in the driveway of the building before going back inside) in a bid to prod Mok to meet with guild representatives. That night, the *Top Model* 12 met with guild officials and by themselves at the WGA West headquarters. They took a secret-ballot vote of their own to ensure that one and all were committed to going through with the walkout. When the *Top Model* workers reported the results of their unanimous vote to WGA staffers and members who were helping them plot their next steps, they received a standing ovation.

The following morning, July 21, the *Top Model* producers declared themselves on strike against Anisa Productions, and they began picketing on the sidewalk outside Mok's West Los Angeles office on busy Sepulveda Boulevard. The red-and-black "Writers Guild on Strike" signs, some of them vintage 1988, featured handwritten slogans tailored to the occasion: "Work it like you have don't have health insurance." "Reality needs a rewrite." "The top show on the CW is the only show that's not union." "Not supporting unionization: That's not model behavior." "What we're asking for is very simple—just a basic contract," striking *Top Model* producer Clint Catalyst told reporters on the first day of the strike.[31]

The WGA carefully stage-managed the *Top Model* walkout. On the first day, the guild arranged a morning rally that included speeches from Screen Actors Guild president Alan Rosenberg and John Connolly, president of the American Federation of Television and Radio Artists, among others. The WGA recruited members and other supporters to join in the picketing in the unrelenting midsummer LA sun. The scene outside the *Top Model* office would become all too familiar for entertainment-industry workers in a little more than a year. But in the summer of 2006, the sight of TV producers hoisting picket signs and chanting pro-union slogans was seen as a novelty by many in the industry.

WGA staff coordinated the picketing and the public relations effort throughout the two-and-a-half-month strike. One photo-op event was held on a blazing-hot August day when ten former WGA West presidents joined the picket line, a visual meant to demonstrate the support among past guild leaders for the reality organizing campaign. But by the end of August, the ranks of the supporters had thinned, and the determination at the top of the WGA to prevail in the *Top Model* campaign appeared to wane, in the view of Blau.

On September 20, the day of the CW network launch, the guild held a "unity rally" at Los Angeles's Pan Pacific Park, located around the corner from the WGA's headquarters and just down the street from CBS's Television City lot. The midday event drew more than one thousand writers, some of them the prominent showrunners who were being so ardently wooed by the guild. Some of those who had not paid any attention to the *Top Model* strike were impressed by the level of organization and political campaign-style messaging on display. The event ended with a march down to CBS's Television City, as an effort to call attention to CBS's role in the dispute as the co-owner of the CW.

The tone of the speeches at the rally made it clear that the WGA's call for "unity" was about much more than the cause of twelve striking workers on a reality show. "We are at, I believe, one of the watershed moments in our history," WGA West board member Phil Alden Robinson, the Oscar-nominated screenwriter of *Field of Dreams,* told the enthusiastic crowd. "This happens every 20 years or so, when a generation of writers sees the landscape changing and is faced with a crossroads, at which we can either stand united and win, or stand apart and lose."[32]

Patric Verrone left little doubt about the scope of his ambition as WGA West president in his address, spelling out what he termed "the Writers Guild doctrine for the 21st century":

> When we win more victories in animation, it will be because we are united. When we win contracts for cable writers in nonfiction and comedy-variety, it will be because we are united. When we win a contract for the "America's Next Top Model" writers, and for all reality writers and editors with us today, it will be because we are united. When we demand our fair share on downloads, when we demand guild wages and benefits on all new media, when we demand that every piece of media with a

moving image on a screen or with a recorded human voice must have a writer, and that every writer must have a WGA contract, (the companies) will know that we are united.[33]

In many ways, the WGA's *Top Model* strike was a practice drill for the much larger campaign to come. But it ended in an unqualified defeat for the WGA and in dismissals for the twelve employees.

The WGA's move on *Top Model* irked the notoriously protective union for Hollywood's craft and technical workers, the International Alliance of Theatrical Stage Employees. IATSE took the position that some of the work done by those who sought WGA coverage actually fell under its purview as the umbrella organization for the union representing movie and TV editors. An IATSE-affiliated local had cut a deal with Mok in 2005 to represent editors working on *Top Model.*

IATSE used the opening created by the show's standoff with the WGA to swoop in and cut a deal, after a federally monitored election, to cover even more below-the-line workers on *Top Model,* from camera operators to grips to sound and lighting technicians. Mok and the CW were open to expanding IATSE representation on the show because they had decided to replace the striking story producers with IATSE-represented editors.

When *Top Model* reorganized its production operation to eliminate the jobs of show producers and associate show producers, the twelve striking staffers were terminated. Mok issued a statement saying that after the story producers walked out, he developed a "new system" for producing the episodes that "puts our material directly in the hands of our editors without the intermediate step of story producers."[34] IATSE's pugnacious president, Thomas Short, ultimately issued a statement chiding the WGA for having "mishandled" the *Top Model* organizing effort "due to zero experience at organizing in the entertainment industry"—a direct jab at Young.[35]

The *Top Model* strike ended on September 29, 2006—one year and a day before the WGA West and WGA East sent tremors through the industry by initiating a membership vote to authorize an industry-wide strike. But by then, Hollywood's nerves were already on edge. Relations between the WGA and the AMPTP were already showing signs of strain. The depth of the distrust on both sides was vividly illustrated in late 2006 after the WGA informed the AMPTP it would not begin contract negotiations in January, as the sides had previously discussed. The AMPTP wanted to start the negotiations well before the October 31, 2007, contract expiration to avoid the pressure of having to sort out so many complex issues on a tight deadline. The WGA wanted the leverage of the clock running out to amplify its strike threat.

The AMPTP lifted the veil on previously private discussions with the WGA on the timing of negotiations by blasting the guild's decision to the media. AMPTP president Nick Counter said he was "shocked and dismayed" by the WGA's change of heart, and he needled the WGA West by pointing to Young's lack of experience in Hollywood contract negotiations. "Mr. Young is new to our business, and he may not have assessed the situation in the best possible way," Counter asserted.[36]

The AMPTP's move brought a sharp response from the WGA, which accused the AMPTP of using scare tactics and engaging in "histrionics," among other things. The exchange over the negotiations date set a pattern for heated verbal volleys between the sides that surprised industry veterans. "The castigations flung by both sides were equally hyperbolic and unprofessional," says Dick Wolf, creator and executive producer of *Law and Order* and its spin-offs. Wolf, one of the most successful TV producers of the modern TV era, was highly critical of the WGA's tactics throughout the strike.[37]

Although the WGA had a long history of spurning early talks and negotiating down to the wire, this time around, with the enormity of the issues on the table, the guild's decision to delay was a warning shot. The WGA said that it wanted more time to see how the nascent markets for paid downloads and Web streaming were shaping up before the guild crafted formal compensation proposals.

Verrone found a colorful way to describe the WGA's tactical approach to the contract talks in a November 2006 interview on the entertainment industry–oriented talk show *Sunday Morning Shootout* on cable channel AMC. "Because we don't have crystal balls, we need to have . . . the other kind of balls," Verrone said.[38]

4

Brinksmanship Across the Table

"Ugly" is the only way to describe the tenor of the relations between the Writers Guild of America and the Alliance of Motion Picture and Television Producers in the months leading up to the October 31, 2007, expiration of its MBA. The verbal sparring between the sides grew steadily in the first few months of the year after the WGA settled on July 16 as the start date for the negotiations—despite the AMPTP's push to begin much sooner. The AMPTP raised hackles in April by floating the idea that a multiyear study of the new media marketplace was needed before any decisions could be made about new residual formulas. The WGA in May went public with details of its contract proposals, some of which bordered on ridiculous in the eyes of the studios. No single incident captures the petty nastiness that poisoned the atmosphere at the negotiating table better than the debacle that became known as the Chair Incident.[1]

Six days before the contract was to expire, AMPTP executives and their entourage of about forty studio and network labor and legal executives traveled to the WGA West headquarters in LA's Fairfax district for another negotiating session. The previous thirteen meetings had been held at the AMPTP's headquarters in the Encino area of the San Fernando Valley—a thirty-minute drive from WGA headquarters in the best of traffic circumstances. The AMPTP had a cavernous conference room that was specially designed for collective bargaining and the dozens of participants that union contract talks typically draw. There was plenty of elbow room around the extra-long rectangular conference table, and several rows of seats on one side to handle the overflow. The seats had schoolroom-style desktops attached to allow for note taking.

There were no comparable amenities when Nick Counter, Carol Lombardini, and the others gathered in the lobby of the WGA West late on the morning of Thursday, October 25. The group was led to a large conference room on the second floor of the guild's four-story building. Shortly thereafter, the group was asked to come up to a conference room on the fourth floor to begin the session. As the executives filed into the room used for WGA West board meetings, it became clear before even half of them were through the door that the space was too small to accommodate everyone.

David Young was sitting next to Patric Verrone and John Bowman at the conference table. He stood up and explained that they had been expecting only half as many people from the AMPTP. With about eight negotiating committee members and a handful of WGA staffers around the table, there were not even enough chairs to go around.

Counter suggested that they go back down to the larger second-floor conference room. Young stiffened and surprised the AMPTP group by responding quickly with an emphatic "No." The WGA representatives were not moving from the fourth floor, Young informed Counter. There was an uncomfortable silence for what seemed like a long time to many in the room. Finally, one of the studio labor executives raised his voice in anger at what he viewed as a power play by the guild. "That led to some yelling back and forth across the table. It was unnecessary and stupid," recalls one participant.

The situation quickly became so heated that WGA negotiating committee member Marc Cherry, creator and executive producer of *Desperate Housewives*, hurried out of the room to hunt for available chairs. When Cherry, a showrunner worth many millions thanks to the success of his ABC series, came back with two chairs in tow, the ridiculousness of the situation was laid bare. "There were people on the (WGA) negotiating committee who were clearly embarrassed," recalls the participant. After Cherry made another run for chairs, this time with help from a few others, Lombardini joked that he would be rewarded with an honorary membership card in Local 44, the IATSE-affiliated union for prop masters and set decorators.

The flap over the chairs boiled down to a lack of communication between the principal players. It was a central problem throughout the negotiations and strike period that hampered both sides' ability to make progress on issues much more important than chairs.

Long before the studios and WGA faced off at the bargaining table, Counter and Lombardini were convinced that the WGA was determined to go on strike no matter what the studios offered. They had paid attention to the extensive member-outreach campaign spearheaded by Verrone and Young. They had watched warily as the guild pressed its reality organizing campaign to the point of the *America's Next Top Model* strike. There was unease among the CEOs about the guild's increasingly activist stance in challenging the growth of product placement and branded integration in television and film.

In September 2005, the WGA organized a small group to crash a conference in New York hosted by the magazine *Advertising Age.* The protesters disrupted a panel session in progress and passed out fliers to a surprised roomful of advertising and entertainment-industry executives.[2] In February 2006, a group of about one hundred WGA and SAG members, including Verrone, protested with picket signs outside the Beverly Hills Hotel, where a similar conference on branded entertainment was taking place.[3]

For two years, WGA leaders had seemingly made every effort to heighten the stakes, and the tension, of the 2007 contract talks. The signs that the guild was preparing for a strike were unmistakable, from Verrone's rhetoric to Young's ascent to WGA West executive director to the backgrounds of the new WGA staffers recruited by Young.

Faced with a union that had promised to get tough with management, the AMPTP's game plan was to come out swinging. Counter opened the 2007 negotiations by putting forth two unusual proposals for structuring the deal, both of which could only be viewed by writers as onerous. One involved a radical top-to-bottom overhaul of the entire residual system, in ways that were far less generous to the middle-range writers. The other was the study proposal, which promised to forestall any new media residuals for at least three years.

At a time when frustration in the creative community over new media compensation was palpable, the decision to open with such a provocative move supports the belief, firmly held among many writers, that the

AMPTP was goading the WGA to strike. "We were set up by the AMPTP," says a WGA negotiating committee member. "They had every intention of making us go on strike, unless they thought we would cave, because they gave us these two proposals that were useless."[4]

On the first day of negotiations, Counter had the floor as he presented the two proposals for the guild to choose from as a starting point for the negotiations. The route the AMPTP favored, Counter made clear, called for the guild and the conglomerates to jointly conduct (and split the cost of) a three-year study of the new media marketplace for entertainment, in all its permutations. The goal would be to measure the value of these emerging markets. Gathering more information over time would allow the industry to determine which business models were likely to take root, and would in turn allow the studio negotiators to construct equitable compensation formulas. The rub was that during this three-year period, compensation terms for new media would be unchanged from the 2004 contract. That meant no payment for Web streaming and continuing with the home video rate for paid downloads.

For the AMPTP to propose that everything remain status quo for writers for another three years after the WGA had so fired up its membership about new media was nonsensical. It indicated that the top brass at the networks and studios had lost touch with the creative community; otherwise, the CEOs would have known instinctively that the study proposal would never fly and that the thorough residuals revamp would be a call to arms.

The WGA brought to the table a twenty-six-point proposal that ran the gamut of the mundane—standard 3.5 percent increases in minimum payments for various types of TV and film work—to the exotic, such as giving writers the right to consult on product-placement deals and the ability to honor other unions' picket lines without consequences from their employers.

There was plenty for the AMPTP to dislike in the WGA's proposals, but the two biggest points of contention—to no one's surprise—were the WGA's demands for new media and home video. For new media, the guild lumped paid downloads and Web streaming as a single residual classification that called for payment of 2.5 percent of distributor's gross revenue for any reuse of a film or TV production via "the Internet, cellular technology and any other delivery system not already covered in the (master contract)." The distinction of seeking a percentage of revenues based on distributor's gross was a bid by the guild to avoid the home video residual scenario of calculating residuals based on producer's gross. For home video, the guild sought to double the long-standing residual formula by increasing the definition of producer's gross from 20 percent to 40 percent of total revenue generated by a title.

As far as the studios were concerned, the WGA's proposal was full of roadblocks to a deal. The AMPTP had no intention of budging on the traditional home video rate—not for writers, directors, or actors. And the 2.5 percent proposal for new media was wildly unrealistic, in the AMPTP's view, because whatever the studios agreed to pay writers, they would also have to pay out to directors and actors. In most instances, Screen Actors Guild residual rates are set at three times the rate paid to WGA and DGA members, according to long-standing industry practice.

In the WGA's view, if the AMPTP's study proposal was bad, the other option was worse—far worse. The AMPTP dubbed it the "recoupment" proposal. To writers it became known as the "thirty-two-page 'fuck you' deal." In a nutshell, the recoupment proposal outlined a framework for a thorough overhaul of the entire residual system, not just for new media. The studios have long resented their obligation to pay writers, actors, and directors residual fees for any reuse of movies and TV shows even if the property has never made a dime of profit for the studio. The recoupment proposal was pitched as a trade-off that would reward successful productions by paying higher residual rates on profitable film and TV shows while freeing studios of the obligation to pay on productions that were still in the red. Residual payments would kick in only after a movie or TV program had made back the money the production entity spent on development, production, marketing, and distribution.[5] This framework ran completely counter to decades of industry practice, and it would ensure that only a small percentage of productions would generate residuals for writers, actors, and directors in a timely manner.

The residual system is particularly nettlesome for studios as it pertains to feature films. During the WGA talks, AMPTP executives frequently cited Warner Bros.' costly 2002 turkey *The Adventures of Pluto Nash* as an prime example of why the residual-fee system was in need of an extreme makeover. The studio paid out tens of thousands of dollars in residual fees to key creative talent in *Pluto Nash* because of its telecasts on TV in the United States and abroad. Because the studios enter into long-term contracts with domestic and foreign TV channels, virtually every movie produced by a Hollywood studio is guaranteed of having some posttheatrical TV exposure. And virtually every movie gets a DVD release in the hopes that sales will help offset losses or, in the best-case scenario, greatly add to profits. From the perspective of the CEOs, if the WGA was determined to break new ground on residuals for new media, they would demand their own changes to the system, established in the 1940s to compensate writers of radio programs that were repeated.

The AMPTP declared its intent to field the recoupment proposal a week before the negotiations began when Counter held a media briefing on the WGA talks. The level of detail offered at that session with reporters indicated the depth of concern within the AMPTP about how the coming battle would play out in the press. Three well-known and well-regarded industry executives were recruited to help Counter spin the studios' side of the contract drama: Barry Meyer, chairman and CEO of Warner Bros.; CBS Corporation president and CEO Leslie Moonves; and Anne Sweeney, president of Disney–ABC Television Group and cochairman of Disney's Media Networks unit. "We've talked about it, we've thought about it but we never really have gone after it. And we think we need to have to really go after it now. We can't wait any longer," Meyer told reporters during the July 11 meeting at AMPTP headquarters. "We're operating under terms and conditions that were formulated 50 years ago. . . . Why isn't (there) a model that says once the investment is recovered, maybe there should be a higher percentage paid of the profits?"[6]

But there was a reason the studios never pushed hard for a radical rethinking of these compensation formulas during previous contract negotiations. Residuals are as sacrosanct for the creative community as Social Security and Medicare are for voters in election years. Residuals are fiercely protected by the creative community because they are such a large component of annual income for all but the most successful WGA, DGA, and SAG members. The reuse payments are crucial for helping creative talent survive lean times in an industry where workers are almost exclusively hired on a project-by-project basis, and even experienced writers, directors, and actors can go months, if not years, between jobs. "When I was really unemployed, the things that really kept me going were residuals and health benefits," Marc Cherry told the crowd at the WGA rally in September 2006 for the striking *America's Next Top Model* producers. "This is a rough town."[7]

In television the credited writer or writers of a half-hour television series on a broadcast network receive about eleven thousand dollars for the first repeat of the show in prime time on the network; for hourlong series the fee is about twenty-two thousand dollars, under the terms of the WGA's 2004 master contract. The pay scale slides with the number of additional repeats. The residual pay scale is lower for broadcast network programs that are rerun on cable, and it is lower still for made-for-cable programs that are rerun on cable, whether on the show's original network or another outlet. Given the sporadic nature of employment in film and television, writers have long insisted that residuals should be viewed not as bonus income but part of a writers' base compensation. "To revamp residuals is to destabilize this entire industry," said writer-director Bill Condon, a WGA negotiating committee member, during the July 18, 2007, news conference that followed the guild's second day of negotiations with the AMPTP. Negotiating committee members were emphatic in their opposition to the recoupment proposal. "All we're asking is to continue to get paid when our work is used and reused," said Condon, whose film credits include the 2004 biopic *Kinsey* and the 2006 rendition of *Dreamgirls*.[8]

The change proposed by the studios would particularly hurt younger writers who most need the residuals to help pay the rent. "Your proposal transfers money from developing, promising writers, actors, and directors who need them the most to established pros who need them the least," WGA negotiating committee chief John Bowman told the AMPTP during the July 18 bargaining session. "It's bad for the business."[9] Bowman cited the career histories of writers like Cherry and David Chase, creator of *The Sopranos*, in making the case for maintaining the existing residual system. Cherry and Chase delivered hugely profitable hit series after working for twenty-plus years as writers with varying degrees of success. Cherry had famously fallen out of favor in Hollywood TV circles at the time he wrote the script that became *Desperate Housewives*. Without residual money to tide them through the inevitable periods of unemployment, writers like Cherry and Chase might well have had to give up on the entertainment industry and find other employment, Bowman argued. As an experienced showrunner, with everything from *Saturday Night Live* to *Murphy Brown* to *In Living Color* on his résumé, Bowman was intimately aware of the pressures on working writers, and he knew that any suggestion of eliminating or scaling back residuals would enrage the creative community.

Moreover, the WGA cited the often comical examples of "Hollywood accounting" as a big reason writers could never agree to wait until the studio determined that a property was profitable. "According to Hollywood accounting, 'The Simpsons' is not in profits. How can we trust that kind of bookkeeping?" Bowman scoffed during the July 18 bargaining session. (*The Simpsons* is among the most popular and long-running TV shows of all time.)

To add insult to injury, the AMPTP's recoupment proposal also included provisions to ease long-standing WGA contract requirements, such as that the screenwriter's name is included in all movie advertising when other talent is listed or that a writer receive first-class transportation accommodations when asked to travel in connection with a project. "Every point that had ever been won (by the WGA), they now wanted to turn the other way," said a WGA negotiating committee member. "That was the really nasty part. . . . What kind of way is that to start a negotiation?"[10]

As with the study proposal, recoupment turned out to be a major tactical blunder for the AMPTP. In an effort to intimidate the WGA's new leadership, the studios wound up giving guild leaders all the ammunition they needed to fire up their foot soldiers. The recoupment proposal allowed WGA leaders to tell the membership that the studios were pursuing massive rollbacks without offering anything on new media.

The first day of formal bargaining on July 16 was largely consumed with opening statements and the exchange of proposals, or what one industry veteran termed the "Kabuki theater" of labor negotiations. The meeting room at the AMPTP was packed with WGA and AMPTP company representatives as well as observers from SAG, the DGA, and IATSE.

There was little back-and-forth between the sides on the first day as Counter presented the AMPTP's two options, the study and recoupment. But they went at it in their dueling statements to the media as soon as the session ended in the afternoon. The threat of a strike had attracted far more attention than guild contract talks typically receive from national media outlets.

The AMPTP continued to portray the guild as being led by radicals with a reckless agenda. The recoupment proposal was a difficult but necessary step to "adapt to the transformative changes that confront us," the AMPTP asserted. "We must change our mindset and our age-old ways of operating. Instead of helping us work toward solutions that would give us the flexibility we all need for the benefit of all, the WGA demands would impose unreasonable costs and Draconian restrictions," the statement read.[11]

The guild stayed on message with its central assertion that it was only fighting to ensure that writers receive a "fair" shake. "The conglomerates always try to paint us as unreasonable and bellicose," the WGA statement read. "Our proposals simply try to ensure that writers keep up with the industry's growth. That's fair and reasonable."[12]

After a one-day break, they reconvened at AMPTP headquarters on July 18. John Bowman's opening statement left no doubt where the WGA stood on the AMPTP's proposals. If forced to choose between two untenable offers, the guild was prepared to do battle on every point in the recoupment proposal. "Fine," Nick Counter said ruefully as he lifted a copy of the study proposal from the table and dropped it with a theatrical gesture on the floor. "I can't believe you guys would do this," he said, laying one hand on the recoupment proposal.[13]

The second day ended with more recriminations. The WGA hastily scheduled a late-afternoon news conference at guild headquarters, where Bowman and other prominent negotiating committee members tried to put a human face on the fight. Carol Mendelsohn, showrunner of CBS's stalwart *CSI: Crime Scene Investigation*, emphasized how much more work had been heaped on the average TV series writer's plate in just the past five years. "As a writer-showrunner, it used to be that you wrote your show," she said. "Now you write your show but there's a whole additional universe that goes with it: Webisodes, mobisodes, computer games, blogs. And all of these need to be written, the same as the scripts."[14]

Larry Wilmore, a showrunner and comedian who created Fox's *The Bernie Mac Show,* reiterated writers' frustration at being asked to wait to see what develops in new media. "We've been asked to wait before. Writers are tired of playing catch-up," Wilmore said. "We're just looking to negotiate a fair deal. So far the companies have been saying: No, no, no— Talk to the hand, not the face."[15]

Bowman disputed the AMPTP's contention that the WGA's new media residual proposals would bankrupt the entertainment industry or that the business models were still too uncertain. "Our operating principle is simple," Bowman said. "If you get paid for the reuse of our material, we get paid. The companies have made hundreds of deals in the new media arena over the past year, which proves that they do have viable business models. . . . We don't need a study, we need a fair share for writers of the revenue our work generates."[16]

After two face-to-face sessions, it was clear that the gulf between the AMPTP and the WGA was as wide as the Grand Canyon. The sides would not meet again until September 19, the day after Patric Verrone was reelected WGA West president by an overwhelming margin.

As the writers and the AMPTP waited out the rest of the summer, the major television networks began preparing contingency plans in the event of a strike. The conventional wisdom in Hollywood still assumed the WGA would wait until the summer of 2008 when the Screen Actors Guild's contract expired. Writers and actors would have maximum leverage with the studios if they linked arms in a joint strike threat.

But for months, labor executives at the networks and studios had been warning their bosses that the WGA could go on strike as early as November 1. The Big Four networks had to be ready to roll with replacement programming. The networks started doing so as far back as 2006 by loading up on unscripted series that would not be affected by a WGA walkout. ABC, CBS, Fox, NBC, and the CW each ordered multiple series that were to be fully produced but held in reserve until they were needed or the strike threat passed.

The networks were comfortable stocking up on unscripted series because they are far less costly than traditional comedies and dramas—sometimes as little as half of the per-episode license fee for a scripted series. And reality shows offered more flexibility in the number of episodes that could be ordered compared to a scripted series. Because of the high costs of mounting a scripted production—from the cost of the stars to the cost of the sets—many studios are reluctant to accept orders for new shows that are anything less than the industry standard of thirteen episodes.

Unscripted programs, on the other hand, can be structured to unfold over a handful of episodes, sometimes as few as four or five. Game shows can be presented as stand-alone entities that could be sprinkled onto the schedule as needed, à la NBC's *Deal or No Deal* or CBS's revival of a game-show chestnut such as *Million Dollar Password*. The malleability made it easier for the networks to bank episodes of unscripted series for an undetermined amount of time. "I don't think I've ever picked up or will pick up over the next six months as many projects as I am doing now," Mike Darnell, president of alternative programming for Fox, said in August 2007.[17]

At the same time, there was a concerted push by both network executives and writers to get scripted pilots and series in the can before the witching hour of the WGA's October 31 contract expiration. Pilots are traditionally green-lighted by networks during the January–April period known as "pilot season," but there was a flurry of orders made in the summer of 2007, as programming executives nervously eyed the calendar. Fox gave the go-ahead to two high-profile drama projects, one supervised by Shawn Ryan, creator of FX's edgy cop drama *The Shield*, the other from the company headed by movie producer Brian Grazer. (Neither pilot ultimately earned a series pickup.) CBS sent its hottest comedy prospect, *Worst Week*, a remake of a BBC comedy, into casting and preproduction in late summer. Hollywood veterans noted the novelty of recruiting crew members and holding pilot casting sessions in the dog days of August. NBC gave a six-episode order to a drama series, *The Philanthropist*, from producers Tom Fontana and Barry Levinson. (The project wound up beset by problems and eventually had a brief run in the summer of 2009.) A similar acceleration of script purchases and green lights was seen on the feature-film side. Studios scrambled to get screenplays turned in and polished before the October 31 deadline in order to have finished scripts to shoot in 2008.

For all the preparations, there was still a strong sense of disbelief among executives and within the creative community that the WGA would actually pull the trigger. The industry had endured strike fever in 2001, when WGA contract talks went down to the wire and the deal was signed two days after the guild's contract expired. In 2004 writers worked for five months after the expiration, even as guild members rejected one tentative agreement in a referendum vote.

Many of the midlevel network and studio executives who deal most directly with creative talent had no past experience with a Hollywood strike. In a youth-centric business, the rank-and-file executives, as well as the legion of talent agents, managers, and publicists who serve as a key conduits between employers and their clients, were too young to have been working in the industry during the 1988 WGA strike. Even with the warnings and anecdotal tales told by their older colleagues, it was impossible for the younger generation of Hollywood players to understand the far-reaching impact that a work stoppage would have until they experienced it firsthand.

By the spring of 2007, *Daily Variety* and the *Hollywood Reporter* were routinely describing deals for new film and TV projects as being "pre-strike" business activity. But the industry remained fixated on the notion of the "mother of all strikes" hitting in the summer of 2008, with writers and actors walking out at the same time for the first time since 1960. It was not until the WGA revealed its October surprise—the initiation of its strike authorization vote among members on October 1—that some close observers of the labor situation began to suspect the guild would make a move sooner rather than later.

After the rocky start of negotiations in July, WGA leaders doubled down in their preparations for a strike. Publicly, Patric Verrone and others insisted that a work stoppage was seen as a last resort and that the guild's focus was firmly on finding a resolution at the negotiating table. Behind the scenes, however, the guild was girding for war. The union veterans recruited by Young to the WGA West reached out to other unions for support and pledges of solidarity. One particularly vocal supporter of the WGA was the high-profile Service Employees International Union, which provided a range of assistance and expertise to aid the writers' cause.

The "contract captains" recruited earlier in the year began to be coached for their duty as strike captains. The guild instituted a "negotiations alert" e-mail bulletin for members, in an effort to ensure that the WGA could communicate directly to members as events occurred, rather than relying on media reports. Picket signs, placards, T-shirts, and baseball caps were ordered by the hundreds, all of them bearing pro-WGA messages and some designed with iconography that evoked the great organized labor battles of the 1930s and '40s. The signs of these materials being delivered to the WGA West headquarters were Hollywood's equivalent of troops gathering along a border.

A few weeks before the AMPTP threw down the gauntlet of its recoupment proposal, a select few guild insiders got an ominous preview of the bare-knuckles brawl in store for the contract negotiations. It started in the late spring with a dispute between the AMPTP and WGA trustees of the guild's health benefits program. The Writers Guild–Industry Health Fund is funded by the AMPTP member companies, chiefly the largest studio conglomerates, as are the medical plans administered by the DGA and SAG. Guild members have to meet predetermined annual-earning thresholds to qualify for benefits. The amount that companies pay is subject to negotiation in the guilds' master contracts. The WGA's 2004 contract called for AMPTP companies to pay an additional 8.5 percent of the total compensation paid to WGA members in each year of the contract to the fund. The fund is overseen by a board of thirty-four trustees, evenly divided among AMPTP- and WGA-appointed representatives.

The fund's charter allows that if both sides agree that the health plan is flush enough to meet all of its obligations to members, the AMPTP companies can reduce the total amount of their contribution to the fund by a half percent in the last six months of the guild's master contract. In 2007, as the six-month window approached, the AMPTP trustees raised the issue of the half-percent reduction, but the WGA trustees were not so sure the plan was funded sufficiently to warrant the reduction. In the event of such a dispute, the fund's charter calls for the sides to try to find an "impartial umpire" to make the call, and if they cannot agree on the impartial ump, then they go to federal court to ask a judge to find them a referee. The studios filed for that arbitration in early July.

What made the situation more unpleasant, in the view of the WGA trustees, is that the AMPTP's complaint included a provision requesting repayment of attorneys' fees and other legalese that made the pro forma filing akin to a lawsuit against the WGA trustees.

The health-fund tussle was a small matter, in the scheme of things, but it was unnerving nonetheless to the WGA trustees. "When we saw they were playing hardball with this issue, we knew we were in trouble," says a WGA trustee.[18]

When the WGA and AMPTP reconvened negotiations in September after a two-month break, Patric Verrone came to the table fortified by a resounding endorsement of his leadership by guild members. He had been reelected president by 90.2 percent of the members who cast ballots.[19]

The WGA East, meanwhile, elected a new president on September 21, news and documentary writer Michael Winship. Winship was not a new-comer to the process—he had been a member of the WGA East's govern-ing council, and he had served as an alternate member of the negotiating committee—but taking the helm when he did was comparable to being dropped into the eye of a hurricane.

The night before the WGA East election results were revealed, the nego-tiating committee and other guild leaders made the decision to stealthily change their plan of attack. If there was to be a strike, it would come sooner rather than later; there would be no waiting until the summer to sync up with SAG. If the AMPTP and WGA could not make a deal by Halloween, picket lines would form in November. In surveying their options, the writ-ers realized that they would have far greater impact if they went out in early November, when the television season was in full swing, rather than in the summer. Also spurring the WGA's decision was the move by the film divisions of the major studios to vastly increase the number of mov-ies set to go into production in the first half of 2008. The studios called it a safety measure; the WGA called it stockpiling. "If negotiations were to fail, moving it up closer to the contract deadline created an element of surprise. There was a feeling that the studios thought we were going to wait for SAG. Plus, there was also the empirical realization that they were stockpiling," Winship says. "We realized that whereas normally there would be about 40–50 films going into production at the beginning of the year, it looked like there were going to be something like 120. So clearly they were trying to stockpile in advance of a July 1 (2008) strike. That was a huge factor in our thinking."[20] The WGA did not broadcast its decision to target a November strike, just as it had never officially announced its previous focus on the summer of 2008. But the assumption was so pervasive that the guild maintained the element of surprise on the timing of the work stoppage even after it began its strike-authorization vote.

The WGA election results and the behind-the-scenes maneuvering only stiffened the guild's resolve when its bargaining sessions with the AMPTP resumed on September 19. The absence of anything like a friendly interchange between the sides during the prestrike bargaining sessions was startling to the AMPTP executives and labor veterans who had many years of experience hammering out union contracts. The WGA team, as the AMPTP often noted in its public statements, was mostly new to the process, although Verrone and Bowman had served on past contract-negotiating committees. From the start, the tone in the room was chilly, with both sides focused on defending their carefully staked-out positions. There was little back-and-forth discussion across the table. Mostly, the sides stuck to prepared remarks and talking points that were usually met with stony silence.

As the process wore on, the public statements from both sides began to include barbs and snide remarks, which only pushed the participants deeper into their bunkers. The sides spent a great deal of time hunkered down in separate rooms during the bargaining sessions. After one side would make a presentation of facts and figures to support their position, the group would often split off into separate rooms to caucus and prepare a response.

At the bargaining sessions held on and off from mid-September through the end of October, the face time between the sides remained cordial, if stiff, but once they broke for the day, the anger was unleashed. This point was especially true after the WGA initiated its strike-authorization vote on October 1. WGA leaders made their case to members in a letter that accompanied the ballot, asking members to authorize the WGA West board and WGA East council to call a strike. "Since talks began on July 16, the companies have refused to engage in serious negotiations. Instead, they have rejected *each* of our proposals and responded with a 'comprehensive' proposal of their own: thirty-two pages of draconian rollbacks that would eviscerate virtually every gain that writers have made in the past 50 years," read the letter signed by the WGA West board, the WGA East council, and members of the negotiating committee. According to the guild's charter, the strike-authorization voting process had to be conducted over a three-week period. The guild took care to send its ballots in the same green envelopes that it used for mailing residual checks, to ensure that members would open the letter.

Once the guild was conducting its strike vote, AMPTP executives felt that the continuation of the bargaining meetings was merely for show. Nick Counter did not hide his fury after the October 5 session. "We have had six across-the-table sessions and have been met with only silence and stonewalling from the WGA leadership. We have attempted to engage on major issues, but no dialogue has been forthcoming from the WGA leadership," Counter said. "This is the most frustrating and futile attempt at bargaining that anyone on the AMPTP negotiating team has encountered in guild negotiation history . . . The WGA leadership is hidebound to strike. We are farther apart today than when we started, and the only outcome we see is a disaster engineered by the present leadership of the WGA."[21]

As Counter fumed, the WGA was so confident in the outcome of the strike-authorization vote that it posted on its website a list of stringent rules that members would have to follow if the strike ensued or face disciplinary action from the guild. A few of the WGA's stipulations raised hackles with other unions and the AMPTP. One was a rule that sought to address the tricky area of writers who also worked as directors and producers, or, as they are known in the entertainment industry, "hyphenates." The WGA's strike-rules memo mandated that guild members who had hyphenate roles were not allowed to perform certain tasks on projects that they wrote, such as cutting for time, changes in technical or stage directions, and other adjustments that inevitably crop up during the course of production. The DGA sounded the alarm with its members over the WGA's rules, as some of those hyphenate functions could be interpreted as part of a director's duties. The DGA sent a missive to its members noting that in accordance with its master contract, DGA members who were also in the WGA could be held in breach of contract if they refused to perform certain services.[22]

The WGA had no choice but to back down and soften its language in the rule about the directing issue. But the flap raised the crucial question of how hyphenates would be allowed to function during the strike. WGA leaders knew from past experience that the decisions made by this key constituency could make or break the effectiveness of the walkout.

Another rule that brought a swift rebuke from the studios was the WGA's contention that writers had to submit to the guild copies of any scripts that had been commissioned by an AMPTP member company but were unfinished at the time the strike ensued. The guild said it needed to know the status of scripts on the eve of the strike to be able to police against strikebreaking activity during and immediately after the work stoppage. The AMPTP raised a stink, noting that the scripts were proprietary to the studios that paid for them and that the WGA's demand violated laws protecting a company's "trade secrets." The AMPTP made it clear in its public statements that writers who submitted scripts to the WGA could face breach-of-contract claims from the commissioning company.[23]

The WGA also asserted that its members would be barred from writing scripts for animated feature films produced by AMPTP member companies during the strike. Because IATSE-affiliated locals had represented animation workers since the early 1950s, writing for animated feature films is covered by IATSE rather than the WGA. Given the bad blood between IATSE and WGA, the guild's statement on animation spurred a threat of quick legal retribution from IATSE president Thomas Short, who had continued to publicly bash WGA leaders for leading the industry to the brink of war. In his pointed statement about animated features being IATSE turf, Short referred to the guild as "the house of hate commonly known as the Writers Guild of America West."[24]

For many WGA members, the circulation of the strike-rules memo was the first concrete sign that a strike was an increasingly likely scenario. But most working writers did not have much time to worry over the dark clouds gathering. They were too busy working frantically to finish scripts in advance of the October 31 contract expiration. Showrunners and staff writers on many prime-time TV series worked around the clock after the strike-authorization vote and began to bank as many scripts as possible. In some cases, the goal was to complete scripts to allow the show to continue producing episodes after the strike began. In other cases, the intent was to ensure that the show could go back into production immediately once the strike was over. As much as the rank and file had been awakened to the need for solidarity, writers had an equally strong sense of loyalty to their shows. Getting a series on the air is no easy feat, even for the most successful hyphenates; it takes a special kind of all-consuming commitment to be a showrunner. For many writers, regardless of the righteousness of the cause, the prospect of going on strike was akin to abandoning a child.

The acrimonious exchanges between the AMPTP and WGA continued as the sides held seven bargaining sessions between October 2 and October 15. On the morning of Tuesday, October 16, however, AMPTP president Nick Counter had a surprise for the guild representatives. In the interest of maintaining labor peace, the studios withdrew the recoupment proposal. "In the overriding interest of keeping the industry working and removing what has become an emotional impediment and excuse by the WGA not to bargain, the AMPTP withdrew its recoupment proposal," Counter said in a statement.[25] Counter was blunt in explaining where the AMPTP stood in his remarks that day to WGA leaders. He complained about the lack of progress and discourse through the sessions to date. "Let no one misconstrue today's action," Counter said. "While the producers will not insist on our recoupment proposal as a condition of reaching an agreement with you, we will not increase residual payments for videocassette and DVD use, including electronic downloads."[26] He also insisted that the studios would draw the line at any effort to gain higher residual rates for shows airing on the CW or MyNetworkTV, pay TV channels such as HBO and Showtime, or basic-cable outlets. The lower rate of pay across the board for pay and basic cable had been an increasingly contentious issue as the volume of original production for those realms increased. But WGA leaders knew they had to pick their battles. This negotiation's go-round was laser focused on new media.

Although the recoupment proposal had been a negotiating ploy all along, Counter's move to scrap it was meant to put pressure on the WGA to make concessions. And once recoupment was off the table, the two sides had no starting point for any sort of discussion. The sides would not hold another bargaining session until the following week—after the guild announced the results of its strike-authorization vote.

There was no room for interpretation in the vote tally. It was a resounding declaration of WGA members' anger and willingness to sacrifice for the larger cause. The strike authorization vote generated the highest turnout in the guild's seventy-four-year history, with 5,507 ballots cast, 90.3 percent of them approving the leadership's call for a strike authorization. With fully half of the 10,500 members covered by the AMPTP film and TV contract taking part in the referendum, the studios could not credibly dismiss the results as being driven by a fringe element. "This historic vote sends an unequivocal message to the AMPTP, loud and clear. We will not be taken advantage of and we will not be fooled," WGA East president Michael Winship said after the vote tally was released.[27]

The AMPTP's about-face on recoupment was too little, too late. WGA members, stoked by aggressive leadership and the studios' hard-line stance, were in no mood to wait. Without a dollars-and-cents offer from the studios on new media, writers were ready to walk.

The guild and AMPTP held five more sessions between October 19, the day the strike-vote results were announced, and October 31, the last day of the contract. After the AMPTP dropped the recoupment proposal, the WGA continued to accuse the conglomerates of stalling by refusing to make a formal offer on the make-or-break issue of new media compensation. The AMPTP continued to slam the guild for its unyielding stance. The finger-pointing went on and on, amid rising angst in the industry. "Their opening offer would have rolled back our compensation by 50 percent. Now they decrease the rollbacks to 45 percent and proclaim that they are truly bargaining. Minor adjustments to major rollbacks do not constitute forward motion," John Bowman said in a statement released after the session on October 25, the day of the flap over the chairs at WGA West headquarters.[28]

The following day, October 26, the sides met again briefly and managed to find common ground on at least one issue: the request by the AMPTP to bring in a federal mediator, Juan Carlos Gonzalez, who serves the Los Angeles area for the Federal Mediation and Conciliation Service. The sides set the first meeting with Gonzalez in the room for the following Tuesday, October 30, at AMPTP headquarters, less than forty-eight hours before the contract expiration.

Despite the last-ditch effort to bring in a mediator, the die was cast the day before the first session with Gonzalez when the WGA announced it would hold a membership meeting November 1 at the Los Angeles Convention Center, ostensibly to update members on the status of negotiations. What guild leaders sought was a final exclamation point from members on its strike threat. The location selected for the meeting was meant to send a message to management and WGA members alike. Emboldened by the turnout for the strike-authorization vote, the guild booked a 63,600-square-foot, 5,000-seat hall at the downtown convention center. Most WGA gatherings were held at the guild's headquarters or at its 540-seat Writers Guild Theater facility in Beverly Hills. David Young admitted after the meeting he had his doubts about whether they would fill the room.

On October 30, the first day of talks with the mediator ended with more recriminations from both sides. The WGA asserted that after meeting face-to-face in the morning and early afternoon, the guild by a quarter to seven was fifteen minutes away from presenting a "comprehensive package proposal" when the AMPTP executives informed the WGA representatives that they would review the proposal the following day.

On Wednesday, October 31, Hollywood stayed glued to cell phones and Blackberrys for any kernel of news as the talks reconvened with the mediator. The longer the doors remained closed at the AMPTP, the more hopeful Hollywood's various constituencies became that a strike would be averted. Shortly after five o'clock, however, those hopes evaporated.

The WGA and AMPTP raced to get statements to the press, each blaming the other for the meltdown of the talks, mediator or no mediator.[29]

The WGA had presented the AMPTP with a proposal that morning that dropped nine low-profile items from the guild's original twenty-six-point plan. The writers eased their stance slightly on DVD and paid-download residual rates by focusing on increases for those titles that surpass one million dollars in sales and dropping the demand for an increase in the residual paid for sales under one million dollars. The sides broke into separate clusters for more than six hours after WGA brass made the morning presentation.

To the AMPTP, making such a minor adjustment to the DVD and paid-download demand was as meaningless as the AMPTP's withdrawal of the recoupment proposal was to the WGA. Nick Counter, Carol Lombardini, and others had informed WGA negotiators in no uncertain terms that there would be no discussion of changing the home video formula. It was a line-in-the-sand issue for the studios. Counter told the WGA in the early evening that there would be no further talks unless the guild formally dropped the DVD and paid-download demand from its proposal. "The magnitude of that proposal alone is blocking us from making any further progress. We cannot move further as long as that issue remains on the table," Counter told the WGA in the early evening, according to a statement released by the AMPTP.

WGA leaders were shocked at how willingly the studios seemed to be spurring the guild's strike option by issuing such an ultimatum. In those last hours leading up to the midnight expiration of the contract, the AMPTP was stubbornly digging in, perhaps out of concern that the studios not appear to be wavering in the face of the strike threat. "After three and a half months of bargaining, the AMPTP still has not responded to a single one of our important proposals," the WGA responded. "Every issue that matters to writers, including Internet reuse, original writing for new media, DVDs and jurisdiction, has been ignored. This is completely unacceptable."

The brinksmanship between the AMPTP and WGA had engendered such fear in Hollywood that it wound up being strangely appropriate that the breaking point in the talks came on Halloween night.

WGA staff had little time to digest the drama unfolding around them. They worked around the clock on Wednesday and Thursday to prepare the convention-center hall for what would prove to be a landmark membership meeting.[30] A long, narrow platform was set up in the front of the room for a dais that would seat the seventeen members of the WGA negotiating committee—plus Patric Verrone, David Young, and Michael Winship—in the front row, and the seventeen negotiating-committee alternates in the second row.

Young's worries about playing to a half-empty room were quickly put to rest. Guild members began filing into the hall as early as five for the seven o'clock meeting. The WGA's final head count was three thousand—three thousand anxious, engaged members who braved rush-hour traffic to hear the latest word directly from guild leaders.

The mood in the hall was serious, but not somber. The heady sense of collective purpose that would fuel the picketing campaign on both coasts was palpable at the convention center that night. Even for those individuals who had heard Verrone and Young make their case on the contract issues at previous gatherings, there was a general awakening that night about the urgency and the moral imperative of the cause. The fight was not just about getting paid now—it was about enshrining the principle that writers would continue to be paid in the future, no matter where technology took the television and film businesses. "When you heard what was really going on at the negotiations, presented in a methodical, intelligent manner, and not in a crazy, rabble-rousing call to arms, you just knew that there was no alternative but to strike if things didn't change," says Mike Scully, an experienced showrunner. "It was a night that really made you feel good about being a writer. It gave you the feeling that you had some real power, as delusional as that might be."[31]

There was a commensurate rush of emotion and realization that guild members shared common bonds through their chosen profession. Verrone missed no opportunity to introduce himself as "I am a writer" or to use the catchphrase "We're all in this together." The emergence of a common enemy in the studios, combined with the tribalism encouraged by guild leaders, fueled powerful feelings of solidarity, idealism, and professional pride in many writers that would tide the WGA through the long three and a half months of the strike.

As the meeting at the convention center was called to order, members of the negotiating committee got a standing ovation as they walked up to the dais. By any measure, they were an impressive group, from the showrunners of top hits—Carlton Cuse of *Lost*, Carol Mendelsohn of *CSI*, Neal Baer of *Law and Order: SVU*, Shawn Ryan of *The Shield*, Marc Cherry of *Desperate Housewives*—to such notable screenwriters as Bill Condon (*Dreamgirls*), Stephen Gaghan (*Syriana*), Terry George (*Hotel Rwanda*), and Susannah Grant (*Erin Brockovich*). In total, they were a much more high-profile group than had been assembled for WGA negotiating teams in the recent past. These people could not be easily dismissed by the studios.

Verrone, Young, Bowman, and Winship did the talking at the start, detailing the guild's frustrating experiences at the bargaining table with the AMPTP and their reasoning for pushing so hard on new media. Microphone stands were set up in numerous spots in the room for members to ask questions and express their views to the assembled leaders. Much of the commentary from the floor during the three-hour meeting was fiery and passionate, but none of it challenged the guild's positions or the very big gamble of going on strike. There was high praise for the courage and resolve demonstrated by Verrone and Young and the negotiating team and much talk of how writers under previous WGA regimes had allowed themselves to be taken advantage of for too long. Screen Actors Guild president Alan Rosenberg was there to pledge the support of his 120,000-member union, in the first of many such guest appearances Rosenberg and SAG would make on behalf of the WGA.

The prevailing sentiment of the night was captured with plain-spoken eloquence in a mostly impromptu observation from Howard Michael Gould, an alternate member of the negotiating committee. Speaking from the second row of the dais, Gould looked like an unassuming college professor in his rust-colored cardigan sweater and blue dress shirt with an open neck. His remarks would resonate with writers long after the meeting ended through word of mouth and through a video clip posted by the WGA on YouTube:

I want to just speak for a minute here to the moderates and the skeptics. I want to speak to you because I am one of you. I have been over the years less militant than some other people. . . . I know that strikes are destructive, and they're painful, and they sometimes have a way of going on longer than you want when you go into one. I've always felt that it's a card we needed to hold and it's a card we'd need to play when there was an issue that just about every member would know in his or her gut was the kind of thing that we just had to take a stand on. . . .

(New media) is such a big issue that if they see us roll over on this without making a stand, three years from now they're going to be back for something else, okay? I might've been the most moderate one up here when we started (negotiations). But I sat there in the room the first day and (the AMPTP) read us those thirty-two pages of rollbacks, and what they wanted us to hear was that if you don't give us what we want on the important thing, we're going to come after you for all those other things. But what I heard was, if we give them that thing, they'll still come after us for those other things. And in three years it'll be "We want to revamp the whole residual system," and in another three years it'll be "You know what? We don't really want to fund the health fund the way we've been." And then it'll be pension, and then it'll be credit determination. And there just is that time when everybody has to see this is one where we've just got to stand our ground.[32]

Finally, Bowman delivered the news that they had all come to hear: the negotiating committee had voted unanimously to recommend that the board of the WGA West and council of the WGA East call for a strike against AMPTP member companies. That announcement brought another standing ovation—delivered with clenched-fist determination.

The following morning, Friday, November 2, the WGA West board and WGA East council held a joint meeting at WGA West headquarters. It did not take long for members of the two governing bodies to vote unanimously to call a strike to begin 12:01 a.m. Monday.

A few hours later, a packed news conference was held at WGA West headquarters. Against the camera-ready backdrop imprinted with the

"Writers Guild of America Contract 2007" logo, Verrone, flanked by Winship and Bowman, read with gravitas a prepared statement announcing what everyone in Hollywood already knew.[33] During the questioning that followed, Verrone was adamant. "It's our sense we can do some economic damage immediately," Verrone said. "I don't think they want this to happen. . . . We don't want it to happen. But the thing we want less is a bad contract, and so whatever it takes to get a good contract is what we intend to do for as long as it takes."

Bowman played the diplomatic card. His grim demeanor betrayed his exhaustion after weeks of marathon meetings and strategy sessions. "We have 48 hours. What we really want to do isn't strike—what we want to do is negotiate," Bowman said. "There still is time."

5

United Showrunners

The morning after the WGA's news conference announcing the strike timetable, about ninety showrunners gathered at the Sheraton Universal hotel, adjacent to Universal Studios, in an effort to make some sense out of the swirl of events.[1]

The anxiety in the room, reserved by the guild for the invitation-only meeting, was palpable. The showrunners who turned out were destined to be the tip of the spear in the WGA's fight. They were the writer-producers responsible for leading the army of 100 to 150 production staffers required to turn out a weekly television series. As industry leaders with much at stake, the response of prominent showrunners would set the tone for how many other WGA members viewed the strike effort.

The WGA facilitated the meeting space at the Sheraton, but the impetus to bring the group together came from an unlikely band of activists, none of whom had been involved much in WGA affairs in the past.

Steven Levitan, a comedy writer known for hitting it big early in his career with the NBC comedy *Just Shoot Me,* had emerged a few days earlier as a leader of the effort by a handful of showrunners to seek a kind of consensus on their response to the strike. "We knew that we as showrunners had considerable muscle in this fight," Levitan says. "We thought it was important that we try to get together as a group and talk."[2]

Levitan, tall and TV-anchor handsome, looked like a talk-show host as he ran around the rows of chairs with a microphone to draw out questions, concerns, and comments from attendees. The majority of those in the room had never experienced a Hollywood strike; many were still in school at the time of the WGA's 1988 walkout.

By the morning of Saturday, November 3, less than forty-eight hours before the guild had vowed to go on strike, showrunners with series in production were grappling with a combustible mix of emotions, from fear and dread to anger and, for some, panic. The timing was particularly cruel for a handful of younger writers who were just getting their first shot in the 2007–8 season at putting a show on the air. But to a person, there were no doubts or dissent expressed about the *need* for the WGA to strike. The shared sentiment in the room was that the conglomerates' hardball tactics and lack of response on new media left the guild no choice. The resolve was strong that writers had to show some backbone to prevent history— and the home video scenario—from repeating itself.

As would be expected from a roomful of writers, there were eloquent speeches and rousing assertions made about the issues at stake being a matter of principle. There was talk of the extra responsibility borne by the most successful WGA members. But for all the impassioned statements, one of the speakers who made the strongest impression on many participants was the least flowery of all.

Greg Daniels is an Emmy-winning showrunner respected for his work on *Saturday Night Live*, *The Simpsons*, and *King of the Hill*, and for deftly shepherding the US adaptation of the quirky British hit *The Office* into a hit for NBC. Soft-spoken and unassuming, Daniels looks the part of a devoted husband and father of three who spends his weekends at soccer games and other family pursuits.

But the stress of the buildup to the strike was evident in Daniels's demeanor. After a slow start, *The Office* was steadily improving its ratings performance for NBC. The show had become the poster child for the promise that new media exposure held for traditional TV programming, as *Office* became a standout success on iTunes and in NBC.com's Web-streaming platform even before its ratings on the network began to spike. The prospect of abruptly shutting down production just as *Office* was hitting its stride was a scary scenario for Daniels and for everyone else involved with the show.

None of this was lost on the crowd as they listened to Daniels, who rose to speak about halfway through the meeting. He did not rant, nor did he bemoan the specific circumstances *Office* faced. Instead, he very succinctly laid out the plan that he and his writing staff had devised to gather before dawn to form a picket line outside the location shoot that the show was scheduled to begin on Monday morning. "When Greg got up and said, 'Here's what I'm doing at 5:30 on Monday morning,' we wanted to cheer," said one participant in the meeting. "Here was a guy who was not a hot-head by any means, and that he would be driven to the point of plotting to shut down his own show—that hit a lot of people."[3]

None of the attendees knew it at the time, but the people in the room at the Sheraton that morning would form the backbone of a WGA coalition that would soon be christened United Showrunners. Just as the group collectively wielded immense clout in the prime-time television business, the people behind United Showrunners would have great sway over the course of the strike.

The November 3 meeting of showrunners was a preview of things to come on picket lines. The sheer number of A-list writers in the room helped ease their collective anxiety. The decision reached by the group hinged on questions of principle, morality, and a concern for the greater good, and it amounted to a commitment to make a sizable financial sacrifice. Individually, showrunners stood to lose hundreds of thousands of dollars, if not more, in a prolonged strike.

Showrunners earn a fee for every episode of their show—typically ranging from thirty to fifty thousand dollars for a broadcast network series (less for cable), but top-tier players earn as much as seventy-five thousand—plus additional compensation if they are a credited writer of the episode. A majority of showrunners receive additional compensation from their studio through exclusive contracts known in the industry as "overall deals." Those fees would stop coming as soon as showrunners stopped delivering new episodes, and there was no guarantee that production of episodes scuttled by the strike would ever be made up. The payments and funding for a showrunner's overhead expenses such as assistants and office space would be suspended immediately once the walkout began under standard force-majeure contract provisions.

The showrunner coalition had been pulled together only a few days before the November 3 meeting by Levitan and his writing partner,

Christopher Lloyd, and a handful of other showrunners, including Dawn Prestwich and Nicole Yorkin, who were at the helm of the FX drama *The Riches*, and Thania St. John, showrunner on the Sci Fi Channel's *Eureka*. They were among the few dozen who attended a WGA-hosted informational meeting for showrunners at the Sheraton Universal on October 28, the weekend before the conflict between the WGA and AMPTP escalated inevitably toward a strike.

In his years as a comedy writer, Levitan had never paid any attention to WGA affairs, or the internal politics of the guild. He had been fortunate enough to be in demand as a writer and showrunner, and he had never given any thought to the possibility that as a union member, he might one day be on strike.

That fall, Levitan and Lloyd were consumed with the task of launching a high-profile comedy series for Fox, *Back to You*, which was fortified by familiar faces from past sitcoms, *Everybody Loves Raymond*'s Patricia Heaton and *Frasier*'s Kelsey Grammer. The pedigree of the stars and the series' creators raised the performance bar for the show. But even with the round-the-clock work that goes into getting a new show on the air, Levitan and Lloyd could not escape the drama of the WGA's contract-negotiation process and the increasingly heated speculation about a strike.

Levitan was surprised by what he heard at the October 28 WGA meeting. The gravity of the situation sunk in as he listened to guild staff discuss the WGA's strike rules, dos and don'ts of picketing, and the types of legal notices that writers under contract to AMPTP signatory companies would have to send to their employers. "My eyes were opened at that meeting," Levitan says. "One thing we heard was that during the last strike some studios would say to showrunners, 'Wink, wink—even if you strike, you guys could still break stories.' That just struck a nerve. I thought, that's really lame for showrunners to keep working if people are out losing their livelihoods."[4]

After the meeting ended, a few people stayed behind to talk to Sarah Singer, the WGA executive who had been tasked with reaching out to showrunners. Singer was an experienced union organizer who had been recruited by WGA West executive director David Young. She had been through many labor actions involving food-service workers, among other sectors.

With her earnest and authoritative manner, Singer quickly gained the respect and the trust of WGA members like Levitan who had no idea what to expect in a strike. As Levitan and others peppered Singer with questions, she repeatedly stressed the importance of WGA members demonstrating their solidarity, particularly among the most successful writers. From that huddle, the suggestion arose that showrunners declare their support for the guild's contract goals in a full-page advertisement to run in Hollywood's hometown newspapers *Daily Variety* and the *Hollywood Reporter*. Levitan, who had worked in advertising early on in his career, volunteered to write the ad copy and do a mock-up on his home computer. The group left the meeting with a mission to enlist as many showrunners as they could reach to lend their names to the ad.

The response they got was overwhelming. More than 130 major players agreed to sign on. In the process, they assembled an invaluable database of e-mail addresses and telephone numbers. "Pencils Down Means Pencils Down," declared the headline of the ad that ran November 1, the day of the guild's membership meeting at the LA Convention Center. The copy vowed that if a strike ensued, "We, the following showrunners, will do no writing and no story breaking—nor will any be asked of our writing staffs—until we get a deal."

The design of the ad was spare—an image of a sharpened yellow pencil that Levitan scanned on his home computer—but that did not matter. The long list of well-known names and shows was more compelling to the industry than a flashy graphic. The list included showrunners from *CSI, Grey's Anatomy, House, Desperate Housewives, The Office, ER, Lost, Family Guy, Two and a Half Men, Law and Order: SVU,* and many other prominent shows. Underneath the names was the tagline "You Have Our Word" and the logos of the WGA West and WGA East.[5]

Around the time that United Showrunners came together, another group of writers who had enlisted as strike captains launched an initiative that would play a crucial role in disseminating information and shaping opinions during the strike. As the October 31 contract expiration deadline approached, the group of about a half-dozen writers realized that WGA members would need a forum for sharing news and information, for discussion and debate, as well as for venting and sounding off. To do so, they harnessed the same tools and technology that lay at the heart of the guild's contract-negotiation fight. A few days before the strike ensued, the group—whose primary members included John Aboud, Jeff Berman, Ian Deitchman, Laeta Kalogridis, David Latt, and Kate Purdy—created a blog devoted to the strike. The blog was dubbed *United Hollywood* after an internal discussion among the founders about whether the name should be specific to writers, or if it should reflect the larger creative community. The founders ultimately opted for the broader approach, reasoning that the WGA was not alone among Hollywood unions in facing difficult contract talks with the AMPTP. By all accounts, the *United Hollywood* moniker was settled on before any of the blog's founders were aware of the United Showrunners campaign, and vice versa.

There were plenty of WGA members and Hollywood insiders who wrote extensively about the strike on websites and blogs, from commentary to breaking news coverage. Nikki Finke, a longtime entertainment-industry journalist, saw the profile of her *DeadlineHollywoodDaily* blog rise exponentially within Hollywood and in media circles as she offered round-the-clock coverage of the strike and related issues.

But *United Hollywood* quickly became the central online hub for writers during the strike. Almost overnight, the blog fulfilled its founders' vision by offering a steady stream of news, analysis, and logistical information, as well as links to and critiques of other media coverage of the strike and relevant topics. It carried a range of essay and commentary articles, mostly from striking writers. The *United Hollywood* team also produced a series of short Web videos, including *The Office Is Closed*, which featured Greg Daniels, Mindy Kaling, Paul Lieberstein, B. J. Novak, Michael Schur, and other members of *The Office* staff picketing outside a planned location shoot for the show on the second day of the strike. Daniels and the others explain in lay terms, and with humor, why Hollywood writers were willing to take to the streets.

The three-minute video was widely seen via YouTube and other video sites. Through videos and blog posts, *United Hollywood* helped distill the issues at stake in the WGA negotiations, and it helped put a human face on the mass of nearly eleven thousand striking film and TV writers. Moreover, *United Hollywood* and other Internet-driven communications during the WGA strike proved to be a groundbreaking model for organized labor in any sector. Never before had union members been afforded such instantaneous access to news and information germane to the dispute. And the fact that those tools were available at minimal cost to the WGA and its supporters only underscored the revolutionary aspects of the digital technologies that were the source of the friction between the WGA and AMPTP. "The very tools that were the basis of the dispute in the strike were the tools that were used to wage the strike," says Aboud, a comedy writer who was one of the most active of the *United Hollywood* bloggers at the outset. "The strike itself was a demonstration of the change that is sweeping through the business."[6]

For the most part, *United Hollywood* operated independently of the WGA. The WGA West's philanthropic arm, the WGA Foundation, provided some money to help fund the production of the videos, to hire an assistant to the founders, and, later in the strike, to hire a consultant to help with viral marketing and distribution of the blog. But the editorial content of *United Hollywood* was under the control of the founders, not WGA officials, though there was an effort made to confirm sensitive information and coordinate the timing of the release of certain items.

The need for an autonomous, albeit pro-WGA, source of information became clear to *United Hollywood*'s founders as the strike deadline drew near. Guild leaders were focused on myriad logistical issues—from coordinating pickets to recruiting other unions and high-profile supporters. But there was no clearly articulated plan that *United Hollywood* founders were aware of to ensure that the WGA had a proactive communications strategy, other than mass e-mail bulletins, statements, and news releases posted on the websites of the WGA West and WGA East.

United Hollywood, on the other hand, was part propaganda machine, part soapbox, and part safety valve. It came as no surprise to its founders that it was so quickly embraced by striking writers, or so widely read within Hollywood and beyond. "Because I'm a writer I know that the only thing writers do more than write is read," Aboud says. "I had every confidence based on our strike captain meetings that we would have a very effective ground war. I knew all of the conventional and traditionally effective labor tools were going to be in place. But what I didn't get a sense of was that the official guild effort was including a strong enough propaganda machine. I just didn't get the sense that they were going to be able to communicate aggressively."[7]

The statement made in *United Showrunners'* "Pencils Down" ad addressed a gray area for showrunners, who shoulder the responsibility for overseeing all aspects of production on their shows. Showrunners are also known in industry parlance as "hyphenates," because of their dual functions as writer-producer or writer-director or in some cases writer-director-producer.

Many of a showrunner's duties—which encompass everything from overseeing the placement of sound effects to music cues to final editing decisions—do not explicitly involve writing. The question of what showrunners can and cannot do during a strike has long been a thorny issue for the WGA. It was the subject of a 1978 Supreme Court decision spurred after the WGA implemented tough disciplinary actions against some hyphenate members following its nearly four-month strike against the studios and Big Three networks in 1973.[8] Ten hyphenate WGA members were expelled or suspended after that strike. Two members were hit with fines of fifty thousand dollars, and four others were fined between five and ten thousand dollars, though the fines were later reduced by a vote among WGA members.

In a five-to-four decision, the Supreme Court made it clear that the guild has no right to prevent hyphenates from fulfilling their nonwriting duties during a strike, especially those supervisory duties that involve the "adjustment of grievances" among lower-level employees. Justice Byron White wrote in his majority decision that the WGA's strict rules and poststrike penalties were a coercive threat to the hyphenates and their employers: "These penalties were meted out at least in part because the accused hyphenates had complied with the orders of their employers by reporting for work and performing only their normal supervisory functions, including the adjustment of grievances, during the strike.

Hyphenates who worked were thus faced not only with threats but also with the actuality of charges, trial, and severe discipline simply because they were working at their normal jobs. And if this were not enough, they were threatened with a union blacklist that might drive them from the industry. How long such hyphenates would remain on the job under such pressure was a matter no one, particularly the employer, could predict. Moreover, after the strike, with the writers back at work, the hyphenates who had worked during the strike still faced charges and trials or were appealing large fines and long suspensions. At the same time, they were expected to perform their regular supervisory duties and to adjust griev-ances whenever the occasion demanded, functions requiring them to deal with the same union that was considering the appeal of their personal sanctions."

Regardless of the Supreme Court decision, during the 1973 strike and the others that followed, there was a deep suspicion among members that some hyphenates used the cover of their nonwriting responsibilities to surreptitiously work on scripts and story outlines. It was surely a divisive point among members as the 1988 strike dragged on and the public dissent of a large number of top TV writer-producers forced the WGA to settle.

But while the guild had no power to ban hyphenates from nonwriting work, WGA members could make the individual choice to withhold all of their services in the interest of putting more pressure on the networks and studios. The WGA's Sarah Singer addressed the quandary with showrun-ners, framing it as both a moral issue and a tactical consideration for guild members. If showrunners continued to put the finishing touches on epi-sodes in various stages of production after the strike began, it would only give the networks and studios more completed material to help them wait out the strike. Another important factor was maintaining the support of other entertainment-industry unions, particularly Teamsters-represented drivers. Hollywood Teamsters officials had put the WGA on notice: writ-ers would have their support, but only if hyphenates also respected their own guild's picket lines and refused to do any work for struck compa-nies. Teamsters drivers and members of the International Alliance of Stage and Theatrical Employees were still bitter from the 1988 experi-ence of losing income because of the writers' strike even as some WGA members continued to pass through studio gates to work. Singer and others strongly emphasized this point in discussions with showrunners. It made an impression on the group that organized the "Pencils Down" ad and the gathering of showrunners at the Sheraton Universal on Saturday, November 3.

Before the meeting started, Levitan, Prestwich, Yorkin, St. John, and others who had helped recruit names for the "Pencils Down" ad—including Marti Noxon, of ABC's *Private Practice;* Matthew Weiner, creator of AMC's *Mad Men;* and longtime *Tonight Show with Jay Leno* head writer Joe Medeiros—arrived early to help set up. Once they surveyed the setup of the room, they hastily started rearranging the chairs from horizontal rows to semicircles in order to better encourage conversation.

As they worked, the idea arose that the organizers of the meeting should ask their peers to commit to doing no work on their shows for at least one week should the strike happen. It was a bold move to undertake without much advance discussion, but the group realized that getting such a commitment from showrunners would be a powerful contribution to the guild's arsenal at a precarious moment. It became clear that at least one person from the organizing group would need to step up and lead the meeting. WGA's Singer was there to help, but she knew the message would be sent much more forcefully if it came from fellow showrunners.

As this point was being discussed, the heads in the room swiveled toward Levitan, who had little choice but to accept the assignment. It marked the first of numerous instances during the strike saga that the multimillionaire comedy writer would survey unfamiliar surroundings and ask himself, "How did I get here?" Regardless of how unprepared Levitan felt at the time, the meeting was successful beyond the expectations of the organizers—and the guild.

There was hesitation from some about committing to stopping all work on their shows, but the setting allowed for a healthy discussion about the reasoning behind the request. The back-and-forth gave attendees time to absorb information about the WGA's tactical approach, about lessons learned from the 1988 strike, and about the importance of having the support from key union allies like the Teamsters. Perhaps most important, the star power in the room convinced showrunners that they had strength in numbers. In the end, the vast majority of those persons in attendance vowed, in front of their peers, to stand down for at least one week if the strike ensued.

The timing was opportune for the WGA. On November 2, a few hours after the WGA's press conference to announce its intent to strike as of November 5, overtures by a well-connected third party spurred the AMPTP and WGA to set the eleventh-hour meeting for Sunday at the Sofitel hotel.

The showrunners' resolve strengthened the WGA's hand as guild leaders and negotiating-committee members went into the make-or-break session. Word of the surprising solidarity among top TV players quickly spread on the industry's e-mail and blog grapevine. Studio negotiators were apprised of what had transpired among showrunners on Saturday long before they sat down with the WGA again on Sunday.

The surest sign of how strongly the guild believed that showrunners would be linchpins in the contract battle was the composition of the WGA West and WGA East's joint contract-negotiating committee. Of the seventeen members, nine were writers who worked primarily in television. Of those nine, seven were prominent showrunners who were carefully selected to represent important shows on key networks: Neal Baer, NBC's *Law and Order: SVU*; Marc Cherry, ABC's *Desperate Housewives*; Carlton Cuse, ABC's *Lost*; David A. Goodman, Fox's *Family Guy*; and Carol Mendelsohn, CBS's *CSI: Crime Scene Investigation*. Representing cable programs was Shawn Ryan, creator and executive producer of *The Shield*, the gritty cop drama that transformed the fortunes of News Corporation's FX cable channel. Another negotiating committee member, Robin Schiff, was an experienced hyphenate known for handling female-lead series.[9]

In the top post of negotiating-committee chair was John Bowman. The veteran comedy writer and showrunner was two weeks away from the premiere of his latest series—the TBS late-night sketch comedy *Frank TV*, starring comedian Frank Caliendo—when the strike began. Bowman was well suited to serve as spokesman for the guild's contract demands and as the head of the committee representing the cross-section of writers whose livelihoods are governed by WGA contracts. Bowman brought not only his years of industry experience but also a Harvard MBA degree to the table. He could not be dismissed as uninformed in the ways of business. He had served on the guild's 2004 negotiating committee, and he was in his second term as a WGA West board member at the time he became negotiating-committee chair.

Guild members came to respect Bowman as a pragmatist who provided a steadying counterbalance to Verrone's fire and Young's idealism. His radio announcer's voice and enunciation added to the air of intelligence and seriousness he brought to the guild's discussion of contract issues and entertainment-industry macroeconomics. The personal stakes for Bowman were high after the strike ensued, as he had to abandon his work on *Frank TV* just as the show was nearing the starting line. All of these qualities resonated strongly with many guild members.

To be sure, the negotiating committee had its share of distinguished film writers, including Oscar nominees Susannah Grant (*Erin Brockovich*) and Terry George (*Hotel Rwanda*) and Oscar winner Stephen Gaghan (*Traffic*). And there were many prominent screenwriters who were vocal and visible in their support of the guild during the strike, notably Akiva Goldsman (*The Da Vinci Code*) and Paul Haggis (*Crash*).

But the highly coordinated response from television showrunners reflects the nature of their work. Showrunners are accustomed to crisis management and juggling myriad responsibilities on tight deadlines. "We're control freaks," Levitan says. "Showrunners are used to getting things done."[10] Screenwriters, by contrast, often work alone, or in relative isolation with a writing partner. Only occasionally do screenwriters have responsibility for overseeing the production of their scripts, unless they have hyphenate status on a production. The differences between film and TV writers had at times in the past been so great as to be highly polarizing for the guild during contract battles, especially when negotiations were stuck on issues that were relevant primarily to one camp. The divide was evident in 1988 when much of the contract fight was rooted in the guild's demand for higher residuals for TV shows that aired in foreign countries.

Twenty years later, guild leaders were careful to try to head off a film-TV divide among members by emphasizing how new media was a universal concern for all WGA members. At the same time, the film and TV writing marketplace was not nearly as balkanized in 2007 as it was in 1988. The explosive growth in job opportunities for writers in both sectors made it easier for writers and directors to move freely between film and TV work.

From the start, the United Showrunners coalition vowed to maintain a businesslike approach to their efforts to enhance the WGA's leverage. Like Levitan, a number of the people involved with United Showrunners had long enjoyed fruitful and friendly relations with top executives of the AMPTP member conglomerates.

Early on in the strike, there was talk among the group showrunners of organizing pickets outside the homes of the CEOs and distributing personal information about the executives, but that idea was quickly dismissed as a low blow that would only be counterproductive in the long run. Experienced showrunners were accustomed to working closely with senior network and studio executives, as business partners. Even during the extreme conditions of the strike, showrunners were mindful of the need to treat the WGA's fight as a business dispute, not a personal battle. They knew it was the only way the CEOs would ever take them seriously.

WGA leaders had good reason to be concerned about how showrunners would react to a strike. Dissent by prominent television writers had altered the course of the guild's work stoppages in 1985 and 1988.[11] The WGA West was a hornet's nest of internal battles among guild officers, executive staff, and board members in 1985 when members voted by a slim margin to authorize a strike in early March. The burning issue at the time was home video residuals and the dispute between the guild and the studios on how payments were calculated. It was the first conflagration over the hated "producer's gross" system under which writers' residuals were based on 20 percent of the revenue generated by video sales of a title rather than 100 percent. At the time, the details of the home video formula were not widely understood—even by the guild officials in charge of collecting residuals.

As home video sales grew in the early 1980s, guild staffers began to notice the discrepancy in residual calculations. The WGA West vehemently opposed the studios' contention that the producer's gross formula was spelled out in its contracts with the WGA as well as the Directors Guild and Screen Actors Guild. In 1984 the WGA filed arbitration claims against the individual studios, hoping to force them to make up years of payments to writers. By the time the arbitration claims were ready to be heard, the WGA's master contract had expired. WGA West leaders were hoping the threat of the home video arbitration would force the studios to settle those claims or make significant contract concessions in other areas.

In the end, the guild folded after a two-week strike. The tensions within the WGA West were too debilitating to withstand; there was fear that the guild would splinter with defections if the strike continued. In addition to the strife among board members and guild executives, the pressure was turned up by a group of a few dozen writers who dubbed themselves the "Union Blues." Most were television writers who were immediately vocal in their opposition to striking over video residuals. It was seen largely as a film writers' issue, and even some screenwriters thought it was not a strike-worthy concern. Some members of the WGA East were also publicly balking at supporting a prolonged work stoppage.

Against this chaotic backdrop, the WGA West's executive director, Naomi Gurian, was swayed by some board members and the Union Blues dissenters to quickly complete a deal with the Alliance of Motion Picture and Television Producers. The guild agreed to withdraw its home video arbitration claims largely in exchange for a $1.25 million influx to the WGA's pension and health fund. The decision cost Gurian her job in the month that followed the strike, amid more fractious battling among board members. And although the guild did hold together, a deep resentment for the actions of the Union Blues emerged among many members. On an emotional level, it did not help that one of the leaders of the Union Blues revolt, respected TV and film writer Lionel Chetwynd, was an outspoken political conservative in a left-leaning town.

Three years later, after the WGA again raised picket signs on March 7, 1988, the erstwhile Union Blues faction reemerged to publicly challenge guild leaders on the rationale for the strike. This time Chetwynd and others dubbed the group the "Writers Coalition," but the effort is scornfully remembered in WGA lore as being the return of the Union Blues.

As the strike dragged on, Chetwynd's group held large-scale meetings to persuade like-minded WGA members to sign a petition threatening to change their status as guild members in a way that would allow them to return to work despite the strike. The group even took up a collection to hire its own lawyers. The divide between WGA members by income strata was so great as to threaten to split up the union. Yet WGA members did reject the contract offer from the studios by a margin of 75 percent to 25 percent in a ratification vote held in mid-June. Writers Coalition leaders were critical of guild leaders for encouraging members to reject the offer.

In mid-July 1988, twenty-one writers aligned with the coalition filed a complaint against the guild with the National Labor Relations Board. The move was ostensibly an effort to affirm their right to change their membership status to the so-called financial core, or a member who is a participant only in the health and pension plan and cannot vote in guild elections or serve as an officer. But the real reason for the filing was to put guild leaders on notice: if the strike was not over in two weeks, hundreds of working writers would effectively resign their guild membership, participating only in the health and pension plan, the Writers Coalition claimed. The strike ended three weeks later, on August 7.

By any measure, the 1988 strike was a debacle that yielded little of substance for WGA members, compared to the millions it cost them in lost compensation and lost opportunities.

It is a widely held belief in the television industry that the decline in the prime-time market share controlled by the Big Three networks was hastened by the 1988 strike, which delayed the start of the 1988–89 season. Although Nielsen ratings data show a slow but steady erosion in viewership for ABC, CBS, and NBC beginning well before the strike, the fall of 1988 is remembered in the creative community as a turning point. It is a fact that the long strike spurred the then-upstart Fox network to develop unscripted alternatives to traditional comedies and dramas. The video-vérité *Cops* and documentary-style *America's Most Wanted* became staples of the network's prime-time schedule.

Steve Levitan was feeling pretty good on the evening of November 4, 2007. A day after showrunners had taken their stand at the Sheraton Universal meeting, WGA and AMPTP negotiators spent the day behind closed doors at the Sofitel hotel. The sporadic communications from insiders on both sides to key interested parties on the outside were that the talks were going well—surprisingly well.

Levitan received two calls that evening at his home in the Brentwood area of Los Angeles that gave him reason to feel optimistic that a crisis had been averted. The first was from negotiating-committee member Carlton Cuse, who called from the Sofitel. Cuse was effusive about how the muscle flexed by the showrunners was the decisive factor in forcing the AMPTP to address the new media issues. Not long after speaking to Cuse, a call came in from David Young, who thanked Levitan profusely for helping to instigate the consensus building among showrunners. It made all the difference in the negotiation session, Young told him. "I was feeling fantastic," Levitan says. "This was exactly why we did (the meeting)—to show that we were strong and united to avoid the fight. That was the whole idea."[12]

About two hours later, Levitan was jolted by another call from someone in the WGA camp. By then the first news reports were breaking online about the angry end to the talks after the WGA East officially went on strike after midnight eastern time. "That was devastating moment No. 1 in this whole process," Levitan says. "I thought, 'Oh boy, we are in deep.'"

As the picketing began the next morning, the vast majority of prominent showrunners made good on their weekend vow not to do any producing work on their shows, even the ones who were not directly involved with United Showrunners. From day one, guild leaders were heartened by the high turnout for picketing, and members were impressed by the solid organizational structure the guild had in place. In Los Angeles, WGA West members were expected to log a full day of picket duty at a preassigned site, starting as early as six o'clock.

Among the first hires David Young made after being named interim executive director was Jeff Hermanson, who had once been Young's boss at the garment workers' union. As the October 31 contract deadline approached, Hermanson and his staff worked with hundreds of volunteers recruited through the guild's member-outreach effort to create the network of strike captains who would serve the guild valiantly until the last days of the strike.

Strike captains had the responsibility of ensuring a strong turnout among members at their assigned picket locations. They worked with Hermanson to scope out the logistics of each site, surveying the area on foot to note all the entrances that needed to be covered, the best available parking options for pickets, and the nearest public restrooms, among other issues. Members were assigned picket sites according to the geographical location of their homes, and also according to where they did the most business as writers. The WGA wanted studio bosses to look out the window and see familiar faces walking the picket line.

Strike captains were tasked with making sure the pickets kept walking in a loop and chanting proguild slogans. After the first week, the turnout was so strong that the daily requirement dropped to four hours a day. But the chanting was mostly given up after a few weeks of complaints about how uninspired the slogans were. "Our chants, which faded away after the first week or two, were pretty lame. 'What do we want? Power. When do we want it? Now.' As writers, it was pretty embarrassing," comedy writer Mike Scully admitted. "We were better off just grumbling quietly to ourselves."[13]

The intensity of the WGA's street theater was nothing like the effort mounted in 1988, when picketing was much more sporadic and focused on one target site at a time. On picket days, large groups would gather in the late morning outside a network or studio, mill around with picket signs for an hour or two, make a little noise, and then break for lunch, or nearby bars. The contrast was not lost on the leaders of the AMPTP. "They were clearly better organized," says Carol Lombardini. "It was a much more serious effort (at picketing) than had ever been put forth in the past."[14]

This time around, writers were "were told where to go and what to do," said a writer who was active with United Showrunners. "People who'd been through the last strike were blown away by our resolve. They kept telling us, 'It was never like this in '88.' When you showed up there was a shift sign-in sheet, and there were shirts and signs, water and sunscreen. It's called 'organization.' And there was a big group-pressure factor at work because everyone was doing it. We were out of work anyway, and we were galvanized by the fact that (the studios) wouldn't talk to us."[15]

Levitan was assigned to picket duty at 20th Century Fox, the studio where he had been under a lucrative exclusive contract for nearly ten years. In the first few days of the strike, the experience of walking a picket line along a busy stretch of Pico Boulevard, enveloped by the sound of honking cars and shouts from passersby, was surreal to Levitan. But in the moment, Levitan did not have a minute to dwell on the oddness—or even the comedic potential—of the situation. He channeled his nervous energy into maintaining and expanding the United Showrunners coalition. Because of the leadership role he had haphazardly assumed, Levitan was inundated after the strike began with calls and e-mails from WGA members looking for information, advice, and counsel. He was overwhelmed by the level of fear and near panic he was hearing from fellow writers, but he remained focused on convincing his peers why it made sense to stand down completely, for the sake of keeping the strike as short as possible. In the first weeks of the strike, Levitan wrote e-mails and placed phone calls seemingly around the clock.

To keep the spirit of solidarity running high, Levitan and the other "Pencils Down" organizers decided to stage an all-showrunners rally outside of Disney's Burbank headquarters on day three. They knew that a strong public display of unity among showrunners would send a powerful message—to writers, to the public, and to Hollywood's CEOs. And they felt showrunners would benefit from seeing that they had strength in numbers, as they had in the November 3 meeting. The United Showrunners leaders were absolutely right that a booster shot of solidarity was in order, but they still had no idea what they were heading into with the mass showrunners rally.

The forest of picket signs said it all: *CSI. Lost. Army Wives. Two and a Half Men. Heroes. House. Desperate Housewives. The Office. Bones. Weeds. Law and Order: SVU. Gossip Girl. ER. The Shield. The Tonight Show with Jay Leno. The Young and the Restless.* The more than 125 showrunners who assembled outside the main entrance to Walt Disney Company in Burbank on the morning of Wednesday, November 7, 2007, carried picket signs with the names of their shows to reinforce just how much of prime time was endangered by the strike. The gathering drew television cameras and reporters from a range of media outlets. The contrast of picket signs juxtaposed against the Seven Dwarfs figures perched on the top of the Disney executive building made for great visuals. WGA leaders could not have planned it better if they had tried.[16]

After a few hours of picketing, showrunners headed to a nearby industry haunt, the Smoke House restaurant, for lunch and a discussion about what else they might do to pressure the studios to resume negotiations with the guild. The AMPTP had held firm on its position that there would be no negotiations while WGA pickets ringed studio lots. The steadfast refusal to meet angered writers and helped galvanize the turnout for picketing in the early weeks.

Showrunners were doing their part that morning, but there was no mistaking them for coal miners. After the mass picket outside Disney, many of them drove BMWs and Mercedes and Lexuses a few blocks to the Smoke House, where they availed themselves of valet parking and headed to a private room in the steak house that sits across the street from the Warner Bros. lot. The scene had the feel of a Hollywood charity event or awards luncheon, but for the jeans and baseball caps and athletic shoes. Writers milled around the room, engaging in the small talk that comes easily to people accustomed to taking part in publicity campaigns and premiere parties. In an opportunistic move to curry favor with top industry names, talent agency Paradigm came forward with an offer to pick up the tab, once the word about the showrunner picket spread the day before.

Levitan was again pressed into service to address the group as they settled in to eat. As he did at the Sheraton Universal, Levitan emphasized that the purpose of the meeting was not to issue an edict but rather to discuss the situation and solicit ideas for how they could maximize their collective clout. David Young and other WGA staffers attended the lunch, but they let Levitan do the talking.

The mood turned somber in an instant as showrunners voiced concerns and raised questions about the strike and the decision to withhold producing services. The room grew louder as people began to talk over one another. As Levitan struggled to field the questions, he glanced at Young, who was shaking his head and gesturing for Levitan to cut off the discussion. Although the room was private, the restaurant was still too public of a setting for such a heated discussion, and they had not carefully monitored everyone who had entered the room. Young then quietly conferred with Levitan, telling him that showrunners would have to reconvene at WGA West headquarters for the meeting—which meant at least a half-hour drive at that time of day. Levitan felt embarrassed but made the announcement with an apology for "flying by the seat of our pants." When Levitan arrived at the guild about an hour later, it was the first time he had set foot in the building.

Levitan and other United Showrunners leaders knew from the preview at the restaurant that nerves were on edge and some tempers were running high. Unlike the previous Saturday at the Sheraton Universal, the meeting at guild headquarters quickly became extremely contentious. Some questioned the WGA's rationale for going on strike and the need for writers to sacrifice their shows, while others who were staunch supporters of the strike blasted the ones they saw as potentially jeopardizing the guild's most potent weapon, the solidarity of its members.

After three days on strike, showrunners were extremely anxious. Most of them were accustomed to working nearly around the clock when shows were in production. Now that they had nothing to do but picket and talk with other writers, they had nervous energy to spare, and it all came pouring out at the meeting, which lasted three hours. To Levitan and the other United Showrunners organizers, conducting the meeting felt like an exercise in trying to juggle chain saws. One militant showrunner declared that anyone who could not afford to go ten weeks without a paycheck "should not be a writer," given the vagaries of employment even in the best of times. Some suggested that a fund be put together by the well-heeled among them to help others make mortgage and rent payments. A number of younger and less experienced writers were unabashed in discussing their fears, lamenting the loss of what could be "my one big chance" to launch a successful show.

Levitan and others tried to maintain a level of civility to the discussion, but voices were raised and insults were traded more than once that afternoon. A turning point came when a showrunner with a high-profile drama series, *Terminator: The Sarah Connor Chronicles*, which was scheduled to debut in January on Fox, rose to speak. Josh Friedman offered a personal perspective on the moral imperative showrunners faced, without any bombast or finger-wagging. Some at the meeting were aware that Friedman had undergone surgery in 2005 for a cancerous kidney, but most were not. "I'm thinking about the fact that I won't get to go to the premiere of my show," Friedman said. "I had cancer last year. I didn't know if I would be here this year. But I am not going back to work. That's what this means to me."[17]

For all of the debate, as the meeting stretched into its third hour, showrunners with only a few exceptions came to a consensus on extending their "Pencils Down" pledge beyond week one of the strike. They also came up with a consensus list of strike dos and don'ts that Levitan wrote down on a whiteboard. "At some point people started to realize that we had such strength in numbers," one participant recalled. "You looked around and realized: Everyone who could replace me (on a show) is in this room. That was a powerful feeling—people felt safe within the group. There was peer pressure involved too. You didn't want to be the one who said 'No.'"[18]

One idea raised at the Smoke House and discussed in greater detail at the WGA meeting was a proposal that showrunners barter their producing services on uncompleted episodes in exchange for the AMPTP resuming negotiations with the guild. Guild leaders were cool to the idea because having showrunners cross picket lines to produce would alienate other unions, and it would only give the networks and studios more material to help them withstand a long work stoppage. And there was no guarantee that the studios would make significant concessions even if they did agree to come back to the table.

Unbeknownst to the United Showrunners contingent, quiet diplomatic efforts were under way to break the stalemate and give the AMPTP a graceful way out of its untenable position that there would be no negotiations while the WGA was on strike. The effort came not from within the AMPTP or WGA but from a third party that had much to lose every day that the strike continued. As the strike went into its second week, leaders of Hollywood's five largest talent agencies felt intense pressure to intervene, if only to protect the viability of their own businesses. Talent agencies rely on the 10 percent commissions and other fees earned when their clients draw a paycheck. With a WGA work stoppage, talent agencies lose money not just on writer clients, but also from actors and directors who have no work because there are no more completed scripts to shoot. "We were afraid we were looking at 1988 all over again," said a senior partner at a top agency. "We were scared."[19]

As soon as the *United Hollywood* blog went live, its care and feeding became a full-time preoccupation for the founders. They collectively shared the job of updating the site with the latest information, news, photos, and links, as well as sifting through submissions. Most of the work was done by each person working alone on home computers and laptops. After the strike began, they had the additional challenge of working around their responsibilities as strike captains. As the strike went on, the volume of material flowing through the blog grew on a daily basis. "The strike was like running into a buzz saw," *United Hollywood* cofounder John Aboud says. "I knew that if the strike happened, there would be a flood. It is intrinsic to the soul of the writer to need to express him or herself in a situation like this."[20]

Aboud had the highest public profile of the *United Hollywood* leaders. He and his writing partner, Michael Colton, were regular panelists on the pop culture–skewering VH1 series *Best Week Ever* and its offshoots, *I Love the '80s* and *I Love the '90s*. Both Harvard alums, Aboud and Colton were also known in Hollywood as the cofounders of the well-regarded comedy Web magazine *Modern Humorist*. *The Comebacks*, the first feature film on which Aboud and Colton received screen credit, was released by an imprint of 20th Century Fox about three weeks before the strike began.

Aboud and the other *United Hollywood* founders were not in the same career strata as the members of United Showrunners. But they were comers, steadily employed on film and television projects, which counts as success in an industry where even established writers can go months without securing a paid job. The *United Hollywood* founders and hundreds of other similarly situated WGA members were alarmed by Patric Verrone's warnings that the Internet posed a grave threat to their future earning potential. Through the guild's outreach campaign, members like the *United Hollywood* founders were quickly schooled in the WGA's history and legacy of hard-fought strikes.

The *United Hollywood* blog reflected the idealism and activist spirit of this important faction within the WGA. In short order, the blog postings expanded beyond strike-related concerns to issues such as media consolidation and Federal Communications Commission policy on media-ownership rules, as well as net neutrality, or the push for a federal regulation barring broadband providers from imposing any limits on the type or volume of content accessed by users.

The tenor of *United Hollywood*'s content reflected many of the characteristics often associated with the "millennial" generation—those eighteen- to twenty-five-year-olds who came of age in the first decade of the twenty-first century. As outlined in a 2007 study by the Pew Research Center for People and the Press, those traits include a strong, if simplistic, sense of justice; being more idealistic than cynical; a willingness to engage in activism on causes that resonate; a tendency to maintain large social circles and to place a high value on the bonds of friendship; an expectation of employment mobility and swift career advancement on the job; and a predisposition to be deeply suspicious about the integrity of big business and many political institutions. This core group of strike supporters believed the studios were being greedy and exploitative of writers in the new media arena, and no amount of facts and figures about the lack of profits for Hollywood on the Internet would shake that conviction.[21] To wit, a sampling of commentary and opinion from *United Hollywood* during the strike, from a December 7, 2007, post by *United Hollywood* cofounder Laeta Kalogridis:

> I've said for a long time that this negotiation wasn't about anything rational on their side. The rational thing is a fair deal that neither side loves but both can accept. For them, this is about greed and the culture of corporate rapaciousness. It's about trying to strip writers (and other unions in this town) of protections it has taken decades to win and to keep.
>
> This fight was coming no matter who our leaders were. A new technology came into play (the Internet) and intersected with a "robber baron" culture that considers stripping away health care, pensions and job

security nothing but good business. The fight was never avoidable. The only question was how we would wage it, and whether we would win.

So now we know where the congloms stand, clearly and starkly: They want the Internet, and they don't want to pay us residuals that come from it or anything but fractions of a penny for downloads. Period.[22]

From *The Office* writer-producer Michael Schur, November 11, 2007:

It's sometimes hard to explain to people that we are not striking to make sure Aaron Sorkin doesn't have to fall out of escrow on his eleventh vacation home, but rather for the vast majority of our union who work sporadically, who average $62,000 a year, and who often find themselves undesirable hirees around age 40 if they never managed to land a job on a hit show.

So how do we get our point across, to people who don't understand why we're doing this? The best way I have found, is to say: everything on the internet? We get zero. They get everything. They get millions and millions and eventually billions and billions, and we get zero. And the "they," here, is basically six of the biggest baddest companies in the world, run by men who annually receive salaries and compensation well north of 50 million dollars.

This attempt on their part to lock down the internet for free . . . this is just good old-fashioned corporate greed, is what this is. This is old-timey Rockefeller union-busting land-grab stuff.[23]

From *Buffy the Vampire Slayer* creator Joss Whedon, February 6, 2008:

The studios are inefficient, power-hungry, thieving corporate giants who have made the life of the working writer harder from decade to decade. They are run by men so out of touch with basic humanity that they would see Rome burn before they would think about the concept of fair compensation. I maintain that they have never revealed their true agenda in the causing and handling of this strike, and to expect them to now is cock-eyed optimism of the most dangerous kind.[24]

The activist spirit that Verrone and Young brought to the guild meshed well with the natural inclinations of this important subset of the WGA. Verrone's status as a workaday TV writer gave him credibility with younger writers on the ascent and those whose incomes would be most affected by gains the WGA was able to secure in its Minimum Basic Agreement. Young brought a great moral authority to every conversation with his blue-collar union background. And the outreach Verrone and Young spearheaded gave writers the chance to consider the deeper meaning of being guild members in a white-collar business and the common interests they shared with other members of the WGA and other Hollywood guilds. "This was an opportunity to get involved with something where you really felt like you could make a difference on an individual level," Aboud says. "This is something where you really had an opportunity to walk the streets and put some shoe leather behind your positions. So it certainly was something that felt of a piece with my political leanings."[25]

The same force of idealism and discontent with the status quo that was marshaled by the WGA would help Barack Obama win the White House a year almost to the day after the strike began. The influence of grassroots efforts like United Showrunners and *United Hollywood* was greatly underestimated by Hollywood's corporate leaders for too long, and at great cost. "There had actually been this sense of community among writers that had already been building for several years," says John Bowman. "We were talking to each other a lot more. There was already a growing sense of frustration with the business side among writers. And then here we had a goal that united us."[26]

6

Angst in the Executive Suite

As 2007 began, Peter Chernin, Bob Iger, Barry Meyer, and Leslie Moonves made a point of talking with one another regularly about the upcoming cycle of guild contract negotiations. None of them had any illusions that the talks with the WGA, DGA, and SAG would be easy this time around.

The four CEOs formed the nucleus of power on the management side of the negotiations. The charter of the AMPTP mandates that its board members, composed of representatives of the studios that founded the organization in 1982, must vote unanimously to approve all contracts. In reality, the shots were called by the four CEOs with the deepest roots in the creative community and the biggest investments in traditional film and TV production. Chernin, Iger, Meyer, and Moonves were creatures of Hollywood in a way that their counterparts at NBC Universal, Sony Pictures Entertainment, Viacom, and MGM were not. Given the complexity of the issues and the looming strike threat, executives at AMPTP member companies were more than willing to leave the responsibility for setting the agenda for the AMPTP's Nick Counter and Carol Lombardini to the men with the most experience.

Chernin, Iger, Meyer, and Moonves had close ties to one another. They had long been friends and business associates, as well as competitors. Moonves, president and CEO of CBS Corporation, and Meyer, chairman and CEO of Warner Bros., have the strong bond that comes from enjoying great success together. Moonves worked for Meyer as president of Warner Bros. Television (and its predecessor, Lorimar Television) in the first half of the 1990s when the studio was the unrivaled leader in TV production with a roster of successful shows that included megahits *Friends* and

ER. Chernin had climbed through the ranks to become Rupert Murdoch's top lieutenant as president and chief operating officer of News Corporation, and he also served as CEO of News Corporation's Fox Entertainment Group unit housing all of its Hollywood-based operations. Chernin and Iger, president and CEO of Disney, became direct competitors in the late 1980s and early '90s, when Chernin was head of programming for the Fox network and Iger held the same job at ABC. In those years, Chernin and Iger did plenty of business with Moonves and Meyer in buying shows from Warner Bros. Television. Beyond their professional contacts, the men had moved in the same social circles for many years.

By the spring of 2007, the foursome was meeting about once a month for breakfast to discuss the prognosis for the labor talks and the general state of the industry. They tended to meet in highly visible spots in Beverly Hills and West LA. It did not hurt their cause for the word to get out that the CEOs were doing some strategizing of their own.

For an earlier generation, the responsibility on the management side for Hollywood's labor relations rested in large part with one studio mogul, MCA/Universal chieftain Lew Wasserman. Wasserman famously took it upon himself to maintain good relations with Hollywood unions and public officials after his conglomerate-building ambition was thwarted in the early 1960s by strident opposition from the Screen Actors Guild and an antitrust probe by the Justice Department. The pressure from the union and Washington, under attorney general Robert F. Kennedy, forced the 1962 breakup of Wasserman's MCA talent agency from MCA's prosperous TV production unit, Revue, right at the moment when MCA was acquiring the ailing Universal Pictures studio. (When faced with the choice of sticking with the talent agency or film and TV production, Wasserman chose production.) After that setback, Wasserman made sure he had the right relationships in place to help fight off future incursions into his business interests. For years, Wasserman had been the one to help lead Hollywood management and labor to equitable compromises in contracts. Wasserman's reign ended in the late 1980s, around the time of the writers' strike in 1988. Since then, no one in a commensurate position of power has been able to wield the same level of behind-the-scenes clout, though several have tried to position themselves as Wasserman's successor.

Jeffrey Katzenberg, the CEO of DreamWorks Animation, tried to appoint himself to the role as relations between the WGA and AMPTP deteriorated in the summer of 2007. Katzenberg went so far as to try to organize a meeting of the WGA negotiating-committee members, and during the strike he would reach out to prominent showrunners. But his efforts were largely brushed off by the key WGA players, who sensed that Katzenberg would have a hard time getting the other CEOs to play ball with him. Katzenberg had a long résumé as a senior executive at Paramount and Disney before cofounding the DreamWorks SKG studio venture with Steven Spielberg and David Geffen in 1994.

By 2007 Katzenberg was running DreamWorks Animation, the publicly traded spin-off company. That meant he did not have a dog in the fight with WGA, as the guild does not have jurisdiction over writing for animated feature films, DreamWorks Animation's primary business. Katzenberg told people he was trying to get involved to spare the industry the pain of a strike, but in an industry that encourages intense competition among top executives, suspicion about Katzenberg's motives were too great to overcome. "Peter Chernin and Les Moonves were not going to let Jeffrey come in and pull off something that they couldn't," said one prominent showrunner who was contacted by Katzenberg. "The egos involved are just too big."[1] Besides, Chernin, Iger, Meyer, and Moonves were savvy enough to realize that there was no turning back to the Wasserman days. The industry had changed too much for such a parochial approach. The dominant AMPTP member conglomerates had divergent interests at times, which made it untenable for the CEOs to cede so much power to a single executive in their midst.

The foursome knew from the outset that the biggest obstacle they faced in trying to maintain labor peace in Hollywood was the perception gap between management and labor on new media. Writers feared they were already being elbowed out of the dot-com gravy train, as they had been on home video, which turned out to be the savior of the entertainment industry in the 1980s and '90s. The CEOs were troubled because they knew the bottom-line reality. For all the attention paid to the innovation of digital distribution, Hollywood's conglomerates had yet to make any real money on new media. As far as the CEOs were concerned, the

Internet was most useful to them as a promotional tool. If exposure on the Internet encouraged more people to watch a program on a regular basis on TV, it would boost ratings and advertising revenue in the venue in which the media conglomerates still made the lion's share of their money. Even with thirty-second commercials embedded in programs streamed on the Web, and even with consumers paying $1.99 per download via iTunes, the total revenue generated through these new platforms in 2007 was minuscule compared to the $25,000 to $75,000 or more that a network commands for a thirty-second commercial spot in a moderately successful prime-time series.

Writers rightly questioned how the conglomerates could call Web streaming of full-length programs a "promotional" use when advertising was included. To their own detriment, studio executives were loath to acknowledge publicly that a large share of that advertising had little inherent value, because so much of it stemmed from larger deals with top advertisers for traditional commercial purchases. In other words, the Internet spots were freebies given away to big spenders as incentives and add-ons.

Original production for the Internet remained primarily a promotional device as far as Hollywood's top studios were concerned. In varying degrees, the studios had experimented with original content or made-for-Internet webisodes tied to hit shows, such as Lost, The Office, and CSI. Hollywood took note that even Google was stymied in how to squeeze profits from videos that became viral sensations on YouTube, which Google acquired in 2006.

Chernin could speak with authority about the struggle to make money in the online realm. News Corporation was hailed for making a wily move in 2005 when it scooped up Intermix Media, the parent firm of MySpace, for $580 million just as the social networking giant's traffic and user base was exploding. But two years later, MySpace was still requiring major investments from News Corporation, which poured money and resources into enhancing the service, boosting its international profile, and expanding the brand name into business ventures such as MySpace Music and MySpace TV. At the time Chernin was preparing with his colleagues for the guild talks, MySpace was not projected to be a significant source of profit for News Corporation any time soon.

After many meetings and brainstorming sessions, the CEOs were in synch on what they did *not* want to do in the next round of guild contracts. There was less of a consensus on the best approach to take with any of the guilds, but particularly the Writers Guild. The CEOs were inclined to resist what they knew was coming from the WGA: proposals to establish new residual formulas covering the reuse of movies and TV programs in new media and unfettered WGA jurisdiction over made-for-Internet productions done by AMPTP signatory companies. The studio chiefs thought it was far too early to be able to determine the moneymaking potential of new media, and therefore it was too soon to lock in new residual formulas.

The tough talk from WGA leaders about the urgent need for Internet residuals irritated the CEOs because from their perspective, the existing system was flawed and had not kept pace with the changes in the marketplace over the past thirty years, let alone the past few years. In some instances, the high cost of residual fees effectively prevented studios from selling rerun rights to programs initially produced for ABC, CBS, Fox, or NBC to local broadcast TV stations. Residual fees have historically been highest for reuse on broadcast TV because the Big Four networks and local broadcast stations so dominated the TV advertising market.

But as broadcast TV's competition has increased markedly from cable- and satellite-delivered channels, local stations can no longer spend as freely as they once did to acquire rerun rights to shows that were only moderate successes in prime time. With B- and C-level shows drawing lower license fees in syndication, residual obligations and other costs, such as music licensing, for a syndication rerun can wipe out what little profit the studio stood to make on the sale. In those cases, the studio has no choice but to seek a cable buyer for a show. The sale to a cable channel will often come at a lower price than what the same property could generate in broadcast syndication, but the studio's residual obligations will also be significantly reduced.[2]

The CEOs hated having their hands tied in deal making by what they viewed as an outmoded residual system. And they were adamant in their refusal to extend the old residual system to new media, for fear that it would hobble these fledgling businesses with untenable costs before they even got off the ground. "We were really afraid that we were going to push all of that business someplace else before we had a chance to develop it," says Barry Meyer. "Certainly we wanted to do it with the writers and directors and actors that we're used to working with, but it can't be under the same old rules and conditions. We've got to have new models for a new kind of business."[3]

Knowing that the WGA would make an aggressive bid to establish a new category of residuals for new media, Counter prepared a forceful response. The proposal to shift the entire residuals system to recoupment-based formulas was meant as a "be careful what you wish for" warning to the WGA. As much as writers wanted to break new ground in residuals, so did the conglomerates.

The studios, however, stumbled right out of the gate. The recoupment proposal put before the WGA on the first day of negotiations in July was as unrealistic in the realpolitik of the situation as some of the items the WGA had in its list of demands. The AMPTP's opening salvo would be the tactical blunder that gave the guild the last big push it needed to rally members for a strike. And it became a source of friction among the CEOs.

Although the CEOs monitored the situation leading up to the July talks, their focus was on defining the AMPTP's agenda in broad strokes—and setting the parameters of what they would and would not be willing to do in terms of new media. The execution of the negotiation strategy was left to Nick Counter. The CEOs had faith in the AMPTP's long-serving president, for his decades of experience as a labor negotiator and for his track record of keeping the studios out of an industry-wide strike for nearly twenty years.

Counter, by many accounts, did not believe the WGA could pull off a strike, not with all the leadership turmoil the guild had been through in the previous few years, and not with the level of personal sacrifice that the WGA would ask for from its most prominent members, particularly showrunners. On a personal level, Counter was incensed by the rabble-rousing and the tactics employed by Patric Verrone and David Young. He believed they were spoiling for a fight, for their own aggrandizement, and he was not about to be cowed by them.

In fact, as the tension mounted with the WGA, the AMPTP quietly approached SAG with an offer to conduct early negotiations on a new contract to succeed the master agreement that expired for actors on June 30, 2008. The overture meant that the studios were offering to allow SAG negotiators to help craft the template for new media that the WGA and DGA would follow. It was meant as a sign of the studios' deep desire to avoid any unrest with actors. A strike by any of Hollywood's core unions is debilitating to film and TV production, but when actors walk, the industry shuts down in an instant. There are no temporary work-arounds; there is no squeezing out one more episode from an existing script if there are no actors working in front of the cameras.

By the time the AMPTP reached out to SAG, though, the leaders of SAG and the WGA had been having regular discussions about working together to maximize the leverage that both guilds could bring to bear on the studios. Patric Verrone had found a kindred spirit at SAG in Alan Rosenberg, who had been elected national president of SAG just three days after Verrone took the helm of the WGA West in September 2005. Both men ran for office as scrappy populists who vowed to fight to protect the livelihoods of the "middle-class" writers and actors who were most dependent on gains achieved through master guild contracts. The WGA had the earlier contract expiration, so the writers had the more immediate strike threat to wield. And the one-two punch of actors walking out on the heels of writers was a formidable club for both guilds to swing.

The WGA and SAG were so much in synch that the WGA's recommendation strongly influenced SAG's decision to appoint Doug Allen as its national executive director in January 2007. Allen had been a strong contender for the same job at the WGA West when the guild was reviewing candidates prior to formally appointing David Young to the post. Allen, who had spent the previous twenty years as assistant executive director of the NFL Players Association, shared Young's philosophy of the need for Hollywood unions to drop their historic gentility and to prepare members for a long and bloody fight over twenty-first-century compensation concerns.

The cohesion between the WGA and SAG was not lost on Counter. Nor was the fact that the DGA, true to form, kept its distance from the heated rhetoric coming from SAG and the WGA. The directors let it be known that they were spending more than one million dollars to commission two separate studies of the size, scope, and profit potential of the new media marketplace to arm its negotiating team with facts when the DGA's turn at the bargaining table came. The DGA was also the only one of the three guilds to have had consistent executive management. Whereas David Young and Doug Allen prided themselves on their status as Hollywood outsiders with deep experience in union organizing, DGA executive director Jay Roth is a longtime Hollywood insider and lawyer who has headed the guild since 1995.

In preparing for battle with a new regime at the WGA, Counter devised the hardball plan to offer the WGA a choice between two proposals that amounted to "bad" (the three-year study plan) and "worse" (the recoupment push). Barry Meyer bore the burden of being closely identified with the recoupment proposal. During the AMPTP's press briefing on July 11, 2007, five days before the start of formal talks between the studios and the WGA, Meyer made the mistake of saying too much. A forty-year industry veteran, the gentlemanly Meyer at times sounded like a lawyer arguing the case for what the studios saw as the need to overhaul the residual system. His reasoned and articulate discussion of the proposal helped the reporters understand why the studios viewed the existing system as unsustainable. He spoke earnestly about their desire to shift to a system that was more generous to writers, directors, and actors in success, while allowing the studios to manage their costs with less profitable productions. When his comments were reported in detail in the trade press, many in the creative community were aghast at what they viewed as an attack on their livelihoods. "We're operating under terms and conditions that were formulated 50 years ago," Meyer said at the briefing. "We have to look at models that allow our investment to be recaptured. And this is the time to do it because of all the new-media issues."[4]

Although Moonves and Disney's Anne Sweeney also spoke about the proposal that day, Meyer's voice was the most resonant. Chernin, who did not attend the briefing, disavowed any advance knowledge of the offer that gave the WGA the last bit of justification it needed to take its members out on strike. It would take two months for the AMPTP to formally withdraw the recoupment proposal from the negotiations platform, but the CEOs knew within days of the press briefing that introducing such an inflammatory concept at such a precarious time had been a big mistake. Meyer got an earful about his choice of words from some of his peers. "As soon as (the AMPTP) said they wanted to completely remake residuals, we said 'Really? How are you going to do that?'" John Bowman says. "And when they starting talking about things like profit-based residuals, that made everybody crazy because we've all gotten profit statements showing that no money has been made by our shows and our movies. 'The Simpsons' has never made any money. So there's absolutely no credibility there for going to a profit-based system."[5]

The CEOs watched with dismay through the rest of the summer and fall as relations between the AMPTP and WGA devolved. The foursome and other top Hollywood executives stayed out of the public eye in relation to negotiations after the debacle of the recoupment proposal, leaving the day-to-day combat duty to Nick Counter and Carol Lombardini. But in the seventy-two hours after the WGA's November 2 announcement that it would strike on November 5, Moonves and Iger, among others, worked the phones in a last-minute stab at diplomacy. They reached out to showrunners on the WGA's negotiating committee that they knew well. By numerous accounts, the executives uniformly pressed the point that Patric Verrone and David Young were recklessly leading writers off a cliff, and that the small amount of money generated by new media for the foreseeable future was not worth the pain and sacrifice of a strike. They were blunt in questioning Verrone's qualifications to lead the guild. They noted that some members of the negotiating committee had known some of the CEOs of AMPTP conglomerates a lot longer than they had known Verrone or Young.

Negotiating-committee members, including *Desperate Housewives'* Marc Cherry, *CSI*'s Carol Mendelsohn, *Law and Order: SVU*'s Neal Baer, and *Lost*'s Carlton Cuse, were also proactive that weekend in pressing the guild's perspective with the top brass that writers wanted the security of gaining a toehold in new media now so as to avoid the home video scenario. Asking for a residual of 2.5 percent of revenue derived from new media exploitation of a production was fair to both sides because writers would make money only if the studios made money.

The conversations went round and round. When WGA and AMPTP negotiators convened at the Sofitel hotel on November 4, the CEOs were in near-constant contact with their labor executives. Just like their counterparts on the WGA side, the executives ran the emotional gamut on that long day—from hope that disaster would be averted to the grim resignation that the onslaught was coming.

As the storm clouds gathered, another key Hollywood constituency, talent agents, was also becoming increasingly alarmed at the state of the WGA and AMPTP negotiations. The entertainment industry's largest agencies had as much to lose as anyone in a prolonged labor action. No work for clients meant no 10 percent commission fees coming in. The savviest agents knew that a strike would have bad long-term implications for a marketplace already in turmoil.

Leaders of the industry's largest talent agencies—Creative Artists Agency, William Morris Agency, Endeavor, International Creative Management (ICM), and United Talent Agency—kept in close contact with one another as the WGA's October 31 contract expiration date approached. Verrone and Young had met with the leaders of some of the top agencies earlier in the year in an effort to introduce themselves and explain their perspective on the importance of the 2007 contract negotiations. Young left the impression on some that he was worried about agents' self-interest and whether they might be a hindrance to the WGA's cause. Several prominent agents offered their matchmaking and deal-making services to Young, given his lack of experience in guild negotiations, but Young "gave off the impression that he didn't trust anyone outside of the union," said one top agent.[6]

By the time the WGA initiated its strike-authorization vote, agency leaders were meeting together on the matter under the auspices of the Association of Talent Agents, the trade organization representing the vast majority of entertainment and literary agencies in Los Angeles and New

York. The ATA by definition has deep experience in guild issues; it is the entity that negotiates the agencies' master agreements with Hollywood unions. These so-called franchise agreements govern the terms of the business relationships between agents and clients who are guild members.[7]

The strike threat prompted an unusually cooperative approach among a group of successful Hollywood rainmakers who are, generally speaking, intensely competitive with one another. Like the CEOs, however, the agents recognized the fragility of the situation and did not want to do anything to alienate the studios or, more important, their high-level screenwriter and showrunner clients.

After the strike began, with only recriminations being exchanged by the WGA and AMPTP and no new talks scheduled, the agency leaders felt they had to be more proactive. In a flurry of shuttle diplomacy, phone calls were made to CEOs, negotiating-committee members, and other prominent WGA members in an effort to figure out what it would take to get the sides back to the table. A handful of top agents had a meeting with Verrone and Young at WGA West headquarters on November 8, the fourth day of the walkout. The key players in this effort were the top echelon of agency partners: Jim Berkus of United Talent Agency, Rick Rosen of Endeavor, Jeff Berg and Chris Silbermann of ICM, Jim Wiatt of William Morris Agency, and Bryan Lourd of CAA.[8]

It became clear to the agency leaders that relations between the sides were so poisoned that it would take a person with great influence and respect to serve as a mediator—the show business equivalent of the State Department sending a special envoy to settle a political crisis overseas. In assessing the situation along with their ATA advisers, the consensus opinion emerged that CAA cochairman Lourd was the right man for the moment.

Lourd is known for his low-key but persuasive charm. He is a soft-spoken Louisiana native, the antithesis of the stereotype of the hard-charging, abrasive Hollywood agent. He personally represents some of Hollywood's top stars, including George Clooney and Sean Penn. CAA, whose cofounders included the onetime superagent Michael Ovitz, was in 2007 the single most powerful talent agency in Hollywood. Competitors have been known to refer to it as the "Death Star."

Lourd did not lobby for the assignment, by multiple accounts, but he was willing to serve when called upon. He wound up putting most of his personal and professional life on hold while he focused on the goal of getting the talks restarted and resolved. The CAA power broker started with a call to David Young on the heels of the November 8 agents' meeting at WGA West headquarters. The two met alone for breakfast early on Sunday, November 11, at a low-profile restaurant near the guild's offices. Both Lourd and Young had every reason to keep the meeting secret, lest the prospect of Lourd as a mediator raise unrealistic expectations in both camps.

Lourd emphasized to Young that he had deep relationships with the CEOs who called the shots for the AMPTP and that he was offering to help the sides communicate better. Lourd and the other agents had quietly reached out to several CEOs, who had agreed to a private meeting. They were eager to put an end to the work stoppage and the spectacle of picket lines outside of studio gates. Peter Chernin had already told Lourd he wanted to meet with Young at Lourd's house as soon as possible with the intent of hashing out the broad strokes of a deal—something Chernin believed could be done one on one on a legal pad in a few hours. Over breakfast, Lourd made his case to Young, using the low-volume salesmanship, in much the same way Lourd had persuaded many an actor to sign with CAA. After Lourd's role became public a few days later, a joke went around Hollywood that the CAA titan had "signed David Young as a client."

The next day, Young called Lourd to take him up on his offer. But Young initially rejected the idea of a private meeting with Chernin, according to multiple accounts. There were times when Young seemed inhibited by his lack of experience in Hollywood and his limited understanding of the intricacies of entertainment industry deal making. He seemed concerned about appearing to look weak in the eyes of Hollywood heavyweights like Chernin.

Lourd pressed the point that such one-on-one conversations over dinner or on a golf course were often the key to getting complicated deals done in Hollywood. But Young seemed wary of taking this route, which suggested to observers that he believed those handshake agreements were part of the reason the WGA had not negotiated aggressively in the past. And the counsel Young kept at the WGA were mostly persons who he had brought in from outside of Hollywood during the previous two years. There was no one in Young's inner circle who had a strong relationship with Counter, let alone any of the CEOs.

At the same time the agency leaders were trying to bring the sides back together, United Showrunners cofounder Steve Levitan was busy trying to arrange a private meeting between John Bowman and Peter Chernin. Levitan leaned on his personal attorney, Sam Fischer, partner in the powerhouse firm of Ziffren, Brittenham, Branca, Fischer, Gilbert-Lurie, Stiffelman, Cook, Johnson, Lande & Wolf, to set up a secret get-together. Levitan had come to realize that as much as the WGA was in the right, a big part of the breakdown between the sides was the fact that the writers did not have an experienced Hollywood deal maker in their camp—a deal maker like Fischer.

Fischer ranks high in the entertainment industry's top echelon of transactional lawyers, with an impressive client list of showrunners such as Levitan and *The Office* steward Greg Daniels. Levitan knew Fischer could get any one of the four key CEOs on the phone in an instant. He also felt that Fischer was perfectly suited for the task of helping to mediate because of his firm's long history in guild affairs. Ken Ziffren, respected as an elder statesman of the industry, had helped settle the WGA's walkout in 1988 and had long represented the DGA. Levitan surmised that Fischer's proximity to Ziffren could only help the WGA's cause.

Levitan had become close with Bowman through the United Showrunners initiative; they spoke on a daily basis during the first month of the strike. In a late-night phone call, Levitan explained why he felt it was imperative for the sides to get some face time with a smart lawyer present to serve as referee and translator. DreamWorks Animation CEO Jeffrey Katzenberg, in his calls to United Showrunners leaders, had emphasized that the CEOs had no regard for Verrone and Young but did see Bowman as someone they could work with.

On the phone that night with Levitan, Bowman committed to attending if a meeting could be arranged. Fischer quickly set up it up for Sunday,

November 11—the same day Bryan Lourd took David Young to breakfast—at Chernin's home in Santa Monica. It was to be held in secrecy, with just Chernin, Bowman, and Fischer attending. Chernin had told Fischer that the issues could be settled in a few hours if both sides dropped their posturing. That statement would gnaw at Levitan for the remainder of the strike.

Levitan was a bundle of nerves as he waited for the results of his stealth diplomacy. On Saturday night, he was asked to attend a meeting of about a dozen younger showrunners—rising stars with a lot to lose in the work stoppage—who were wavering in their pledge to withhold their producing services. Levitan was troubled as he drove across Los Angeles from his home on the west side to a writer's home in the Los Feliz neighborhood east of Hollywood. He was worried that if some broke ranks from the United Showrunners coalition, others would follow. Yet he would not risk telling them about the Chernin-Bowman meeting, for fear that rumors would spread and hurt any chance of progress resulting from the meeting. Levitan wound up telling the group as earnestly as he could that some potentially important "stuff" was in the works and that it was important for showrunners to stay the course with the guild. He was not sure if his audience believed him.

The following morning, Levitan got a call from Bowman. He was backing out of the meeting. Bowman indicated to Levitan that the decision was made by Young and Verrone, which was true. But the reason was not intransigence on the part of the WGA leaders; it was because the WGA had just agreed to accept Bryan Lourd's offer to help broker a deal. WGA leaders did not want Lourd to feel undercut before he even got started. Bowman could not tell Levitan about Lourd, for the same reason Levitan did not tell anyone about the meeting arranged by Fischer. Rumors and media coverage would only complicate Lourd's assignment.

Levitan was crushed by Bowman's call. Although he understood that Bowman was in a difficult position in having to answer to multiple constituencies, Levitan was embarrassed for having put his lawyer in an awkward position. He was also upset that with the best of intentions, his effort wound up as a snub of the top executive at the studio that had him under a lucrative exclusive contract. The incident left Levitan incredibly frustrated, but on Monday morning he was back on the picket line outside of 20th Century Fox.

The talent-agency leaders spent the second week of the strike working the phones as they sought to assuage the concerns of WGA leaders, the CEOs, and Nick Counter about the hurdles in getting the sides back to the negotiating table. Finally, a private meeting was set for Friday, November 16, at Bryan Lourd's home in Beverly Hills. Patric Verrone and David Young would meet with Peter Chernin and Bob Iger, with Lourd serving as host and mediator. Incredibly, the plan for the meeting managed to stay quiet until after it was over. The WGA and AMPTP issued a brief joint statement late in the day announcing that formal negotiations would resume November 26, the Monday following the Thanksgiving weekend, with Lourd serving as mediator.

Lourd and the other agents were floored by what they learned during the process of trying to set up the meeting. Both sides were guilty of violating the tenets of Hollywood Deal Making 101. There were no personal relationships to speak of between the new regime at the WGA and the CEOs or Nick Counter. No one on the management side had made the kind of friendly meet-and-greet overtures that they would have undertaken in the pursuit of any other high-level business transaction or acquisition. The situation might have been different if Verrone had been more of a known commodity as a writer. In spite of all the time Verrone put in on 20th Century Fox–produced series, Chernin was unfamiliar with him before he was elected president of the WGA West.

Moreover, the rhetoric and the tactics Verrone and Young adopted were immediately off-putting to the CEOs. They tended to think of writers in terms of the ones they knew best—successful showrunners who were anything but low-paid workers. Once the strike began, the feeling among the CEOs was that the two men at the top of the WGA West were outsiders (despite Verrone's twenty-year career as a writer) who did not understand the entertainment business and, worse, were callous about the strike's repercussions on the broader industry workforce—including writers.

Because of the lack of communication and trust, neither the WGA nor the AMPTP was armed with the ultimate resource in a negotiation:

a sense of the high and low ends of what would constitute an acceptable deal to the other side. And because of the strong emotions stirred by the strike, it was difficult for both sides to understand the other's perspective on the most contentious issues—another important factor in a successful negotiation.

The experienced agency leaders were also surprised to learn that the WGA did not appear to have gathered much independent research on the size and scope of the new media marketplace. The AMPTP had every incentive to downplay the actual earnings, but the agents believed that the WGA would have been better prepared for negotiations if it had considered more outside information to shape its thinking on what added up to "a fair share" for writers.

Early on, Lourd had members of his staff prepare a detailed presentation on CAA's experience in making deals for its clients in new media and in backing several Internet ventures that never turned a dime, despite big investments of money and manpower. As Hollywood's largest talent agency, CAA had a good understanding of the scope of profit potential in new media. To Lourd's obvious dismay, few questions were asked after the lengthy presentation was made to WGA officials and some negotiating-committee members. They were unshakable in their resolve that it was now or never, and no amount of evidence that big profits were still far off would change that view. Guild leaders were firmly convinced they had to claw out residuals and jurisdiction in new media in the next contract or writers would be shafted while the Internet evolved into the dominant distribution platform of the future. Meanwhile, the studios were just as insistent on pushing back hard on new media demands, because there was so little profit to share.

As the agents labored behind the scenes, the WGA's picket lines grew stronger and showier during the second week of the strike. Marc Cherry organized a "Picketing with the Stars" event on November 13 outside Universal Studios, where his ABC hit *Desperate Housewives* was filmed. Cherry knew he could count on the support of his *Housewives* troupe, but he was pleasantly surprised by the turnout of dozens of prominent actors. Under an azure-blue sky, the crowd at its peak spilled off the sidewalk and onto busy Lankershim Boulevard, which borders the western edge of the Universal complex. Screen Actors Guild leaders had encouraged actors to support the WGA strike in their off-duty hours.[9] But the turnout for "Picketing with the Stars" was more than a response to the SAG leaders' directive. It was a show of solidarity and gratitude, a recognition that actors rely on writers to deliver the characters and the stories that define their careers. At the same time, it allowed SAG to demonstrate that it intended to zero in on the same issues as the WGA in its contract negotiations.

Among the notable names who stood shoulder to shoulder with showrunners that morning were Sally Field, Ben Stiller, Calista Flockhart, Rob Lowe, Ray Romano, Hugh Laurie, Felicity Huffman, Lisa Kudrow, Brad Garrett, Rachel Griffith, Jon Cryer, Neil Patrick Harris, Zach Braff, Marg Helgenberger, Seth Green, and Matthew Perry. It was an uplifting experience for Cherry and many other writers. The presence of so many famous faces drew media coverage from local, national, and international outlets. Every interview with a star, every shot of a picket sign, helped the WGA's cause in the court of public opinion, casting the strike as a battle between Hollywood's hardworking little guys and Big Media. "You guys are the tip of the arrow," former *Seinfeld* star Jason Alexander said of the WGA members walking the picket line. "This is the most important thing you've fought for in our creative lives. You're on the side of the gods."[10]

Sarah Silverman, the actress-comedian who is also a WGA member, was characteristically blunt in her on-camera interviews that day. "It's so *crazy* ridiculous. All the writers want is a small percentage of the money that the producers are making on the things that they're writing," she said. "I keep trying to think (of) the other side. Because nobody's *evil*. They must be thinking they're doing the right thing, right? I think they're just being dicks."[11] The backdrop for the TV cameras was perfectly set with a group of writers and actors, including a few supporting players from NBC's *The Office*, gathered in a circle with acoustic guitars and a washboard to sing union songs.

The day before "Picketing with the Stars," the WGA delivered some strong visuals by organizing "Kids Day" on the picket line, to coincide with the November 12 school holiday in observance of Veterans Day. The sight of moms and dads holding an infant in one hand and a picket sign in the other could not help but elicit sympathy, from both industry insiders and passersby on the street. Toddlers and preteens sporting such slogans as "I download SpongeBob" and "I stream Hannah Montana" drove home the WGA's message as well as anything.

The WGA's street theater would continue throughout the strike with an array of themed picket events, including the "Gay Gate" gathering of gay and lesbian writers outside the *Ugly Betty* production facility and a day for dogs to join their owners on the picket line outside 20th Century Fox. Multiple generations of *Star Trek* writers convened one day outside of Paramount. Horror writers chose to gather at Warner Bros., where in a nod to the studio's 1973 classic *The Exorcist*, an "exorcism" was held to rid the AMPTP of its demons. (It was complete with writers dressed as priests and nuns walking around the studio compound while chanting, "Out, demons, out!")

In their frustration, the CEOs and AMPTP executives would angrily point to these gatherings as a sign that the picketing had become a social event for writers who were having fun while the rest of the creative community suffered. But ultimately, the high public profile of the conflict put pressure on the CEOs to act. There was no denying the WGA's marketing savvy. It is hard to fight children and dogs.

In preparing for the November 16 meeting at Lourd's house, the CEO foursome chose the participants from their side carefully. CBS's Leslie Moonves had two conflicts. For one, he was based out of New York, which was not conducive to an assignment that would require a lot of face time for bridge building with the WGA. More important, he was seen as too much of a dove. CBS Corporation is the smallest of the AMPTP's dominant congloms, and its main profit engine is the CBS television network. Moonves had the most to lose as the strike went on and CBS was forced to make do without fresh episodes of *CSI* and *Two and a Half Men* and other cornerstone scripted series. As much as he shared the sentiments of his peers, Moonves still had every incentive to find compromises that would bring the strike to an end. News Corporation, Time Warner, and Disney were larger companies with more diverse operations that could better withstand the sudden shutdown of TV production.

Warner Bros.' Barry Meyer had the experience and the legal training for the task, but he carried the stigma of having been a cheerleader for the recoupment proposal. He was seen as too much of a hawk.

Peter Chernin was a logical choice. Chernin is a natural-born leader with a razor-sharp intellect, a quick wit, and a disdain for pretense that has served him well in his professional life. As the CEO representing Fox and News Corporation's interests, Chernin had a stake in every aspect of the businesses that the WGA and AMPTP were at war over, from film and TV production to broadcast and cable networks around the world to the then-fledgling Internet video distributor Hulu. When the strike began, News Corporation had just launched the service, designed to offer a legal source of full-length TV programs, in beta form, as a partnership with NBC Universal.

Iger was a good complement to Chernin, in personality and in his perch as CEO of the company that opened the floodgates of digital distribution for television programming. Soft-spoken and thoughtful, Iger has a warmth and a sensitivity that endear him to many who work for him. He gained respect among his executive peers for his business acumen with a series of bold decisions, including the iTunes licensing and Web-streaming initiatives, after becoming Disney's CEO in 2005. Iger showed his tough side in the trial by fire he endured for more than a year before clinching the job as Michael Eisner's successor.

Amid high expectations, the midday meeting of Chernin, Iger, Verrone, and Young at Lourd's house on Friday, November 16, was cordial but stiff. Chernin and Iger told the WGA duo that the AMPTP was preparing a comprehensive new proposal that would address their demands on new media, without getting too specific. Verrone and Young reiterated that they had not been the ones to walk away from the negotiation process. They agreed to convene a formal bargaining session on November 26 at a neutral location, which turned out to be the Renaissance Hotel in Hollywood. They agreed that the WGA and AMPTP would issue a joint statement about the resumption of talks but then commit to a "news blackout," to prevent the sides from bashing each other in the media.

Lourd and the other agency leaders were encouraged that the meeting had yielded a date for new talks. The creative community was hopeful and relieved, albeit cautiously so, after the joint statement was released about seven thirty that night. "We're on the 10-yard line. Let's drive it home," read an e-mail message sent by United Showrunners leaders to supporters shortly after the WGA-AMPTP statement was issued.

As the days passed, however, Lourd's optimism ebbed. He had observed the body language from both sides in his own home. Getting the AMPTP and WGA back in a room together was a first step, but it would not amount to anything unless they were able to find some common ground on which to build. Until then, the collateral damage would only grow. On the same day the sides agreed to resume negotiations, layoff notices were sent to the one-hundred-plus production staffers on NBC's *Saturday Night Live*.

The jockeying between the WGA and the studios continued during the ten days between the announcement and the November 26 bargaining session. Although the WGA tabled its regular picketing schedule for the week of November 18 because of the Thanksgiving holiday, the guild staged a midday demonstration on November 20 that drew more than four thousand writers and union members, some far removed from the entertainment industry, for a three-block march down the heart of Hollywood Boulevard.[12] The mass gathering had all the trimmings of a political protest rally as it moved past the tourist traps near the intersection of Hollywood Boulevard and Highland Avenue. Singer Alicia Keys and her band performed two songs from the back of a flatbed truck to kick off the event. She greeted the crowd as a fellow writer. "There are no songs without any words. There are no stories without any words," she said to the sea of picket signs that faced her. "United we stand, divided we fall." The sky was overcast, but the weather that Tuesday afternoon was otherwise cooperative—much to the envy of the striking writers in New York who routinely braved freezing temperatures.

The brief march that followed Keys's performance was led by Teamsters trucks and LAPD officers on motorcycles and bicycles. At the front of the crowd, a group of notables—including Patric Verrone, John Bowman, SAG president Alan Rosenberg, actresses Julia Louis-Dreyfus and Sandra Oh, and writers Steve Levitan, Shonda Rhimes, and Akiva

Goldsman—carried a twenty-foot banner proclaiming "Solidarity with Writers" and "We Are All on the Same Page."

The presence of union members from other sectors—teachers, nurses, airline pilots, service workers, and non-Hollywood Teamsters—gave many writers a strong feeling of moral support, and it reinforced that they were fighting for a cause that transcended the entertainment industry. "On strike! Shut 'em down! Hollywood's a union town!" was one of the chants that spread through the crowd as it migrated west on Hollywood Boulevard toward the end point, across from Grauman's Chinese Theater and its famous cement archive of movie star autographs, handprints, and footprints.

As the WGA and its supporters were swarming Hollywood Boulevard, several of the CEOs tried to appear magnanimous by sending a carefully worded message to their employees, ostensibly to update them on the status of the strike. But there was no doubt that the message was directed to the WGA's negotiating team and the media. "Sitting down for serious discussions [on November 26] is an important first step in the resolution of our differences. These differences are substantial, but we continue to believe that with hard work, patience and understanding from both sides, they can be overcome," Leslie Moonves wrote to CBS Corporation employees on November 20. Barry Meyer sent a nearly identical memo to Warner Bros. employees the same day. "One crucial fact that has been somewhat overlooked during the strike is that we, the members of the AMPTP, as producers of television programs and motion picture entertainment, have always believed that writers should be compensated when their work is distributed through new media and that they deserve to share in whatever success new technologies create," Moonves wrote. "In fact, the industry has already paid millions of dollars in residuals for permanent and pay-per-view downloads. So, while the terms of those payments may be on the table, the basic principle that writers should be compensated in this arena is not."

The speakers at the rally that closed out the Hollywood Boulevard march were considerably more colorful than the CEOs. Oh, a star of ABC's medical soap *Grey's Anatomy*, had the crowd chanting "share" as a message aimed at "giant media conglomerates." Leo Reed, the local Teamsters leader whose vocal support of the WGA was crucial at the start of the work stoppage, praised WGA members for "acting like a union" and instructed them to "keep that line up until you get a decent contract." John Bowman was forceful but careful in remarks he directed at the AMPTP. "Show some soul. We'll show some flexibility," Bowman said. "Let's get this done by Christmas." In his closing remarks, Verrone indulged in his fondness for historical analogies and quotations—in this case, Hollywood's version of Los Angeles history, as interpreted by Robert Towne, screenwriter of the 1930s period drama *Chinatown*. "When they ask you years from now what it was we went on strike for," Verrone instructed the crowd, "I want you to quote Robert Towne. You say, 'The future, Mr. Gittes.'"

The Hollywood Boulevard march, like the rally outside the Fox Plaza, was an eye-opening demonstration of the WGA's newfound muscle. It rattled the nerves of the CEOs, even as they dismissed Verrone and Young as modern-day Bolsheviks. They could not dismiss the duo's commanding ability to engage and mobilize members of a guild that just a few years before had been the butt of industry jokes for its leadership failures. There was a creeping realization among the key CEOs that Counter had badly miscalculated the handling of the negotiations, and he had underestimated the guild's collective resolve to strike. Moreover, in the face of the WGA's highly effective propaganda machine, the AMPTP had no strategy for competing in, let alone winning, the PR war.

The AMPTP had not needed a strategy in the past, because most of the arm wrestling was done behind closed doors. But this time around was very different, and the CEOs began to feel that Counter had not prepared adequately for the challenge. That was one reason the CEOs welcomed the involvement of Bryan Lourd. Even Young's biggest detractors could not deny his skill at organizing and executing the work stoppage, from working with members to playing the public opinion card just right.

Verrone saw the AMPTP's disarray as a symptom of its arrogance and its initial underestimation of the WGA's ability to wage a strike. "The process (the AMPTP uses) to bargain that has been successful for them for a quarter of century has been to stand back and let the union bargain against itself, and wait until the weaker union comes out and make a deal with them," Verrone said in an interview with *American Prospect* magazine. "That having failed this time, they're now in a position where they have to figure out how to deal with a strike, and I think the advisers who negotiate these contracts are not used to this kind of action," he said. "These generals haven't fought this kind of war in a long time. So they must be at a bit of a loss."[13]

The problems within the AMPTP created divisions among the CEOs. Moonves had the most urgent need to get back to business as usual, and he was amenable to making a few compromises to spur an accord. Iger felt that pressure for ABC, as did Peter Chernin for Fox, albeit not nearly to the same degree. Fox was well positioned to endure the strike because it had the top show in prime time, *American Idol,* coming back for its sixth year on the network in January.

The leaders of the two AMPTP conglomerates that did not own broadcast networks, Barry Meyer of Warner Bros. and Michael Lynton of Sony Pictures Entertainment, were prepared to wait out a long strike. They were taking a hit in TV production, but they had ramped up movie production in 2006 and 2007 as a hedge against a strike. And Sony and Warner Bros. have vast film and TV libraries to lean on for steady cash flow. By all accounts, NBC Universal's Jeff Zucker, who made no secret of his distaste for how Hollywood conducts business, advocated a hard line against all of the WGA demands, especially after the strike began. These fissures among the CEOs were ominous because of the AMPTP's charter, which requires unanimous approval among its board members on all contract offers and deals. The AMPTP's board seats are held only by the companies, and their successors, that founded this iteration of the studio negotiating body in 1982.

For all the divisiveness, though, the CEOs were unwavering in their commitment to two key principles. For one, they could not allow the WGA and other guilds to apply the same terms of the outmoded residual system to the new media realm. The leaders of the AMPTP member companies were convinced that the burden of obligations to pay writers, directors, and actors fees commensurate with what they received for traditional TV and movie work would snuff out the potential of new media. This point was as much a gospel truth to the CEOs as "Don't let them screw us in new media like they did in home video" was to picket-toting writers.

The second vow that the CEOs adhered to was the need for the AMPTP conglomerates to hang together and maintain their membership in the collective bargaining unit. Just like the writers, the CEOs knew there was strength in numbers. If the studios were to negotiate individually with the guilds, the guilds would heap pressure on the weakest one to extract the most favorable terms—and then insist that the other studios accept those same terms. Chernin was particularly emphatic, and persuasive, with his peers on this point.

In many ways, the strong hand played by the WGA forced the CEOs to become more involved in the negotiation process. That participation in turn forced them to collectively focus on their top priorities amid the near paralysis caused by the strike.

By the time the sides returned to the table, with hand-holding by Lourd, on November 26, the CEOs and Counter had devised a stronger game plan. They were ready to play offense if the WGA refused to bend. But there was no doubt that the studios' armor had been dented by its fumbles against a wily WGA. "The studios in the early stages of (the strike) were really flatfooted, because it never occurred to us that somebody at the WGA would be that good as an organizer," Chernin says. "David was actually good for the studios because it forced us to get our act together."[14]

7

Rallies, Retrenchment, and Late-Night Returns

By the time WGA and studio negotiators faced one another again in a conference room at the Renaissance Hotel, Bryan Lourd was working every angle he could think of to help the sides reach an agreement. He gathered facts and perspectives from a slew of informed sources, from industry executives to prominent WGA, DGA, and SAG members to fellow talent agents, managers, and lawyers.[1] To facilitate his role as mediator, Lourd had his own nerve center stocked with telephones and laptop computers set up in a tiny room at the hotel. It was adjacent to the larger conference room and the separate WGA and AMPTP caucus rooms that had been booked for the week of November 26. Lourd made sure his room was situated so he could see who came in and out of the WGA and AMPTP rooms. At his side for most of the four days that they were holed up at the Renaissance was Michael Rubel, Lourd's top business lieutenant at Creative Artists Agency.

Lourd began his diplomatic mission on the assumption that his biggest contribution would be to symbolize a fresh start. He soon found out that he was meant not only to get the conversation started but also to serve as the conduit for communication between the sides. Nick Counter would come to Lourd's room to lay out his response to a suggestion or statement made by the WGA, and then Lourd would walk twenty-five feet across a hallway to deliver Counter's message to David Young, and vice versa. The experience struck Lourd—who has plenty of firsthand experience with high-maintenance clients—as juvenile in the extreme on both sides and shockingly irresponsible in the face of the crippling strike. As the week went on, Lourd came to realize that both sides were looking to him more for cover than for breakthrough ideas. The depth of the dysfunction was revealed to Lourd when a WGA staffer angrily confronted an AMPTP counterpart because a phone call was not promptly returned.

The first day the sides spent most of their time together recapping where they had left off when the talks ended abruptly on November 4. It was another strategic mistake for the AMPTP. The lengthy discussion given to relatively inconsequential contract items such as the Showrunner Training Program, an educational apprenticeship program funded by the major studios, gave the WGA cause to accuse the AMPTP of using stall tactics. Counter and the network and studio labor executives knew there were a handful of issues that would settle the strike, and funding for the Showrunner Training Program was not one of them. Lourd, by many accounts, realized that although he had been successful in getting the writers and the studios to talk again, there was no guarantee that the discussions would be substantive enough to make progress.

Lourd had no experience in labor negotiations, so he learned the protocol of bargaining sessions on the fly. He was surprised on the first day at the Renaissance to be informed that SAG president Alan Rosenberg and SAG national executive director Doug Allen were sitting in the WGA's caucus room. Lourd's instinct was to ask them to leave, but he was informed of the tradition that the WGA, SAG, and DGA allowed one or two representatives of the two guilds into their negotiating sessions as observers, given the AMPTP's practice of enforcing uniform contract terms on the guilds where possible.

Allen, who had been with SAG less than a year, asked to meet Lourd before the joint session began. Although Lourd was intensely focused on planning how to open the session, he obliged. When he walked into the WGA's room, he was greeted by Allen, who still looks the part of having been a linebacker for the Buffalo Bills in the mid-1970s. "It's nice to meet you," Allen said, extending a hand to Lourd. "I understand that you represent the majority of my big stars." Lourd appeared surprised by Allen's remark. He smiled as he straightened up to look Allen squarely in the eye. "I didn't know they were your stars. I thought they were our stars," Lourd said. Allen's demeanor turned serious. "They might be your stars now, but they're going to be *my* big stars by the time I'm done," he told Lourd. Lourd was clearly taken aback. After a pause, he turned up his palms and said with mock sheepishness, "Well, good. I've been looking for a way out of this job."

Lourd appeared to be trying to ease the tension. But Allen was determined to deliver a stern message to the CAA power broker. "I'm serious about why I'm here," Allen said with bravado. "By the time I'm done, this town is going to look a lot different. It's going to take me a while, but these unions are going to be very different unions, like you've never seen before. They're going to be a power base. And it's going to be bloody, but when I'm done it'll all be a different game." This time there was no pause from Lourd. "Well, Doug, I wish you well," Lourd said with uncharacteristic sarcasm. "I've only been here for twenty-three years, so I'm not pretending to know what I'm talking about." Lourd gave a hard stare to the SAG leaders before returning to his war room down the hall.

The exchange had lasted only a few minutes, but it left a deep impression on Lourd. He would later confide in friends that it opened his eyes to the extreme influence that anticorporate ideology had on the leadership of SAG and the WGA. And it troubled him that WGA leaders seemed inordinately concerned with how their decisions were perceived by their counterparts at SAG. "Bryan could see then that as bad as the writers' situation was, these two guys (from SAG) were coming right behind them," a Lourd confidant said, "and for him it was like, 'Oh my God, this is going to be a nightmare.'"

During the four days of talks at the Renaissance, there were numerous media reports that the AMPTP and WGA negotiators were making great progress. Some reports and blog posts went so far as to suggest that the sides were closing in on a deal that would end the strike. These reports fueled optimism in the creative community but had little basis in reality.

The most positive aspect of having Lourd in the room was that the sides made an effort to be more respectful and engaging with one another, at least on the surface. But beyond the niceties, gamesmanship still ensued. The studios dragged their heels in presenting the WGA with an amended offer addressing their new media demands in a comprehensive way. The staging by WGA members of the "exorcism" picket event outside Warner Bros. on November 27, the second day of the talks at the Renaissance, perturbed Counter and others to no end.

On the third day, the WGA presented the AMPTP with its "economic justification" of its contract proposals. By the guild's math, the entire package of compensation increases, including standard 3 percent to 3.5 percent bumps for script fees as well as its new media proposals, would amount to $151 million over three years.[2] The studios, however, could evaluate such a proposal only in the context of how much it would cost not only for the WGA but also when the DGA and SAG sought similar payments.

After a long joint session, the negotiators broke off into their caucus rooms. Bryan Lourd wore down the carpet in the hallway as he bounced from room to room, trying to help each side understand the other's perspective, and trying to see where there was wiggle room for negotiation.

The process of evaluating and discussing proposals was complicated by their location. The Renaissance Hotel was ill-equipped for a meeting that needed to be held very much in private. Making copies of the myriad documents that the sides exchanged was a hassle. Representatives on both sides had to take an escalator up one flight to the hotel's business center, then hover over the copier to make sure that no stray copies were left lying around by accident. The lack of regular office amenities taxed the patience of the negotiators at a time when they needed every ounce they could muster.

By the fourth day, WGA representatives were getting antsy. They had been assured by Lourd that a significant new proposal was coming from the AMPTP. On that Thursday morning, November 29, the offer was finally unveiled with much fanfare and a formal title, "New Economic Partnership." If the terms of the plan had been well received by the guild, it is unlikely the moniker would have drawn much attention. But because it was lambasted by the guild as a rollback in disguise, the name took on overtones of a Soviet-era central planning initiative designed to herd peasants onto collective farms. Even as the offer was being presented,

WGA representatives were told that other elements of the plan were still being worked out by AMPTP staffers and would be put on the table shortly—specifically the studios' proposed compensation terms for paid Internet downloads.

The initial offer included two breakthroughs. First, for Web streaming of TV programs, the AMPTP proposed to pay writers a flat fee of about $250 a year for unlimited runs of an hourlong show and about $140 for a half-hour show. But there would also be a six-week free "promotional window" for programs before the payment obligation kicked in. Among the many objections the WGA had to this proposal was the evidence that most Web streaming of programming was done within a week or so of an episode's debut on the network, so networks and studios would have little incentive to make episodes available for streaming beyond the six-week window. The AMPTP's insistence on carving out a residual-free window for Web streaming of programming would remain a contentious point for the WGA until the last hours of the strike. The notion of allowing program repeats without payment obligation went against the grain of decades of WGA contract precedent.

The Web-streaming proposal in the "New Economic Partnership" was not the first time the AMPTP had addressed Web streaming, but it was a more detailed structure for Web-streaming compensation than had been previously offered. In the talks at the Sofitel hotel on November 4, the AMPTP had floated the idea of a percentage-based residual using the hated "producer's gross" formula that would include only 20 percent of a program's total receipts, as in the case of home video. That idea was such a nonstarter with writers that there was not much time spent on the proposal on that marathon day. Nearly a month later, the AMPTP revisited the Web-streaming issue with its low-ball flat-fee offer.

The second sign of compromise on the AMPTP's part was the provision that would give the WGA jurisdiction over made-for-new media productions derived from existing TV and film properties. Getting the AMPTP to acknowledge that the WGA would have the right to cover all writing activity for a fast-growing subset of entertainment was vital to the WGA. Granting the guild blanket jurisdiction for this distinct new job category—known as derivative made-for-Internet production—would head off disputes like the 2006 webisodes fight with NBC that wound up at the National Labor Relations Board.

Achieving jurisdictional gains in new media, reality, and animation were among the WGA's primary goals for the 2007 negotiations. But the WGA was not about to settle for jurisdiction over just one slice of the new media pie—derivative programming. Patric Verrone and David Young had vowed they would fight for unqualified WGA jurisdiction over all new media production. If AMPTP signatory companies produced content for new media, they would be obligated to work under WGA contracts, which meant that the guild and the AMPTP would have to agree on a compensation framework for new media. It would also open WGA membership up to a potentially large number of inexperienced writers, because having jurisdiction means that with few exceptions, anyone employed in the capacity of a writer by a signatory company has to join the WGA.

All told, the deal points in the "New Economic Partnership" proposal represented some movement by the studios. But it was coming at a snail's pace—deliberately so, in the eyes of WGA negotiators. The financial components of the offer were woefully inadequate, and WGA negotiators knew that Counter knew it would be rejected. Writers felt that with the strike about to enter its second month, the AMPTP was showing reckless disregard for the creative community in forcing the sides to negotiate inch by inch on the key terms that would settle the walkout. They were long past the pointing of bobbing and weaving with low-ball offers. The frustration among WGA negotiating-committee members was building up like steam in a basement boiler room.

The WGA was anxious to see the other elements of the proposal that had been promised. By late Thursday afternoon, Counter and Lombardini still had not presented any additional proposals. WGA negotiators, meanwhile, decided the best way to answer the AMPTP's intransigence was with their own analysis of the "New Economic Partnership" and to draft a counterproposal that would offer an entirely different formula for calculating compensation for Web streaming. Lourd facilitated an agreement that afternoon that in order to give the AMPTP time to present the rest of its proposal and to give the WGA time to respond to what had already been presented, the sides would take a break and resume negotiations the following Tuesday, December 4. Within an hour, however, the politesse of the previous four days went out the window. The WGA and AMPTP were back to jabbing at each other through the media.

It is telling that the key participants have never been able to agree on the sequence of events that evening that led to the breakdown. What is undisputed is that around five thirty, the AMPTP issued a 140-word statement confirming that they had made "groundbreaking proposals" in the "New Economic Partnership" document presented to the writers that morning. The statement also asserted that the WGA had requested the four-day break. "While we strongly preferred to continue discussions, we respect and understand the WGA's desire to review the proposals," the AMPTP said in its statement. "We continue to believe that there is common ground to be found between the two sides, and that our proposal for a New Economic Partnership offers the best chance to find it."[3]

WGA leaders were apoplectic when they learned the AMPTP had issued a statement. They disputed the assertion that the WGA had asked for the break, and they accused the studios of blindsiding them by violating the news-blackout agreement. Within an hour, Patric Verrone and the WGA East's Michael Winship sent a 550-word letter to guild members and a handful of media outlets. Verrone and Winship left little doubt about where the WGA stood on the "New Economic Partnership" offer. "It amounts to a massive rollback," Verrone and Winship wrote. "We must fight on, returning to the lines on Monday in force to make it clear that we will not back down, that we will not accept a bad deal, and that we are all in this together."[4]

AMPTP officials were adamant when pressed by reporters that the WGA had requested the four-day break. And the studio negotiators maintained that they felt free to issue the statement because guild officials had told them they felt an obligation to send a message to their members after four days of silence, in light of the numerous speculative media reports that a deal was near.

The WGA presidents' letter deliberately sought to temper the expectations of members that had been rising since the talks resumed. "Our inability to communicate with our members has left a vacuum of information

that has been filled with rumors, both well intentioned and deceptive,"
Verrone and Winship wrote. "Among the rumors was the assertion that
the AMPTP had a groundbreaking proposal that would make this negotiation a 'done deal.' In fact, for the first three days of this week, the companies presented in essence their November 4 package with not an iota
of movement on any of the issues that matter to writers." The AMPTP
countered that the WGA had acted in bad faith by trashing the studios'
offer barely an hour after the sides agreed to a four-day break to give the
guild time to study the proposals.

The posturing between the AMPTP and the WGA only worsened the
following day, with more statements and rebuttals issued. After a week of
official silence, the return to sniping sparked renewed interest in covering
the strike among media outlets outside of the industry press. The fact that
the sides did not coordinate in advance what would and would not be said
to the media during the four-day break period only exemplified the lack
of effective communication.

By the time the second round of accusations and denials was flying on
Friday, what little progress made in the previous four days had disappeared,
replaced by suspicion and pessimism. Several of the CEOs were furious at
what they viewed as an outright lie by the WGA to deny that it had asked
for the break, because they had been assured by their labor executives that
it had come at the guild's request. The guild continued to insist that the
AMPTP had violated the blackout agreement by rushing out a statement.

With pent-up frustration and anger boiling over, the only certainty
about the situation was that Bryan Lourd's job as mediator had become
that much more impossible. "Both sides were counting on him to soften
up the other side. What he found out pretty quickly was that neither side
wanted to make the first move," John Bowman says. "That wasn't how
Nick operated. Nick never made the first move. He never had to."[5]

As the sides bickered, the WGA staged its Friday mass rally on November
30 outside of the Sony Pictures Entertainment lot in Culver City, a hal-
lowed ground of golden-age Hollywood that was once home to Metro-
Goldwyn-Mayer and producer David O. Selznick's Selznick International

studios, where most of *Gone With the Wind* was filmed.[6] Dubbed a "Hollywood Homecoming," the morning gathering was meant to demonstrate the support for the strike by older members of the guild. But the rainstorm that hit LA at sunrise depressed the turnout to about two hundred hardy pickets, and only a few old-timers.

Nonetheless, the rain, the pickets, and the iconic MGM backdrop made for great symbolism. The rally was held in a small covered area inset from the sidewalk and behind the beaux arts colonnade that was once part of MGM's main entrance off Washington Boulevard. Although the studio lot has long since been reconfigured and remodeled, the fluted columns and ornate wrought-iron gates still stand as a representation of filmdom's illustrious past. The WGA's red-and-black picket signs made quite a contrast with the alabaster columns and the high studio outer wall that runs more than two blocks along Washington.

The "Hollywood Homecoming" rally was not a major event in the course of the strike, but it illustrates how adept WGA members were in commanding the public relations battle. The writers were naturally skilled at getting a message across that they were fighting corporations to preserve their livelihoods and to ensure that they would continue to receive a fair share of the profit generated by their work, in whatever medium it might be. There was no better way to telegraph guild members' principled resolve than the image of members picketing in the rain—or sleet and snow, in the case of the East Coast effort. "I'm out here because I want to be able to look the Teamsters in the eye," said Joseph Dougherty, a TV writer who braved the wet weather to attend the rally.

A few weeks into the strike, there was clear evidence that the guild's PR campaign had been as well orchestrated as its picketing operation. A survey conducted among *Variety* subscribers in mid-November found 54 percent of respondents agreeing that a strike was "necessary at this time," and some 69 percent of the 999 respondents agreed that the WGA was being "more honest and forthright" about the issues at stake in the contract negotiations than the studios.[7]

Beyond the guild-organized events, there was an incredible outpouring of commentary, advocacy, and reporting on strike-related issues by writers and others in the creative community—the vast majority of which was distributed via the Internet. Idled writers clearly needed the outlet. *United Hollywood* delivered a steady stream of short videos—some funny, some poignant, some unabashedly propaganda efforts—that distilled the issues from the perspective of workaday writers. A number of prominent film and TV writers who had established blogs also helped put a human face on the issues, and they reinforced the determination of writers at all career levels to fight the WGA's battle.

Ken Levine, a veteran comedy writer, pens the *By Ken Levine* blog that is well read in the industry and beyond. During the strike, Levine filed dispatches from the picket line that were enlivened by his comedic voice and also by his perspective of having been through three WGA strikes in the 1980s. A sample posted December 4, 2007:

> So on Tuesday I switched over from 20th to Sony. Alas no tequila. But more shade! There's a different vibe at Sony. At 20th it's primarily a large group marching out front in a circle. At Sony there are little pockets of picketers at each of the entrances. And the groups have settled in and have become little families. Years from now the members will hear horn honks and get nostalgic.
>
> Wednesday I'm hitting CBS Radford. I wonder if Gary Sinese is still making homemade cookies.
>
> Members of the negotiating committee have been going to the various picketing sites updating us on the situation and answering questions. John Bowman filled us in at 20th on Monday. It's pretty clear the AMPTP is made up of Bond villains, Gordon Gecko, J. R. Ewing, Mr. Spacely of the JETSONS, and Henry F. Potter from IT'S A WONDERFUL LIFE.

Levine and other writer-bloggers—among them Jane Espensen (JaneEspenson.com), John August (JohnAugust.com), Josh Friedman (*I Find Your Lack of Faith Disturbing*), Craig Mazin (*The Artful Writer*), Ron Moore (RonMoore.com), and the trio behind *Kung Fu Monkey* (Michael Alan Nelson, John Rogers, and Mark Waid)—were understandably consumed with blogging about the strike activities, the state of negotiations, and contract offers.

There were other Web-based WGA support campaigns that blossomed in the days after the strike ensued. The website Fans4Writers (tagline: "When the writers went on strike, the fans went with them") was organized by a disparate group of TV aficionados. Fans4Writers wound up raising money for the guild's strike-assistance fun, sending food and supplies to picket lines and even funding a pro-WGA skywriting effort above the Rose Parade on January 1, 2008. The website LateShowWriters OnStrike.com was born of picket-line brainstorming by the writers of CBS's *The Late Show with David Letterman*. Overnight, the LateShowWriters OnStrike site became an important voice for the East Coast strike effort. Through the run of the strike, LateShowWritersOnStrike served up short videos from the picket lines and humorous posts designed to illuminate the issues fueling the strike. A sample, posted November 26, 2007:

BREAKING NEWS—EXCLUSIVE—THE AMPTP'S CONTRACT PROPOSAL
BY JOE GROSSMAN

Today, the WGA and AMPTP resumed negotiations, and inside sources say the producers finally offered the writers a contract that would pay us using a simple, straightforward formula. Here's how it works.

The pay-per-letter contract:

$0.00 for every use of the letters A, B, C, D, E, F, G, H, I, J, K, L, M, N, O, P, R, S, T, U, V, W, X, Y, Z.

.0125¢ for every Q and anything with an umlaut.

The volume of blogging and commentary unleashed by the strike underscored the force of the Internet as a distribution mechanism. For the price of a $150–$200 annual subscription to a blog- or website-hosting service, writers were afforded the opportunity to speak their minds with complete freedom, in real time, to anyone with a computer and an interest in the subject. "We were able to communicate with the membership so much more readily than we could 20 years ago. It was such an effective mobilizing tool," says WGA East president Michael Winship. "We were able to use the very thing that we were on strike about. And the fact that we were able to use new media so effectively in this sort of asymmetrical warfare way helped us."[8]

Another Internet-driven response to the strike was a series of vignettes produced by documentary filmmaker George Hickenlooper and writer Alan Sereboff. The *Speechless* shorts were designed to illustrate the importance of scripts to the filmmaking process. Prominent actors were depicted as being hamstrung or forced to improvise because no scripts were available. One of the most widely viewed in the series was an eighty-second entry that featured Woody Allen sitting silently in front of a fireplace drinking a cup of tea, with each sip punctuated by the roar of a laugh track. The shorts, ranging from one to five minutes in length, were shot in an arty black-and-white style. The project attracted top talent—Sean Penn, Josh Brolin, Laura Linney, Harvey Keitel, Felicity Huffman, William H. Macy, Martin Sheen, Tim Robbins, and Susan Sarandon, among others—which reinforced the widespread support in the creative community for the writers' cause. It was a perfect illustration of the WGA's catchphrase, "We're all in this together." The *Speechless* series began running November 22, 2007, Thanksgiving Day, and grew to a total of thirty-seven installments widely disseminated via YouTube, *United Hollywood*, DeadlineHollywoodDaily, LateShowWritersOnStrike, and other sites.

This tidal wave of Internet discussion and organizing efforts—from the commentary of bloggers to breaking news bulletins from Deadline-HollywoodDaily to the WGA's own e-mail blasts—was a force the studios could not reckon with, let alone compete with. It was a flowering of communal spirit that was utterly confounding to many on the management side.

The power of the vast online community created by the strike had an influence over events in ways that no one, not even the WGA's top brass, could have predicted. It was akin to the "tenth man" effect of a cheering crowd on a baseball team, and it was largely an echo chamber for the WGA's official positions. Mainstream media outlets were scrutinized and heavily criticized for what many writers viewed as reports that were inherently biased in favor of the studios, if only because the AMPTP member companies spend so much money on newspaper, magazine, and TV advertising. For thousands of idled writers, the Internet matrix of news and commentary became a vital support system during the months of uncertainty. And it spurred a sense of unity and resolve not seen since the Depression era when SAG, the WGA, and the DGA were founded.

Studio and AMPTP executives initially sought to dismiss this outpouring as "noise" that grabbed attention but could not change the dynamic at the negotiating table. But over time the plethora of pro-WGA messages, which seeped into mainstream pop culture, did weigh on key players in the negotiations. Industry executives were alarmed by the "us against them" sentiment the strike had provoked in the creative community. Executives resented being vilified as greedy corporate bosses, particularly individuals such as Leslie Moonves and Peter Chernin, who were proud of having come up through the creative ranks rather than the business side. All of a sudden, they were cast as arch villains.

After the debacle of unveiling the recoupment proposal to the media back in July, the AMPTP's public relations strategy had largely been limited to issuing pointed press statements and publishing the occasional "open letter to the industry" that ran as full-page ads in *Variety,* the *Hollywood Reporter,* the *Los Angeles Times,* and the *New York Times.* Meanwhile, the pro-WGA blogs and websites had a worldwide platform, for anyone who cared to seek them out.

Management was handicapped by another problem when it came to selling its side of the story: the facelessness of modern media conglomerates. After a decade of mergers and consolidation, the seven companies that called the shots for the AMPTP were sprawling multinational entities with disparate operations far beyond Hollywood. Outside of the entertainment industry and Wall Street, and elite circles, the only media titan easily associated with his empire is Rupert Murdoch, who stayed far away from the WGA scrum, leaving it to Chernin. The leaders of Hollywood studios no longer rule unequivocally from their spacious lots. They answer to corporate managers and in some cases are one management layer or two removed from the CEO of the parent firm. As *Variety* editor in chief Peter Bart noted in a December 2007 column, "As the events of '07 remind us, Hollywood is a mere plaything of the international congloms, and Hollywood product represents a relatively minor sector of the product line. Today's managers are a far cry from the Louis B. Mayers or Lew

Wassermans of old. Indeed, to a growing degree, they don't even want to be part of the scene."[9]

By the end of November, mounting concerns within the AMPTP member companies spurred the studios to organize more of a concerted effort to score victories in the court of public opinion. Until then, communications from the AMPTP had been overseen by Barbara Brogliatti, the longtime head of corporate communications for Warner Bros., and the AMPTP's in-house media relations executive, Jesse Hiestand, a former labor reporter for the *Hollywood Reporter* and PR executive at the DGA.

Brogliatti had retired from Warner Bros. in 2005, but she was enlisted in early 2007 to help guide the AMPTP's communications because of the depth of her experience in dealing with guild issues and her strong relationships with many reporters at key media outlets. In dealing with the unprecedented dynamic of the 2007 WGA negotiations, Brogliatti faced many of the same challenges that vexed Nick Counter at the negotiating table. The landscape had been upended by changing times and new technology. In her dealings with reporters, Brogliatti barely hid her contempt for the WGA's propaganda machine.

Four weeks into the strike, Brogliatti was done. She had had enough of being on call 24/7 for reporters desperately trying to follow up on the torrent of rumors and specious claims that pinged around the Internet. Brogliatti in late November shifted to a senior adviser role, and the AMPTP opened its checkbook to retain three heavy-hitter spin doctors from the political realm, Chris Lehane, Mark Fabiani, and Steve Schmidt. Recruiting a trio of high-priced consultants schooled in the art of winning political campaigns was a sign of how desperate the AMPTP was to counteract some of the WGA's tenth-man advantage.[10]

At the same time, the heads of corporate communications and media relations at the various studios and major networks began to engage in PR triage. They conferred through conference calls and reached out to prominent reporters in an effort to give management's perspective on events. They sought to cast doubts and present countervailing facts to combat what their bosses viewed as the most egregious distortions of fact and misinformation swirling around the Web.

The timing of the AMPTP's move to step up its PR efforts was not coincidental. Counter and his closest associates knew that the AMPTP would need the PR reinforcements in place to mitigate the blowup at the bargaining table that was just around the corner.

As November turned into December, the anxiety level increased dramatically for top executives at the Big Four broadcast networks and many cablers. If the strike dragged on through the holidays, executives knew that the second half of the 2007–8 season would have to be written off. Programming executives had been hedging their bets against this doomsday scenario—which also promised to disrupt the development of pilots for the 2008–9 season—for months by ordering a slew of unscripted series that could be called on to plug the holes in prime time.

Although they were prepared, programmers still hated to resort to stopgap measures with something as important as the prime-time schedule. The lack of fresh episodes of popular scripted series would put the networks in the position of turning away customers. It would also encourage more loyal viewers to break their traditional habit of tuning in to ABC on Thursdays at 9:00 p.m. for *Grey's Anatomy,* or keeping a Tuesday 10:00 p.m. appointment with NBC for *Law and Order: SVU,* or a Monday 9:00 p.m. date with CBS for *Two and a Half Men.* The timing of this jolt to traditional viewing habits could not have been worse for the broadcast networks, given all the other upheaval in programming and scheduling.

CBS by mid-November was already planning to kick-start a new edition of its durable reality-competition show *Big Brother.* The show had been a staple of CBS's summer lineup since 2000, but it had never aired during the regular September–May season. But *Big Brother* was a natural choice for CBS as it needed to plug hours, as the format for the show calls for episodes to run three times a week. Ironically, *Big Brother 9* premiered February 12, the day the strike ended. Episodes of the show, which challenges a group of strangers to live sequestered from their regular lives in a house wired with microphones and cameras, filled thirty-five hours of CBS's prime-time schedule between February 12 and April 27. Although viewership was low, an hour of *Big Brother* cost CBS less than half of what it would typically pay in a license fee of about $2.5 million for a scripted drama series.

By mid-February, the Big Four's airwaves were chock-full of unscripted programs. NBC unleashed a slew of mostly short-lived shows that it had stockpiled as a hedge against a strike, including *1 vs. 100, American Gladiators, My Dad Is Better than Your Dad, Baby Borrowers,* and *Celebrity Apprentice.* Fox was fortified with the fortuitous timing of having *American Idol,* the most dominant show in prime time, rolling out in its regular January debut. Fox felt the loss of its scripted programming—the network's signature drama series *24* had to sit out the 2007–8 season entirely—but not as much as its competitors.

CBS found another creative solution to its programming drought by borrowing a hot prospect from its sibling pay-TV cable network, Showtime. *Dexter,* an offbeat drama about a Miami police blood-splatter expert who moonlights as a killer of murderers who escape the law, had just concluded its second season on Showtime with its star on the rise in the pop-culture firmament. CBS programmers made the decision to air episodes that were edited for content—mostly coarse language—and for length to allow for commercials. It was a bold step that predictably drew the ire of conservative media-watchdog groups. But CBS braved the brickbats because it helped the network in a time of need, and it gave *Dexter* (and by association, Showtime) invaluable exposure to millions of viewers who might otherwise never have seen the show. In the wake of CBS's airing twelve episodes of the show in the Sunday 10:00 p.m. slot, starting February 17, five days after the end of the strike, *Dexter* earned an Emmy nomination for best drama series, and Showtime's subscriber growth rate gained steam.

NBC borrowed from its USA Network cable sibling, airing episodes of light detective dramas *Monk* and *Psych.* And in its desperation for programming, NBC gambled with a deal to license a drama series, *Quarterlife,* produced independently for the Internet by Marshall Herskovitz and Ed Zwick, the prominent pair behind such acclaimed TV series as *thirtysomething, My So-Called Life,* and *Once and Again.* An ensemble about twentysomethings in Los Angeles, *Quarterlife* launched with great fanfare as an example of top Hollywood creatives sidestepping the major studios to produce directly for the Internet. (A few years before, Herskovitz and Zwick had produced a pilot for *Quarterlife* for ABC that did not get picked up as a series.) The thirty-six *Quarterlife* webisodes ran in eight-minute seg-ments that were stitched together into six hourlong episodes for NBC. But only one of them ever aired on NBC. By the time *Quarterlife* was ready for prime time on February 26, the strike had been over for two weeks, and the show's fate on NBC was sealed by a minuscule opening-night rating.

The strike disrupted the programming plans of some of the larger cable networks as well, particularly HBO. The pay cable channel was forced to delay the planned premiere of vampire drama *True Blood* and new seasons of the drama *Big Love* and comedy *Entourage* in 2008 because production on those shows was unable to get under way as scheduled in the fall of 2007.

All of these haphazard programming and scheduling decisions took a steep toll on viewership of the major networks. The prime-time audience for the Big Four networks combined dropped 10 percent in the first quar-ter of 2008, compared with the first quarter of 2007.[11]

The state of prime time was not the only source of angst for network exec-utives as the strike went into its second month. Viewership of late-night programming was plunging after four weeks of repeats. The hosts them-selves were getting restless and feeling an obligation to their production staffs as the holiday season approached.

Conan O'Brien made headlines on November 29 when word spread that he had committed to continue paying the salaries of about eighty of his idled crew members out of his own pocket.[12] The same day, Car-son Daly, the host of *Last Call with Carson Daly*, which follows *Late Night* on NBC, announced that his show would resume production on Decem-ber 3, citing concern for the livelihoods of his production team. O'Brien and Daly's moves came one day before NBC gave pink slips to several hundred production staffers on *Late Night* and *The Tonight Show with Jay Leno*. In the wake of O'Brien's decision, Jay Leno faced some carping by purported members of his staff in the strike blogosphere before he also publicly agreed to cover the bill for *Tonight Show* staff salaries.

Daly's move to resume production on *Last Call* was the first fissure in the united front among late-night hosts since the strike began. But it was not a big blow to the WGA's campaign because Daly's half-hour program has a lower profile than the other late-night shows. And Daly, unlike Leno, O'Brien, David Letterman, and the others, is not a member of the WGA. Still, when *Last Call* began taping new episodes at NBC's Burbank studios, the WGA deployed groups of pickets to greet the host and guests on the program as they drove onto the NBC compound.

With Daly back on the air, there was movement among other late-night hosts and producers to collaborate on a strategy for resuming their shows. This conversation, instigated by Conan O'Brien and Jon Stewart, was highly unusual for a group of comedians and producers who are fiercely competitive with one another.[13] But this time, the hosts were all facing the same thorny problem. As much as late night's front men were supportive of the WGA's cause, they could not stay off the air indefinitely. There was precedent for resuming production after a respectful pause during a WGA strike; Johnny Carson returned to *The Tonight Show* stage nine weeks after the start of the five-month 1988 walkout.

The consensus at the end of November among the hosts and key producers was that they would not make any waves while the WGA and the AMPTP were in the middle of touchy negotiations. December, moreover, is generally a down month for television ratings because of holiday-related distractions. But if it looked like the strike would drag into January, the hosts vowed to reevaluate. And after many conversations among the core group, it became clear that there was strength in numbers if they made a unilateral decision. Not long after Daly went back to *Last Call*, a competitive issue would surface that gave Leno, Stewart, O'Brien, and ABC's Jimmy Kimmel every incentive to return to their desks as 2008 began.

The tension in the room was as thick as LA smog when the WGA and AMPTP reconvened on Tuesday, December 4. The setting had changed, but the attitudes had only hardened after a few days of sparring via the media. As the week went on, the suspense built as both sides waited for the other to make a dramatic move.

For the second round of talks, Bryan Lourd moved the group to the InterContinental Hotel near the 20th Century Fox studio in Century City. He was frustrated by the limited facilities at the Renaissance Hotel in Hollywood, and he hoped that the change of scenery would do some good. By week's end, Lourd's pessimism was deepening, despite his best efforts to help the sides find a path to common ground.

Lourd came to realize that his diplomatic mission was doomed by the depth of the disconnect between David Young and Nick Counter. Counter was of another generation than Young, accustomed to getting deals done over dinner without much in the way of theatrics. He was used to facing off against people who talked tough and asked for the moon but were ultimately prepared to horse-trade to achieve a few carefully defined objectives in a contract.

Counter had long been able to stay two steps ahead in negotiations because of his encyclopedic knowledge of the industry—not just the master guild agreements but also the terms and conditions for most Hollywood contracts, from compensation to movie and TV licensing and distribution deals to below-the-line pay structures. It helped him anticipate problems and identify hidden advantages and weaknesses in guild agreements for his bosses at the major studios. But by 2007, "Nick had lost his fastball," in the words of one studio executive. He was confounded by the challenge he faced in Young, a staunch trade unionist with no background in the entertainment industry. At Counter's direction, the AMPTP tried to bully the WGA, even after the strike was well under way, without fully appreciating how much leg work Young and Verrone had done to prepare WGA members for a work stoppage.

When the WGA and AMPTP negotiators reassembled on December 4, the WGA did most of the talking. The guild presented a counterproposal to the "New Economic Partnership" offer, primarily focusing on the issue of Web streaming. The studios had offered a flat fee of about $250 for an hourlong series in its first year. The WGA took a different approach in suggesting that writers be paid according to the number of views generated by a given program. In the first year of a program's availability via Web streaming, the credited writer of an hourlong episode would receive a payment of $632.64 for every one hundred thousand hits the program generated online. The $632 fee was derived from 3 percent of the residual that a writer would receive for a traditional on-air rerun. After one year, the fee would shift to a flat 2.5 percent of the distributor's gross receipts from the Web-streaming plays.[14] The WGA believed the incremental fee structure would be welcomed by the studios because it would allow them to pay writers based on the popularity of a program—the same kind of pay-for-performance flexibility the studios had sought with the recoupment proposal.

As the negotiations resumed, WGA leaders and negotiating-committee members were being warned by industry insiders, including some sympathetic studio executives, that Counter was poised to make a move that would give the AMPTP an excuse for walking out on the bargaining process. It was well known by December 5 that the AMPTP had retained the public relations team of Chris Lehane, Mark Fabiani, and Steve Schmidt. Lehane and Fabiani had been hired a few years before by SAG at a fractious moment for the guild, and that experience tainted the duo's reputation in the eyes of Hollywood's staunch unionists.[15]

Meanwhile, Counter and the other AMPTP representatives were on edge about the WGA's aggressive public relations campaign. The CEOs were aggravated at how successful the guild had been in framing the public perception of the issues on the table. The unpredictable nature of the picketing and the protests and the discussion in the blogosphere had many within the AMPTP looking over their shoulders out of concern about what the WGA might try next. Despite the negotiations, the WGA had a rally scheduled for Friday, December 7, in Burbank, outside the offices of *American Idol* producer FremantleMedia North America, to promote the push for expanded jurisdiction over unscripted series.

All told, the combustible mix of suspicion, frustration, and anger growing between the WGA and AMPTP made it impossible for the sides to focus on hashing out a complex contract, as Bryan Lourd regretfully realized. Counter was stubborn, and so was Young, who continued to rarely deviate from prepared remarks during joint sessions. It was an understandable response for someone who had little experience with Hollywood deal making. But by multiple accounts, Lourd was exasperated that WGA leaders balked at his efforts at bring about compromise. In one instance, according to multiple accounts, WGA leaders led Lourd to believe that the guild was prepared to offer an olive branch after the negotiations resumed on November 26 of dropping its proposal for expanded reality and animation jurisdiction. But no such movement materialized.

Lourd, according to knowledgeable sources, considered it a symptom of the guild's internal politics among negotiating-committee members, the executive leadership, and the influence of the hard-liners on the WGA West board of directors. The miscues and slow pace of discussions in the sequestered hotel environment made Lourd doubtful that anything could be accomplished as his second week as mediator wound down.

The WGA, on the other hand, had every incentive to find the silver lining in the state of the negotiations. With the strike heading into its second month, the guild needed to project a hopeful attitude about the bargaining in order to maintain the active support of its key members. The guild could not risk having members demoralized by the feeling that the talks were doomed.

After the WGA presented its response to the "New Economic Partnership" proposals, the AMPTP suggested the sides break into smaller groups to focus separately on the various aspects of the WGA's contract demands. Guild representatives reminded the AMPTP and Lourd that they had been promised additional proposals covering compensation for paid downloads, among other matters. But even after the four-day break, the AMPTP still had nothing new to present to the WGA.

As it turned out, the AMPTP would be the one to unleash the negotiating-room surprise that week. But not before Counter and the studio representatives conducted a lawyerly, methodical review of the WGA's demands and priorities for the negotiations. The small group sessions that took place on Tuesday and Wednesday dealt with substantial issues and seemed to spur guarded optimism on both sides, at least on the surface. "For the last two days, we have had substantive discussions of the issues important to writers, the first time this has occurred in this negotiation," the WGA said in a statement released after the sides broke on Wednesday evening.[16] The AMPTP also sent a positive signal with its Wednesday statement: "We believe that there is common ground to be found between the two sides that will put all of us in the entertainment industry in a better position to survive and prosper in what is a rapidly changing modern, global marketplace."[17]

By Thursday morning, however, WGA leaders were getting concerned about the additional proposals from the AMPTP that had yet to materialize. The guild negotiators spent most of Thursday by themselves, waiting for the material that the other side had promised would be forthcoming. By the early evening, Lourd told the WGA camp that the AMPTP planned to work late into the night on the offers and would have something to present at ten o'clock on Friday morning. A few on the WGA team stuck around for a little while afterward, and they thought it was fishy when they saw key studio and AMPTP executives leaving the hotel at around six forty-five.

The rumors about the AMPTP breaking off talks were so strong that Verrone and Winship issued a letter to members early Friday morning addressing the speculation and offering a detailed rundown of their version of what had transpired during the week. The WGA leaders raised the specter of the rumors that "the companies are prepared to throw away the spring and fall (2008) TV season, plus features, and prolong the strike." They cited reports to WGA members from "highly placed executives" that the AMPTP was poised to "abruptly cut off negotiations" and then "accuse the WGA of stalling and being unwilling to negotiate."[18]

That is exactly what Counter would do by the end of the day. Yet Counter and the CEOs were incensed that the WGA would issue such an inflammatory statement to members on the morning of a bargaining session. It was viewed as more evidence that guild leaders were unprofessional and maddeningly unpredictable.

The WGA was prepared for the light but steady rain that fell in Los Angeles on the morning of December 7. Picket signs specially made for the Fremantle rally were wrapped in clear plastic sheeting, and the e-mail advisory on the rally asked members to bring along red umbrellas if possible.[19]

The turnout was several hundred strong. The WGA had obtained a permit to shut down a short stretch of West Alameda Avenue in front of the Fremantle office building for the demonstration. A small stage with a canvas awning was erected for the speakers and a brief performance by Tenacious D, the rock-comedy duo composed of actor Jack Black and Kyle Gass. The crowd was punctual, and the area in front of the stage was filling up with writers long before the noon start time of the rally.

Picket signs and T-shirts carried messages of support for the WGA's reality-organizing campaign. Fremantle was a natural target for the WGA's public pressure campaign as the producer of the most-watched program in prime time, *American Idol,* among other successful series. "Unscripted? Yeah, Write" read one sign. "Fremantle: We're Aiken for Health Insurance" read another, in a play on the surname of the onetime *Idol* contestant Clay Aiken.

The reality-organizing effort had been and would continue to be a tough sell for the WGA to many members, who viewed unscripted programs as the enemy that had infiltrated hours of network prime-time schedules that were previously been filled by scripted series. But the heightened sense of activism spurred by the strike had made some members more understanding of the guild's reasoning that organizing reality producers would help prevent the networks and studios from using unscripted shows as leverage against the WGA.

As the crowd grew, WGA staffers and strike captains led a succession of large groups on walks around the blocks surrounding the Fremantle building. The pickets were vocal, but not boisterous, as they moved past storefronts and restaurants and office buildings on the block that paralleled West Alameda Avenue to the north. Burbank residents were already highly aware of the WGA work stoppage, as the city was home to three prime picket sites: Warner Bros., NBC Universal, and the Walt Disney Company.

As with the WGA's other public events, the Fremantle rally was well organized. The presentation from the stage began at 1:00 p.m. sharp, not long after Patric Verrone arrived at the site. As he surveyed the scene, he was cornered at every turn by guild members and reporters who pressed for information on the state of the talks. Verrone reiterated the points made in the letter to members that morning, making it clear that the WGA was growing increasingly skeptical of the AMPTP's intentions.

As Verrone took the stage to introduce Tenacious D, the WGA representatives at the InterContinental Hotel in Century City were still waiting for word on an offer from the AMPTP. Despite the dire situation warned of in the WGA statement that morning, the guild had a small contingent on hand, with David Young, John Bowman, a few support staffers, and four negotiating-committee members: Neal Baer, Bill Condon, Carol Mendelsohn, and Ed Solomon. The lunch period came and went, and still there was no movement from the AMPTP room and no news delivered by Bryan Lourd.

Right around the time the speeches began in Burbank, however, the AMPTP fired back at the WGA with a lengthy statement to the media responding to some of the "factual mistakes" made by Verrone and Winship in their letter. The AMPTP statement tread familiar tit-for-tat ground, and it accused guild negotiators of arriving late to joint sessions and wasting time in private meetings among themselves.[20] The most noteworthy aspect of the AMPTP statement was a bit of semantics that stood out immediately to WGA leaders and to the reporters who were following the strike. The AMPTP repeatedly referred to WGA leadership as "organizers," with the inference being that they preferred to focus on organizing picketing and rallies rather than negotiating a contract agreement.

Just like the WGA's morning missive, the AMPTP's statement was an extraordinary move to make while the sides were ostensibly still trying to cut a deal. It was also the first salvo from the studios to reflect the spin-doctoring of Chris Lehane and Mark Fabiani, who by that time had spent more than a week immersing themselves in the details of the contract battle. The use of the word *organizers* was the press-release equivalent of a jab in the chest on the playground, and it worked. The WGA camp took it as the insult it was meant to be.

Back in Burbank, Verrone was in his element: on the stump in front of a friendly crowd and serving as emcee at a guild rally. Even his biggest detractors cannot question the veracity of Verrone's commitment to advancing the cause of union representation and the welfare of WGA members, and that dedication comes across when he speaks in public. To striking writers, his was the voice that reassured them that they were doing the right thing for a just cause. On the day of the Fremantle rally, the righteousness of the WGA's quest seemed reinforced by the fact that the rain stopped and the sun slowly began to stream through the clouds just as Verrone took the stage.

In discussing the reason for the rally, Verrone repeated the guild's familiar points on reality organizing: harsh working conditions and a dilution of the WGA's strength in governing prime-time programming. As the crowd cheered, Verrone's tone grew more strident. He was critical of the AMPTP's intransigence but promised that the guild would never bail out of the negotiations. "We will stay at that table day and night for as long as it takes to get a good deal," he said. And he assured the crowd that expanded jurisdiction over reality shows "will be in our next contract."

Verrone's statement did not sound particularly profound in the moment. He kept his overall remarks brief and seemed to take delight in introducing Black and Gass, who accompanied themselves on acoustic guitars. The opening number of Tenacious D's three-song set went over well with the crowd. Specially written for the occasion, "Fuck the Bullshit" included the refrain "They're going to gobble up your Internet cream pie." A swift rotation of speakers followed, including Kai Bowe, one of the *America's Next Top Model* strikers; Aaron Solomon, a producer who walked off his job on the Fremantle-produced game show *Temptation* after the company balked at his demand to work under a WGA contract; actress Alfre Woodard; and writer-director Paul Haggis, an Oscar winner for *Crash*.

The event concluded shortly before two, with Verrone, Haggis, Solomon, and WGA West first vice president David Weiss walking into the lobby of Fremantle's building with a petition signed by more than one thousand WGA members. The petition demanded that Fremantle implement WGA contracts for appropriate production staff members on its shows. Building security stopped the foursome from taking the elevator to Fremantle's offices, but a company public relations executive did come down to accept the petition and pay lip service to their concerns. "We both agreed that we're all very concerned about working conditions for their employees," Verrone told a group of onlookers after he and the others left the building.

Verrone seemed pleased with the results of the rally as the crowd thinned out and a handful of reporters peppered him with questions about the strike and the state of the negotiations.

Right around the time that Verrone was wrapping it up in Burbank, WGA and AMPTP negotiators convened in the joint meeting room at the Intercontinental at about two thirty.[21] Although both sides were aware that the

December 7 session was likely to be momentous, it was a relatively small group that met across the table that afternoon. Nick Counter and Carol Lombardini were joined by two long-serving labor relations executives, Keith Gorham of NBC Universal and Hank Lachmund of Warner Bros. The four negotiating committee members—Baer, Condon, Mendelsohn, and Solomon—were on hand for the guild alongside John Bowman and David Young. The atmosphere in the room was civil, but there was an extra feeling of wariness that made their exchanges more stilted than usual. The exchange of accusatory statements earlier in the day had only heightened the tension.

By the time the sides gathered for the joint session, the AMPTP executives were aghast that Verrone would forgo a pivotal bargaining session in order to preside over the Fremantle rally. The WGA representatives were bracing for the AMPTP to declare that it was once again breaking off the talks. Those expectations were realized as soon as the AMPTP laid out its response to the counteroffer on new media that the WGA put forth earlier in the week. As usual, Lombardini did most of the talking for the AMPTP. She stuck more closely than usual to the text of her prepared remarks because of the volatility of the situation. Although the sides would go through the motions of waiting for the WGA to deliver a formal response to her presentation, Lombardini already knew exactly how the guild would respond.

She started by laying out the AMPTP's rejection of the guild's proposal for a tiered residual for Web streaming based on the number of views for a program. She reiterated that the residual formula for paid downloads would remain the same as the home video rate, and she reiterated that the AMPTP rejected the guild's demand for jurisdiction over original production done for the Internet by AMPTP signatory companies. She did not pause much before launching into the second half of her presentation, which she knew was even more incendiary than the first. She directed the WGA negotiators' attention to a list of guild demands that the AMPTP deemed "an absolute roadblock to any further progress in these negotiations." Lombardini glanced around the room as she paused for a breath. She was not surprised to see the WGA representatives sitting more stone-faced than usual, particularly Young and Bowman. "We have had some frank discussion with you about some of these proposals over the past three days. Unfortunately, these discussions have only reinforced our conviction as to how far apart the parties remain," she continued. "These proposals are completely unacceptable in their present form, or in any altered form."[22]

More silence. Lombardini proceeded to outline, in a lawyerly manner, the reasons six of the WGA demands were deemed roadblocks. She could feel the WGA side fuming as she spoke. Of the six items cited, two were the kind of fungible things included in a negotiation platform so as to be easily removed later in a gesture of concession. The WGA had demanded that AMPTP submit to a "fair market value" test by an outside arbitrator when rights to TV shows and movies were sold in order to guard against sweetheart-deal making. The guild also sought the "sympathy strike" right for WGA members to honor the picket lines of other unions and withhold their services without penalty. Three of the remaining four related to the WGA's push for greatly expanded jurisdiction over reality and animation production. Lombardini called those proposals "a clever disguise to what amounts to a top-down union organizing campaign." The final item on her list went to the heart of the WGA's battle to keep the hated home video residual formula from becoming entrenched for new media. "Distributor's gross" was the WGA's shorthand for ensuring that new media residuals be based on 100 percent of revenue generated by a title. On this issue, both sides were in agreement: distributor's gross was a line in the sand. The WGA would not do a new media deal without it, while the AMPTP called it flatly "unacceptable."

After reading the AMPTP's objections to the six points in detail, Lombardini delivered the closing salvo. "Your determination to continue to pursue these initiatives prevents us from making any movement in any other area," she said. "Therefore, unless you advise us immediately that these proposals are withdrawn, we see no purpose in continuing these talks."

The WGA negotiators broke their stoic silence with a terse "Thank you." They quickly relocated to their room to draft a written response. Once they were behind closed doors, Bowman, Young, and the others let their exasperation show. The WGA team was not surprised by the

AMPTP's move, but they were surprised at how definitive Lombardini had been in her speech. *"We* reject *your* ultimatums," Neal Baer said to no one in particular as he and Bowman huddled over a laptop computer to begin drafting the response.

About an hour later, Counter knocked on the door of the WGA's room. "Well? . . . What have you decided?" he asked. Counter was turned away with Young's assertion that they were still formulating their response. Counter wanted a yes or no on whether they would agree to drop the six demands. But protocol dictated that he give them time to prepare a written response.

Around five, Counter was visibly agitated when he returned to the WGA's door with the same question and was turned away with the same response. Young said he did not know yet if the guild would drop any of its proposals because they were still working on their letter. Lourd observed the brief exchange through the open door of his room.

Finally, a few minutes after six, Counter was back at the WGA's door. "Obviously, you're not going to accept our offer," he said to Young. The WGA representatives in the room stared incredulously at Counter. "When you do, write me a letter and we'll schedule another session."

Counter went back down the hall but returned minutes later. This time he asked to speak to Young in the hallway. Young motioned to Baer to join him as a witness. Lourd was also in the hallway, grim faced in his role as referee. Flushed and visibly agitated, Counter spoke in a low voice to Young. "Are you going to withdraw any of those issues?" Counter demanded. Young gave Counter a steely-eyed stare. "Is that your final decision?" Counter pressed. "We're still working on our letter," Young replied. "Fine," Counter said, thrusting a single-page letter at Young. "We're done."

Counter turned and quickly returned to the AMPTP's room. Young and Baer stared at the letter for a moment and then slipped back into their room. There was no yelling, no slamming of doors, but it was clear to all that the negotiation process had once again imploded with the sides further apart than ever.

Lourd stood alone in the hallway for a few more seconds, thinking about what had just happened and what he knew was coming next.

8

Cue the Directors

By the time the AMPTP engineered the December 7 blowup, the CEOs had given up any hope of bridging the gap with the WGA. Counter and the AMPTP stewards shifted their focus to Plan B: cutting a deal with the Directors Guild of America that would provide a basic template for contracts with the WGA and SAG. The CEOs knew that the DGA had taken a more measured approach to evaluating the size and scope of the new media marketplace, and they knew the DGA's leadership would be far easier to bargain with compared to the stridency of Young and Verrone. The WGA had seen the DGA as serving as a stalking horse for the studios all along; the year 2007 was not the first time this dynamic had played out between the two guilds during tough contract negotiations.

DGA leaders were sensitive to the perception in the creative community that the guild had a history of caving in to studio pressure in contract talks, making it virtually impossible for the WGA or SAG to hold the line on their demands. The DGA historically has negotiated its contract agreements as much as a year or more before it faced an expiration deadline. This time around, with the WGA's decision to start its talks in July 2007 and the complexity of the new media issues at hand, the DGA broke with its tradition of early negotiations for the successor to the contract scheduled to expire on June 30, 2008. The DGA was more than happy to let the WGA be the guinea pig. However, true to DGA form, there were informal conversations among DGA executives, the CEOs, and AMPTP executives. The guild and management sought to feel each other out as to what were acceptable parameters for the coming contract talks.

After the strike began, DGA leaders were concerned about the prospect that the DGA would be seen as undercutting a fellow union if it moved to begin its negotiations. No matter how strongly DGA leaders disagreed with the WGA's strategy and tactics, they did not want their guild to be the bad guy in this Hollywood melodrama.[1]

But as the strike persisted and the AMPTP-WGA talks faltered, the studios pressured the DGA to come to the table. By early December, DGA leaders felt a responsibility to protect their members by initiating what were sure to be tricky negotiations. But DGA brass made it clear to the AMPTP that the guild would not do so while the AMPTP was in active talks with the WGA. That stipulation, meant to protect the DGA's reputation, hastened the AMPTP's decision to hand the WGA its ultimatum on December 7.

Having the DGA alternative was a strategic advantage for the studios at a pivotal moment in the WGA strike. But it did not mean that the negotiations with the DGA would be a cakewalk. Directors had the same concerns about the loss of residual income as TV shows and movies migrated to Internet-based platforms. The AMPTP had to hack through the same thicket of issues to address the demand for new categories of residuals. They just got to do it with a very different cast of characters.

DGA national executive director Jay Roth is the 180-degree opposite of his WGA counterpart, David Young, in his professional style and background. Roth was an experienced labor lawyer who specialized in entertainment law before taking the helm of the DGA in 1995. He had maintained strong relationships for years with Nick Counter and Carol Lombardini, the studio CEOs, and their labor executives. And his style was anything but confrontational. He addressed issues that arose for the DGA with the studios in private settings, not at rallies and press conferences.

Gilbert Cates, the head of the DGA's negotiating committee, was even more seasoned than Roth in guild contract negotiations. He had been active in DGA affairs for decades. He served as president from 1983 to 1987 and was a prime mover in steering the guild through difficult negotiations in the 1980s on home video and cable TV compensation issues. Beyond his DGA credentials, Cates was prominent in the entertainment industry as an accomplished director and producer in film, TV, and stage. When the WGA strike began, Cates was knee-deep in preparations for overseeing ABC's live Academy Awards telecast set for February 24, 2008. It would be his fourteenth time serving as executive producer of the Oscars since 1990.

Michael Apted, who had been the DGA's elected president since 2003, is a distinguished film and TV director, known for 1980's *Coal Miner's Daughter* and the long-running *7 Up* series of British TV documentaries chronicling the lives of a group of Britons in seven-year intervals.

Roth, Cates, and Apted were of the same mind when it came to contract negotiations. They believed that there was nothing to be gained from public saber rattling or showy efforts to negotiate in the press. The DGA triumvirate viewed the displays put on by the WGA as unprofessional and counterproductive. But they had no illusions about what was at stake for their members. DGA leaders were unhappy with the studios' unilateral decision on the residual formula for paid downloads, and they were none too pleased with the rapid growth of the residual-free Web streaming.

Knowing that these issues would be tackled in the 2008 contract negotiations, the DGA set out to be armed with information. In the spring of 2006, Roth organized a weekend retreat for top guild officials at a Santa Monica hotel. Most of the time was devoted to presentations from outside analysts and media experts on how new technologies were likely to shape the future of the entertainment business. On the heels of that weekend, the guild commissioned more detailed forecasts from several of the experts who made presentations. It also commissioned a separate study of the new media marketplace from a prominent consulting firm.

The guild wanted independent research to give its negotiators a soup-to-nuts look at new media as a business proposition for DGA members. It wanted information on how Hollywood was making money on the Web in 2007 and how those revenue sources were projected to grow over five to ten years. The guild also hoped to identify the cutting edge of new media, so as to put safeguards in its agreement for compensation on platforms that might not yet exist. The DGA reasoned that conducting multiple research initiatives at the same time would help them piece together an accurate picture of where the market was headed. The guild allocated more than one million dollars to fund the research project, which took more than a year to complete. Lawyer Ken Ziffren, a longtime adviser to the DGA, took part in the retreat and offered his vast institutional knowledge to the various consultants.

What did the DGA get for its money? Extensive reports that boiled down to the same conclusion: there was no pot of gold for Hollywood in new media, at least not yet. The studies found that the licensing fees and advertising revenue generated through new media platforms were still negligible for studios and networks compared to their traditional profit centers. And although digital distribution revenues were growing, there was no indication that they would become a significant source of studio income in the next five years.

The DGA studies underscored Hollywood's digital dilemma, at least in the short term. New media platforms were steadily eroding the industry's traditional business models without generating a commensurate source of profits. The disruption caused by consumers' embrace of DVRs, Web streaming, and paid downloads was coming at the networks and studios much faster than those companies had been able to figure out how to adapt to the new order, let alone monetize it. The AMPTP and CEOs applauded the DGA's research initiative, because the DGA's findings jibed with their own internal projections.

Even as DGA leaders took the conclusions of their studies to heart, however, the guild still faced a huge challenge. The writers' strike had completely changed the dynamic of the DGA's contract negotiations. Roth, Cates, and Apted were no longer merely negotiating what they believed to be a good deal for DGA members. Once the studios opted to force the WGA onto the sidelines, DGA leaders faced the unwelcome assignment of negotiating a deal that would also be palatable to the WGA, and thus lead the industry out of the paralysis caused by the strike.

On the plus side, the strike gave the DGA far more leverage with the studios than it would otherwise have had, because the AMPTP was eager to punish the WGA by reaching an agreement with the DGA. The CEOs wanted to forge a path to ending the strike, and they also wanted to embarrass the WGA leadership by making it clear to the creative community that the DGA's reasoned approach had been far more effective than picket lines and charged rhetoric. The CEOs knew they had erred by vastly underestimating the WGA's ability to wage war under David Young's leadership. After being knocked on their heels in November, the CEOs were determined to ensure that the studios got their act together in December, starting with the push to marginalize the WGA by negotiating with the DGA.

Because the stakes were so high, the core CEOs engaged in the strike—News Corporation's Peter Chernin, Disney's Robert Iger, Warner Bros.' Barry Meyer, and CBS Corporation's Leslie Moonves—took a more hands-on role in steering the negotiations with the DGA. In short order, Chernin and Iger became the appointed emissaries to communicate with the DGA. The AMPTP's governing CEOs had lost a lot of faith in Counter's ability to finesse these crucial talks at a moment when the clock was ticking for the entire industry and there was little margin for error. By mid-December, Chernin and Iger were consumed with meetings and conference calls with Roth, Cates, and other DGA point persons that would extend through the holiday season and into early January.

The DGA on December 13 announced its intent to begin formal negotiations with the AMPTP in January, citing the "dire" state of relations between the WGA and the AMPTP. But there was some artifice in the tentative-sounding nature of the statement released by Apted and Cates that day. Formal or not, discussions between the sides about the parameters of a deal had been ongoing since before the WGA strike. "Because we want to give the WGA and the AMPTP more time to return to the negotiating table to conclude an agreement, the DGA will not schedule our negotiations to begin until after the New Year, and then, only if an appropriate basis for negotiations can be established. If that's the case, then the DGA will commence formal talks in the hope that a fresh perspective and the additional pressure we can bring to bear will help force the AMPTP to settle the issues before us in a fair and reasonable manner."[2] By the time the DGA's bargaining sessions with the AMPTP began on January 12, most of the high hurdles had already been cleared.

Negotiating with the DGA was the first prong of the AMPTP's offensive maneuvers at the December 7 blowup. The second was an effort to castigate Patric Verrone and David Young as ideologues who were exploiting WGA members to advance their own social agendas.

The CEOs and AMPTP executives had not been shy about questioning Verrone and Young's motives. But the gloves came off on December 7, when the AMPTP issued a lengthy statement minutes after Counter declared the talks over in the hallway confrontation with Young. The speed with which the AMPTP issued its press release that Friday evening convinced the WGA, beyond a shadow of a doubt, that the AMPTP had never been serious about resuming negotiations with the guild. The AMPTP's lengthy statement had a disparaging tone crafted by PR consultants Chris Lehane and Mark Fabiani. "While the WGA's organizers can clearly stage rallies, concerts and mock exorcisms, we have serious concerns about whether they're capable of reaching reasonable compromises that are in the best interests of our entire industry. It is now absolutely clear that the WGA's organizers are determined to advance their own political ideologies and personal agendas at the expense of working writers and every other working person who depends on our industry for their livelihoods."[3]

As if waging a political campaign, the AMPTP's strategists zeroed in on wedge issues with the potential to divide the opposition. The wide variances among the income and job status of the WGA's members made it vulnerable to factionalism, something that had complicated the WGA's contract negotiations in the past. The AMPTP found its wedge issues in items 13 and 14 in the WGA's original list of contract proposals: the push for expanded jurisdiction in reality shows and film and TV animation. From December 7 on, the AMPTP hammered the point that "reality and animation," as it became known in shorthand, were the biggest impediment to restarting negotiations. In public statements and in private settings, AMPTP and studio leaders painted Verrone and Young as power mad in their effort to secure blanket WGA jurisdiction over reality programs. It was as much self-aggrandizement, the AMPTP line went, as it was a bid to increase the guild's leverage in the industry. "The conditions statement [handed to the WGA on Dec. 7] accurately reflected the position of the studios at that time. It was really done to be sure we were all on the same page as to where a deal could be struck," Carol Lombardini says. "The companies were unified in the belief that further conversation was getting us nowhere, and that the Writers Guild needed to know exactly where we stood."[4]

Verrone unwittingly played right into the AMPTP's master plan by declaring at the Fremantle rally that reality jurisdiction "will be in our next contract." The AMPTP seized on that quote as an example of Verrone's inflexibility, as well as evidence that the WGA West president was more interested in being onstage than doing the hard work of negotiating a contract.

The reality-jurisdiction issue was a hot potato for the WGA because many members were still skeptical of inviting reality producers into the writers' tent. There was also concern about the potential for thousands of new WGA members on the lower end of the earning scale putting pressure on the guild's pension and health benefit funds. As much as the WGA pressed the "If you can't beat 'em, organize 'em" point that nonunionized reality shows were a handy safety net for networks in the event of guild strikes, its leaders knew that showrunners and others would not stay on strike for the sake of expanding the WGA's reality jurisdiction. So did the AMPTP.

Animation was less divisive within the WGA, but the guild's push for more turf stirred the fury of the International Alliance of Theatrical Stage Employees, which has historically covered animation writing for film and some TV. IATSE president Thomas Short was quick to bash the WGA for "unethical poaching" in a statement issued shortly after the AMPTP announced the breakdown of the talks on the evening of December 7. Short went so far as to compare the WGA's leadership to "a huge clown car that's only missing the hats and horns."[5]

The guild sought to counterattack by accusing the AMPTP of using reality and animation as a red herring to draw attention away from the real obstacle, namely, the studios' unwillingness to pay up for new media. "Distributor's gross was the one thing they were really trying to get rid of," John Bowman said. "But we were willing to fight for it. It might seem odd to fight for an accounting formula, but we all knew how devastating the alternative would be."[6]

Publicly, the guild claimed the high ground of being willing to stick with the negotiation process, while the AMPTP unilaterally shut it down.

"The AMPTP insists we let them do to the Internet what they did to home video," Bowman said in a statement issued December 7, about ninety minutes after the AMPTP's release. "We reject the idea of an ultimatum. Although a number of items we have on the table are negotiable, we cannot be forced to bargain with ourselves. The AMPTP has many proposals on the table that are unacceptable to writers, but we have never delivered ultimatums."[7]

The AMPTP accused the guild of reneging on an agreement to drop the reality and animation provisions before the talks resumed on November 26. It issued a lengthy "fact sheet" later in the evening on December 7 that called the WGA's reality-jurisdiction push "underhanded and legally dubious."[8]

The finger-pointing and name-calling between the sides would continue for the rest of the month. On December 10, Michael Winship sent an eloquent letter to WGA East members blasting the AMPTP for its duplicity. The opening lines became an oft-repeated example of the enmity between the sides.

> They lie.
> And then they lie again. And then they lie some more.
> Because the AMPTP wants to create confusion, doubt, fear and dissension. They want to divide and conquer, to undercut our proven solidarity. . . . They refuse to negotiate until we accept their ultimatum. We refuse to bow to such supercilious, bullheaded intransigence, designed solely to destroy us. Yet we remain reasonable women and men willing to talk, bargain and negotiate anytime, anywhere.[9]

The more each side attacked the other, the more the sides dug in to their positions. Internally, however, the reality and animation issue was a source of frustration to some members of the WGA negotiating committee who saw the focus on jurisdictional gains as distracting to the guild's primary mission on new media. In this view, the reality and animation proposals were unattainable in this round of negotiations, which meant that they were destined to be taken off the table eventually. However, guild leaders were broadly unified that any concession in the face of the AMPTP's ultimatum was a bad move—which meant the AMPTP had effectively boxed guild leaders into the dilemma of having to publicly support a polarizing issue.

The strike would hit its nadir in the weeks after the December 7 blowup, as WGA members toughed out the holiday season with no idea when their employment crisis would end. The mood on many picket lines turned from spirited to gloomy, from determined to angry. Yet in spite of the mounting nervousness and the club wielded by the AMPTP, the WGA's public display of solidarity held fast to a remarkable degree. There were precious few public expressions of dissent or dissatisfaction with guild leadership. Certainly, there was nothing like the Union Blues breakaway group that complicated the 1985 and 1988 strikes.

It was in these difficult weeks that the triumvirate of Patric Verrone, David Young, and John Bowman showed their leadership mettle in the eyes of many members. After December 7, the trio, along with negotiating-committee members and WGA West board members, fanned out to picket sites to speak with members and make it clear that guild leaders were committed to staying the course. They hoped to counter any suggestion of panic or disarray at the top. "All of (the AMPTP's) press releases were clearly designed to demonize Patric and David," Bowman says. "What they didn't know was that Patric and David had talked to almost every member of the guild in a number of informal gatherings in the two years preceding the strike. Everybody knew who they were, what they stood for, and felt comfortable with them."[10]

Strike captains also got face time with Verrone, Young, Bowman, and others every Friday in meetings held at the Writers Guild Theater, the auditorium in Beverly Hills owned by the guild. The meetings generally focused on procedural and logistical issues involving the various picket sites. It was at these sessions that WGA members with no experience in labor actions were schooled by the seasoned union organizers that Young had brought in to the guild. The experience and confidence these veterans of blue-collar unions—including Jeff Hermanson, Rebecca Kessinger, Sarah Singer, and Ann Farriday—imparted to the strike captains on a weekly basis were crucial to maintaining morale on the front lines. So was the presence of the top leaders, who earned the respect and trust of the strike captains by speaking candidly about the state of the strike.

"They were always so clear cut and direct. They would just cut through the rumors and give you a real sense of what we were doing and why we were doing it," says John Aboud, the *United Hollywood* cofounder. "Everyone would leave those meetings feeling more confident than when we went in. They were very open with us. They knew that among the membership (communication) had to be very honest and very open. Because that's when people start to really have doubts—when they don't know what's going on. In an information vacuum, you start to crack."[11]

Steve Levitan was driving to the Beverly Hills–area home of a friend, actress Jami Gertz, for a Hanukkah dinner on the evening of December 7 when he heard the news about the breakdown in the talks between the AMPTP and WGA. Until that moment, he had been cautiously optimistic that the strike might be over by year's end—hope that was encouraged by all the rumors that the sides were moving closer to a deal.[12] As he arrived at Gertz's home in the ritzy gated community of Beverly Park, Levitan realized that the breakdown meant there would be no more negotiations until January at the earliest. He also knew it meant that his dinner conversation was likely to be interesting. Among the other guests that night were Robert Iger and Sony Pictures Entertainment chairman Michael Lynton. When Levitan spotted the studio chiefs, he telegraphed his despair over the latest setback with a shrug of his shoulders and a wince that was sympathetically acknowledged by the executives. The wordless exchange reflected the exasperation felt on both sides.

After dinner, Levitan waited for the right moment to pull Iger and Lynton aside. Speaking in a low voice, Levitan asserted that what had transpired between the AMPTP and WGA earlier that day was "insanity." He pressed them on what it would take to get the talks back on track. The executives responded almost in unison: get Patric Verrone and David Young out of the process. Surprised by the forcefulness of their reply, Levitan shot back that Nick Counter was just as much a part of the problem. He got no argument.

Levitan then raised the suggestion that his lawyer, Sam Fischer, could be cast in the role of peacemaker. Fischer's knowledge of the industry and his even temperament and experience with difficult negotiations made him well suited to the task. Iger was quick to endorse the idea, so quick that Levitan felt a rush of excitement. The trio's huddle broke up soon afterward amid the natural ebb and flow of party guests. But Levitan left Gertz's house that night with a new mission: to play matchmaker between Fischer and Young.

Early the following week, Levitan requested a meeting with Verrone and Young. A handful of other showrunners met him in the lobby of WGA West for what the others thought was a chance to press the leaders in private on the guild's next moves. But Levitan had his own agenda. As they waited to be led into a meeting room, Levitan warned the group about his plan to spring his Fischer proposal on Verrone and Young. Levitan thought that some of them might be uncomfortable with such a confrontation, but none of them backed out.

Although Verrone and Young were visibly worn out from the strain of working around the clock, the WGA West leaders were cool and calm as they discussed their analysis of the December 7 blowup with the group. But the conversation went on for only a short time before Levitan interjected with his request that the guild hire Fischer to help get the negotiations restarted and to close a deal. "I'm begging you to let this happen," Levitan said. "Sam is the perfect guy for this."

The room got quiet. Verrone and Young appeared taken aback for a moment, but the discussion continued. The WGA chiefs stressed the importance of the guild holding firm in the face of the studios' ultimatums. They emphasized how the AMPTP was hoping to splinter writers' solidarity by declaring reality and animation jurisdiction as the primary roadblocks standing in the way of a contract. Levitan responded that the guild could only benefit from using Fischer's strong relationships with key CEOs to cut through such posturing to get to the real issue of new media. He gently suggested that Verrone and Young take a half-step back from the process and let Fischer try to work under the radar for a while. The tone of the conversation was cordial, but it was still a tense exchange. Young agreed to meet with Fischer, but it was as far as he would commit.

Fischer was not destined to play a role in ending the WGA strike. But Levitan's attempt nonetheless marked a quiet turning point. It signaled mounting concern among key showrunners that the WGA needed its own

Ken Ziffren–style deal maker on its side. Levitan's effort to enlist Fischer was the precursor to a forceful push to come from an even more influential WGA constituency.

Among the ripple effects of the December 7 meltdown was the sense of urgency it stirred among the late-night TV hosts. Publicly, David Letterman, Jay Leno, Conan O'Brien, Jimmy Kimmel, Jon Stewart, and Stephen Colbert remained highly supportive of the guild. Letterman and O'Brien and members of their staffs engaged in a playful contest to grow "strike beards" by giving up shaving for the duration of the walkout—a move that generated sympathetic media coverage for the WGA.[13] Privately, as the strike went into its second month with hostilities escalating and the AMPTP shunting the WGA aside in favor of the DGA, the hosts and their producers focused on setting a date for production to resume, even without writers.

The hosts faced pressure from their networks to return; ABC, CBS, and NBC lost millions of dollars with each week of reruns. But the hosts undoubtedly were nervous about their own long-term fortunes. The longer the shows were off the air, the more viewers would fall out of the habit of keeping that nightly date with *The Tonight Show* or *Jimmy Kimmel Live* or *The Daily Show with Jon Stewart*. The lesson of prime time's irrevocable audience losses after the 1988 strike was not lost on any of them. And the media landscape had only become more defuse, and the alternatives to TV more numerous, in the ensuing twenty years.

It was no surprise that O'Brien's camp spearheaded the effort to find consensus on a return date. O'Brien had committed to pay the salaries of about eighty people on his production staff after they were pink-slipped by NBC at the end of November. Jay Leno and David Letterman were doing the same for their idled staffs, but those two hosts also banked far higher annual salaries—$10 million to $20 million more—than O'Brien. O'Brien wound up paying about $450,000 out of his own pocket during the four weeks that he covered his staff payroll.

The other motivating factor for Leno and O'Brien came from the WGA itself. After December 7, the guild opted for a two-pronged strategy designed to take advantage of the divisions among AMPTP signatory companies large and small. Guild leaders would publicly pressure the studios to conduct separate negotiations with the guild. The WGA knew the chances were slim that one of the conglomerates would break away from the AMPTP organization and negotiate a separate deal. But it was a way to keep the studios on the defensive about their refusal to negotiate.

The other tactic was to clear the way for smaller production companies to resume working with writers by encouraging the companies to sign "interim agreements" with the guild. In signing an interim contract, the companies would ostensibly agree to abide by the WGA contract demands that had been laid out in the bargaining with the AMPTP. The pursuit of interim agreements with prominent independent production entities was a more attainable goal, one that the guild had used in past strikes, than the push for one-on-one negotiations with the major studios.

If the WGA amassed enough interim agreements, it would widen the divide between large and small AMPTP signatory companies, allowing smaller entities to resume work on new and existing projects while the studios were stuck in a holding pattern. But there was some stagecraft to those interim agreements because they included a fine-print clause that allowed the company to eventually revert to the terms of the AMPTP-negotiated contract when it was finally completed. As such, the companies that signed the interim agreements knew they would not be bound by those terms for too long. Moreover, most of the thirty-one companies that signed deals during the strike were film-oriented production companies, which meant the bulk of the WGA deal terms involving new media, jurisdiction over reality TV, and animation had little practical bearing on their operations.

O'Brien's attention was piqued by the fact that one of the first companies to discuss an interim agreement was Letterman's production company, Worldwide Pants. Letterman's company had the freedom to pursue such a deal—unlike the other hosts—because Worldwide Pants owns CBS's *Late Show* outright, along with its companion, *The Late Late Show with Craig Ferguson*. As such, Letterman's company had the autonomy to agree to the WGA's terms without CBS's involvement.[14]

Letterman's full ownership of the two shows is a testament to how desperate CBS was to recruit the former NBC *Late Night* host after Letterman was passed over as the successor to Johnny Carson on *The Tonight*

Show in 1992. Letterman used his leverage with CBS to secure total owner-ship of his program and any program that followed *The Late Show* in the 12:35 a.m. time slot.

The deal that Worldwide Pants ultimately reached with the WGA allowed Letterman and Ferguson to resume production at full strength, while the other hosts had to wing it. What's more, Letterman and Fergu-son had an advantage in booking stars who would not appear on the other shows while the strike was ongoing.

Letterman's pursuit of an interim agreement with the WGA did not stay quiet for long. Before the holidays, Leno inquired with guild leaders about the rumors of a Worldwide Pants deal. By multiple accounts, he was assured by David Young and others that there would be no deal with Let-terman's company. Still, the prospect of Letterman and Ferguson going back on the air galvanized an effort by O'Brien's camp to reach a consen-sus among the hosts on a return date for the late-night shows—Letterman included.

After a flurry of conference calls and at least one face-to-face meeting between O'Brien and Stewart at the former's office in Rockefeller Center, NBC announced on December 17 that Leno and O'Brien would be back with new episodes as of January 2, 2008. The next day, Jimmy Kimmel announced his ABC show would also return on January 2. Two days after that, Jon Stewart and Stephen Colbert confirmed they would be back in action on Comedy Central as of January 7.

Letterman and Ferguson were officially mum about their plans, but Worldwide Pants' discussions with the WGA were widely reported in the media. Letterman's camp let it be known to production staffers and to CBS executives that *The Late Show* and *The Late Late Show* would be back in business on January 2, with or without an interim agreement.

NBC's news release included a heartfelt statement from O'Brien that conveyed how conflicted he was about the decision:

My career in television started as a WGA member and my subsequent career as a performer has only been possible because of the creativity and integrity of my writing staff. Since the strike began, I have stayed off the air in support of the striking writers while, at the same time, doing everything I could to take care of the 80 non-writing staff members on "Late Night."

Unfortunately, now with the New Year upon us, I am left with a difficult decision. Either go back to work and keep my staff employed or stay dark and allow 80 people, many of whom have worked for me for fourteen years, to lose their jobs. If my show were entirely scripted I would have no choice. But the truth is that shows like mine are hybrids, with both written and non-written content. An unwritten version of "Late Night," though not desirable, is possible.[15]

The WGA cast the late-night moves as the result of arm-twisting by top network executives. On the day of NBC's announcement, the guild quickly issued a timely "notice" to members about the strike rules barring any WGA members from doing any work on struck productions, including "all writing by any guild member that would be performed on-air by that member (including monologues, characters and featured appearances) if any portion of that written material is customarily written by striking writers." The memo was not directly addressed to O'Brien and Leno, but it might as well have been.[16]

The movement among the late-night hosts came on the heels of the DGA's announcement of its intent to begin formal negotiations, and it coincided with the WGA's decision to suspend picketing activity until after January 1 because of the holidays. The WGA needed a win to combat any gnawing suspicions among members that the guild's momentum had stalled. An interim agreement with a prominent figure like David Letterman was a perfect solution.

Letterman's handlers saw the possibility of a WGA deal as a rare window of opportunity to gain an advantage over *The Tonight Show*. It would confer a special status on Letterman that the other hosts could not claim. But because Worldwide Pants would be the first company to sign such an agreement in the 2007 strike, the deal terms and potential consequences were vetted by Letterman's lawyers for weeks. The agreement was finally made public on December 28.[17]

The WGA used the announcement to again criticize the studios' intransigence and call for renewed AMPTP-wide negotiations. The Letterman deal also gave the guild an opening to single out NBC Universal for particular criticism. It was expedient for them to target NBC at the moment when the major competitors to the network's highly profitable *Tonight Show* and *Late Night* franchises had just been handed a leg up. And NBC Universal CEO Jeff Zucker had been strident in his rejection of the WGA's reasoning on new media. The guild's strategy of pressuring NBC would become more apparent the following month when it waged war over the network's telecast of the annual Golden Globe awards ceremony.

Meanwhile, as the WGA's talks with Worldwide Pants became common knowledge, Jon Stewart began pushing the WGA for an interim deal of his own. Stewart had numerous conversations with WGA East president Michael Winship, urging the guild to find a way to reach a deal to cover *The Daily Show* and *The Colbert Report*. But as many times as it was discussed, the answer was always the same. Stewart's production company was responsible for both shows, but he did not have full ownership of them. Ultimate control rested with Comedy Central, a unit of Viacom, which refused to agree to an interim agreement with the WGA even at the insistence of the cable channel's signature star. And even if Viacom had submitted to deals for *The Daily Show* and *The Colbert Report*, the WGA could not afford to set the dangerous precedent of cutting deals with select TV shows or movies. Doing so would only chip away at the leverage the guild enjoyed through its blanket coverage of studio film and TV production.

Nonetheless, it was not easy for the WGA to turn down Stewart. Writers for *The Daily Show* and *The Colbert Report* had been staunch supporters of the East Coast strike effort. They were regulars on picket lines, and several of them produced short Internet videos featuring *The Daily Show*'s trademark biting satire to help the WGA's cause.

It was even harder a few weeks later when the WGA had little choice but to organize picket lines outside of the Manhattan studio facilities where *The Daily Show* and *Colbert* were taped. They did the same outside NBC's Rockefeller Center headquarters because of *Late Night with Conan O'Brien*. And on the other side of the country, pickets were a fixture outside the street-level studio of *The Tonight Show with Jay Leno*, facing a busy intersection in Burbank's business district. "It was difficult having to make the decision to picket those shows," Winship said. "The (hosts) had been very supportive. It was difficult having to say, 'Look, this is a strike. It's nothing personal, but we have to continue this strike and now that you're back on the air, without your writers, that means picketing your studios—not as an attack on you specifically, but as an attack on the companies that produce you.' That was a very hard decision to make, but we made it."[18]

In late December and into early January, it seemed there was no rapprochement in sight for the WGA and the studios. But this was the period when the foundation for the strike settlement was laid with horse-trading and hard bargaining between DGA negotiators and the CEOs—chiefly Peter Chernin and Robert Iger.

The strength of the relationships and the reservoir of trust among the key players around the table were most beneficial amid the difficult process of coming to an agreement on compensation terms for new media. It was, at times, a philosophical debate about what constituted a fair share for directors in a highly uncertain marketplace. At other times, it was painstaking negotiating over every fraction of a percentage point incorporated in the master contract. Through it all, the weight of the expectations of writers and actors hung heavy over every conversation.

The prep work the DGA had done stealthily in the weeks before the WGA went on strike proved crucial to focusing the talks on the most substantive issues of compensation rates. The formula for how the pay rates for paid downloads and Web streaming would be calculated had already been agreed to in the early fall. DGA negotiators had faxed their AMPTP counterparts a few pages' worth of proposals with blank spaces where the specific financial terms would be filled in. DGA and studio representatives spent no time debating various options for those formulas in the formal bargaining sessions, as the WGA had, to great exasperation on both sides. The DGA's formulas were easy to understand—for those individuals schooled in the arcana of residuals—and rooted in a rationale that was acceptable to the CEOs.

Given the significance of this consensus, it is surprising that word of the DGA-AMPTP understanding did not leak out in the strike blogosphere or to any mainstream news outlets. That it did not is more evidence of the DGA's close-to-the-vest contract-negotiation strategy as well as the lack of communication between the DGA and the WGA.

In the first wave of conference calls and meetings after the DGA's December 13 announcement, Jay Roth and Gil Cates came up with a list of issues that still needed to be sorted through. The thorniest of them all, by far, was how the sides would define distributor's gross, as distinguished from the producer's gross 20 percent formula. The AMPTP cited the WGA's insistence on distributor's gross as one of its six deal breakers in the December 7 blowup.

DGA leaders were determined to hold the line against the use of producer's gross in any form in its new media contract language—even if the studios offered an increase over the 20 percent standard. The goal was to ensure that a discounted producer's gross would never be a factor in the new media realm. No matter how modest the percentage-based residual might be to start, it was important that the contract language specify that it would be based on 100 percent of revenue.

But in Hollywood, slicing up the money generated by movies and TV shows is never easy. Entertainment lawyers often spend months working on profit-participation definitions for creative talent and others with the clout to command a share of any profits generated from a production. (Of course, the definition of "profit" is famously nebulous in Hollywood.)

Roth and Cates persuaded Chernin and Iger that the sides needed to try to agree to a distributor's gross definition on paper before the formal sessions began in January, or they would run the risk of bogging down the talks. The CEOs agreed to assemble a working group to tackle the problem.[19] That decision sent a signal that the AMPTP was not going to be as inflexible on distributor's gross as it seemed to be on December 7.

Chernin turned to Howard Kurtzman, executive vice president of business affairs for News Corporation's prosperous prime-time television production unit, 20th Century Fox Television. Iger enlisted the president of Disney's ABC Studios production division, Mark Pedowitz. The DGA was represented by Ken Ziffren and the guild's general counsel, David Korduner. It was another group that had a long history of doing business together.

Pedowitz and Kurtzman kept quiet about their assignment even among their own staff members. The foursome needed to hammer out a difficult issue without any pressure from media attention or lobbying from other interested parties in the industry. The goal for the distributor's gross working group was the same as the overriding discussions on new media: reach a consensus on a formula that was fair to both sides. By nature, Pedowitz and Kurtzman were not the type to beat their chests about being recruited for such an important and delicate task.

Pedowitz and Ziffren had a few conversations about the parameters that might be acceptable to the studios. In its public battle with the WGA, the AMPTP repeatedly asserted that the WGA's definition of distributor's gross went well beyond traditional boundaries to include a cut of any advertising revenue that the new media platform derived from commercials inserted into programs and other sources. This point was, in large part, a red herring, a way for the studios to justify rejecting the demand. The DGA was determined to avoid that trap through diplomacy.

After Ziffren and Pedowitz's discussions, Ziffren and Korduner did what good show business lawyers do best: they drew up a preliminary proposal and presented it to Pedowitz and Kurtzman. Each of the four men brought his own deal-making history to the table, and their refinements to the draft language went back and forth over conference calls and meetings until the foursome had signed off on five pages of mostly legalese that defined distributor's gross inside out, upside down, and sideways.

The heavy lifting was done by the time the DGA's formal negotiations commenced on January 12. The issue that had been dismissed by the AMPTP as unacceptable in concept became a pillar of the tentative contract agreement that was unveiled six days later. The DGA took pains to highlight the inclusion of "distributor's gross" language as a major victory. "We would not have entered the agreement on any other basis," the guild stated matter-of-factly in its January 17 press release announcing its tentative contract agreement.[20]

Whereas DGA representatives worked mostly in secret, the WGA stayed in the public eye in an effort to maintain solidarity among its members in the face of uncertainty. On December 17, the day that Conan O'Brien and

Jay Leno announced their intent to return to production, the WGA issued a press release confirming it had denied requests from the producers of the Golden Globes and Academy Awards for waivers that would allow WGA members to work on scripted material for the live telecasts. The WGA West board had broad authority to grant a work waiver that would allow writers to work on a production even in the midst of a strike. But the guild had far more to gain by denying the award shows any fresh material from seasoned comedy writers.

For one, the stars courted for appearances on these shows want the security of prepared material as they go live before a worldwide audience. NBC stood to make as much as fifteen to twenty million dollars from its Globes telecast; the Academy Awards are an even more profitable franchise for ABC. Furthermore, WGA leaders knew that disrupting award season would reinforce to the industry and alert the general public that the WGA was no paper tiger. The WGA West board voted unanimously to deny the waiver requests for the January 13 Globes telecast and the February 24 Oscar telecast. "Writers are engaged in a crucial struggle to achieve a collective bargaining agreement that will protect their compensation and intellectual property rights now and in the future," Verrone wrote in a letter sent to the heads of the Academy of Motion Picture Arts and Sciences (AMPAS) and the Hollywood Foreign Press Association (HFPA), which administers the Golden Globes ceremony. "Granting exceptions for the Golden Globes or the Academy Awards would not advance that goal," the guild said in its statement.[21]

Verrone's letter was not the last word that the WGA, AMPAS, and the HFPA would exchange about the award shows. To reinforce its message to the studios, the WGA did grant a waiver request to producers of the Spirit Awards, an annual event that recognizes independent films. The WGA wanted to make it clear that it was at war with the major studios, not award shows.

On the evening of December 17, the WGA held a membership meeting at the Santa Monica Civic Auditorium. The scene inside the three-thousand-seat venue was reminiscent of the LA Convention Center meeting that preceded the strike. WGA West board members and negotiating-committee members sat two rows deep on a dais bordered on either side by long, narrow banners depicting a graphic of crisscrossed pencils and the slogan "Stronger Together." At least one thousand members turned out for a status report from John Bowman, David Young, and Patric Verrone, among others. SAG president Alan Rosenberg once again offered a rousing pledge of continued support from actors.

There were long lines in front of the microphones set up on the floor for questions and comments from members. There were queries about strategic and logistical issues, from the DGA's moves to the picketing operation to the rumored deal with David Letterman. To the surprise of some who sat on the dais, there was still no dissent voiced at the meeting, no serious challenge to the leadership decisions of Verrone and Young. The solidarity forged by the sense of collective purpose among the writers who manned the picket lines was indomitable. Even after six tumultuous weeks, the members most engaged in strike operations had unqualified faith in the Verrone regime. That bedrock of support for guild leaders was a force that the studios could not dismiss. As the CEOs and Nick Counter focused on negotiations with the DGA, the demands of the WGA's foot soldiers were never far from anyone's thinking. The WGA's carefully crafted events only reinforced that power.

The morning after the membership meeting, the WGA staged a stunt featuring a group of crime-drama writers issuing an "indictment" that charged the studios with "trying to steal the Internet and misappropriate the future of writers." The "Scene of the Crime" rally was held, as a light rain fell, outside the AMPTP's headquarters on a well-trafficked stretch of Ventura Boulevard in the Encino area of the San Fernando Valley. For maximum visual effect, the bushes that ring the parking lot of the office complex were wrapped in yellow crime-scene tape, as were spots outside 20th Century Fox, Disney, Universal, Paramount, and five other picket sites. *CSI: Crime Scene Investigation* star Marg Helgenberger, who at the time was married to SAG president Rosenberg, made a show of reading the indictment for the enthusiastic crowd of about a hundred, many of them carrying picket signs covered in clear plastic sheeting.

On December 19, Bowman and dozens of guild members attended a hearing held by the Los Angeles City Council's housing, community, and economic development committee to examine the economic impact of the strike on the city. The event was a purely a symbolic exercise with local politicians who held no sway with studio CEOs. Once again, though, it was an opportunity for the WGA to present its case in public in a sympathetic forum, and it was a means of having third parties urge AMPTP officials to return to the negotiating table.[22]

Bowman and others testified about the strike's toll on the industry's rank and file, from writers to prop-house owners. Economists and government number crunchers spoke of the huge opportunity costs of the shutdown, as highly paid cast and crew members curtailed their discretionary spending in the face of uncertainty. "The pain is growing each day the strike goes on," said Jack Kyser, chief economist of the Los Angeles County Economic Development Corporation, who estimated that the strike as of December 19 had cost the LA region some $220 million in lost discretionary spending by individuals. Officials with the Los Angeles film permitting office, FilmLA, estimated the strike had cost about ten thousand jobs, with the halt of production on fifty-two drama series and nineteen sitcoms.

The AMPTP did not send a representative to the hearing. The Motion Picture Association of America, the lobbying outfit that represents the major studios in all governmental affairs, sent a statement to be read into the record. The MPAA pegged the lost wages since the stoppage began at "upwards of $350 million," including $120 million for WGA members, $205 million for IATSE members in the Los Angeles area, and $50 million for the Teamsters and other craft unions.

Comedy writer Betsy Thomas got a big reaction by testifying with her infant son, Owen, perched on her chest in a baby sling. Thomas told the committee that most WGA members earned middle-class incomes and "drive Hondas and Toyotas."

After the hearing ended, Bowman and Los Angeles City Council president Eric Garcetti held a news conference outside city hall. A few dozen writers, most of them wearing red WGA T-shirts, stood several rows deep on the steps behind the podium for maximum photo-op effect. Garcetti called for the AMPTP to resume negotiations with the WGA for the sake of the local economy. Bowman reiterated his assertion that the studios were to blame for the economic damage caused by the strike. Bowman's face showed the strain of working around the clock for months under intense pressure, but his demeanor reflected the same intellectual confidence that he had on the first day of negotiations back in July. His baritone voice and enunciation made him a commanding spokesman for the guild in public forums like the city hall news conference.

After he went through his standard talking points, Bowman dropped a big hint to the handful of reporters who continued to lob questions at him. The guild expected to sign its first interim agreements with smaller AMPTP signatory companies within a week or so. The negotiations with David Letterman's company were no secret—the WGA had issued a statement the day before confirming it was in discussions with Letterman's Worldwide Pants. But Bowman indicated that there were several more in the works. He even allowed that the strategy of seeking interim agreements was risky for the guild, because it could chip away at the solidarity of the membership—the WGA's single most potent weapon—if some members were able to go back to work but not others. But the guild decided it was a gamble worth taking because it believed that there were a good number of companies open to interim agreements. If enough production activity got under way at smaller entities, the studios would feel some pressure to catch up.

Bowman's comments about the interim deals were designed to dispel the perception that the WGA was boxed in and stuck without a strategy to end the strike other than capitulation. But he was not exaggerating. The WGA's interim deal with Worldwide Pants was confirmed nine days after the city council session, on December 28, and several more followed in the first half of January.

The Worldwide Pants deal had great significance for the WGA, beyond its power to send David Letterman and Craig Ferguson back to work with their writers. There was no innovation in the deal terms per se; they were virtually identical to the WGA's initial proposal to the AMPTP. The WGA bandied this point as a sign that its demands were acceptable to some companies—even if the fine print allowed Worldwide Pants to revert to whatever terms were ultimately reached in the industry-wide accord. Despite that safety net, the agreement had been carefully studied by Letterman's legal team at one of the entertainment industry's most prominent law firms, Jackoway Tyerman Wertheimer Austen Mandelbaum Morris & Klein.

Jim Jackoway, Letterman's longtime personal attorney, is well known for being a formidable negotiator who is skilled at securing record-setting fees and generous profit-participation terms out of studios for his A-list clients. (After a grueling contract renegotiation for Letterman in 2002, Jackoway was, at least temporarily, banned from setting foot inside CBS.) Jackoway and his associates sought to make sure there would be no unintended consequences for Worldwide Pants. There had been some debate within Letterman's inner circle about whether signing the agreement was a good idea. *Late Show* producers who thought it would give Letterman a competitive advantage against his archrival on NBC, Jay Leno, won out.

A lot of the heavy lifting in the review was done by one of Jackoway's partners, Alan Wertheimer. Wertheimer generally focused on representing top-tier feature-film talents, particularly writers and directors. He had a deep familiarity with guild agreements and writer contracts, which made him a logical choice to assist in the contract review for one of the firm's most important clients. In the process, Wertheimer had numerous conversations with WGA officials, including David Young. Young was eager to land the Worldwide Pants deal for strategic reasons, particularly because it would help drive a wedge between CBS and NBC. The discussions went down to the wire through the week of the Christmas holiday as the sides raced to get a deal completed before Letterman and Ferguson were scheduled to return. During this period, Young and Wertheimer became comfortable with each other.

Wertheimer's name was not mentioned in the press release announcing the Worldwide Pants interim agreement, nor was Jackoway's. But in short order, it became clear that Wertheimer's behind-the-scenes involvement was the most meaningful result of the contract that would be rendered null and void in six weeks' time.

From the January 2, 2008, edition of *The Late Show with David Letterman*, the top-ten demands of striking writers (as delivered on air by WGA members):

10. Complimentary tote bag with next insulting contract offer. (Tim Carvell, *The Daily Show with Jon Stewart*)

9. No rollbacks on health benefits, so I can treat the hypothermia I caught on the picket line. (Laura Krafft, *The Colbert Report*)

8. Full salary and benefits for my imaginary writing partner, Lester. (Melissa Salmons, daytime TV writer)

7. Members of the AMPTP must explain what the hell AMPTP stands for. (Warren Leight, *Law and Order: Criminal Intent*)

6. No disciplinary action taken against any writer caught having an inappropriate relationship with a copier. (Jay Katsir, *The Colbert Report*)

5. I'd like a date with a woman. (Steve Bodow, *The Daily Show with Jon Stewart*)

4. Hazard pay for breaking up fights on *The View*. (Nora Ephron, screenwriter and director)

3. I'm no accountant, but instead of us getting four cents for a 20 dollar DVD, how about we get 20 dollars for a four cent DVD? (Gina Gionfriddo, *Law and Order*)

2. I don't have a joke—I just want to remind everyone that we're on strike so none of us are responsible for this lame list. (Chris Albers, *Late Night with Conan O'Brien*)

1. Producers must immediately remove their heads from their asses. (Alan Zweibel, comedy writer)

9

Deal or No Deal?

Alan Wertheimer was having lunch at a restaurant in Park City, Utah, on January 20 when his cell phone rang. It was the third day of the Sundance Film Festival, the annual gathering that brings a glossy mix of Hollywood and independent-film types to the ski-resort town about thirty-five miles east of Salt Lake City. Wertheimer was there partly to scout for potential clients, but mostly to indulge his love of movies at the festival that is the premier showcase for independent films and up-and-coming talent.[1]

The call that interrupted Wertheimer's lunch that Sunday afternoon was from WGA West executive director David Young. Young was characteristically forthright during the brief conversation. The WGA wanted to retain Wertheimer as an outside counsel as guild leaders prepared to go back into contract negotiations—this time directly with News Corporation president Peter Chernin and Disney CEO Robert Iger.

Young's call to Wertheimer came three days after the DGA and the AMPTP revealed the basic details of a contract agreement that included new categories of residuals for new media and other precedent-setting provisions. It established a residual rate for paid downloads that was double the comparable rate for home video. The deal also cemented the DGA's jurisdiction over made-for-Internet productions with precise parameters. And it included a groundbreaking obligation for AMPTP members to disclose contract documents and other information pertaining to licensing and distribution in new media, in an effort to help the DGA understand how business models in the new media realm would evolve during the three-year term of the contract. In the DGA's public statements regarding the deal, however, no single element was touted more than the fact that the residual formulas established for paid downloads and Web streaming were based on distributor's gross, and nothing less. The DGA had achieved the provision that the AMPTP had said was a deal breaker in its negotiations with the WGA.

The DGA sealed its tentative contract agreement January 17 after six days of formal negotiations with Nick Counter, Carol Lombardini, and studio labor executives at AMPTP headquarters. But the bulk of the work had been done by a handful of key players in the weeks leading up to the formal bargaining sessions. Chernin and Iger had several meetings at Chernin's home in early January with Gil Cates, Jay Roth, and other DGA officials to fine-tune the basic framework of new categories of residuals for paid downloads and Web streaming, as well as the parameters of the DGA's jurisdiction over productions done for the Internet. Chernin and Iger worked on big-picture issues; the nitty-gritty of the numbers and percentages in the final deal was left to Counter, Lombardini, and their team. This approach, coupled with years of preparation by the DGA, allowed the sides to tackle tricky matters that could have easily been bogged down in debates and jockeying among the larger group of executives in the formal bargaining sessions.

The day the DGA agreement was announced, the studios made the same offer to the WGA to engage in informal discussions "to determine whether there is a reasonable basis for returning for formal bargaining," the AMPTP said in a statement. "We hope this agreement with the DGA will signal the beginning of the end of this extremely difficult period for our industry."[2]

In their phone conversation, Young told Wertheimer that if he wanted the job, he would have to return to Los Angeles immediately because the first meeting with the CEOs was set for the following Tuesday, January 22. Wertheimer was on a plane within hours.

Among the individuals who were most relieved when Wertheimer said yes was John Bowman, who was starting to feel the clock ticking. As soon as he saw the basic terms of the DGA deal, he knew the strike was essentially over. His gut told him it would be impossible to maintain the support of prominent screenwriters and showrunners if those deal terms were put on the table for the WGA.

The single biggest selling point of the DGA agreement was the gains in the residual rate secured for paid permanent downloads, or the new media equivalent of a DVD purchase. It also established the DGA's unequivocal jurisdiction to enforce guild rules and contract terms for members working on made-for-new-media productions, whether wholly original or derived from an existing TV or movie property. DGA negotiating committee chairman Cates was not shy about heralding the deal's precedent-setting elements. "Two words describe this agreement—groundbreaking and substantial," Cates said in the five-page press release announcing the deal.[3]

The deal more than doubled the traditional home video rate of pay for popular television programming, and it marked an 80 percent improvement for feature films. Most important, residual payments were all based on a distributor's gross formula. For television programs that generated more than one hundred thousand paid downloads, the residual rate was set at 0.7 percent of distributor's gross. For movies that achieved more than fifty thousand downloads, the rate was set at 0.65 percent of distributor's gross. For TV programs and movies that fell under the one-hundred-thousand and fifty-thousand download thresholds, the pay rate remained at the traditional home video level of 0.3 percent until worldwide gross receipts reached one million dollars, when the rate increased to 0.36 percent.

DGA leaders knew the AMPTP would respond favorably to a formula rooted in past contract precedent, so they proposed that payments be calculated as a flat fee based on a fixed percentage of the traditional residual base for a television program for a twenty-six-week exhibition period following the premiere telecast of the program. Distributors would have the right to pay the flat fee again for another twenty-six weeks of streaming. But once a year had passed since the premiere telecast (whether the distributor had exercised both twenty-six-week options or not), the fee shifted to 2 percent of distributor's gross. The sides settled on 3 percent of the traditional residual base for the first two twenty-six-week periods, which worked out to about $600 for a prime-time broadcast network drama and about $320 for a half-hour broadcast network program.

There was more struggle between the DGA and AMPTP on an issue that was vital to the studios, which insisted on carving out a residual-free "promotional" window for Web streaming of programs. The AMPTP argued that streaming was still largely done for promotional purposes, to help bring new viewers into the show, rather than for advertising revenue. There is precedent in guild contracts for residual-free promotional uses of programming and other materials, on the understanding that a producer's investment in promotion was an effort to enhance the profitability of a TV program or movie.

The AMPTP dug in its heels for a promotional window of seventeen days after the initial telecast of a program, or twenty-four days in the case of a show in its first season. Residuals would be due only if the program was still made available for streaming after a seventeen- or twenty-four-day window. This provision was unpopular for directors as well as writers and actors because there is clear evidence that the vast majority of online viewing of full-length TV programs is done within a few days of the initial TV telecast, as viewers catch up with shows at their own convenience. DGA and WGA members were already frustrated by the relatively low residual base for new media, compared to traditional TV and movies, and saw the promotional window as a means of cheating them out of the lion's share of the action in Web streaming. Despite the best efforts of DGA, WGA, and eventually Screen Actors Guild negotiators, however, the promotional window remained an ironclad element of the AMPTP's new media–deal template.

The issue of jurisdiction was an area where the DGA and the AMPTP shared some of the same concerns about how—and for whom—guild coverage should be applied on original made-for-Internet productions. It was taken as a given by both sides from the start that Internet productions derived from an existing TV show or movie—à la *The Office* webisodes that spurred the National Labor Relations Board ruling—would automatically be considered covered work.

The question of original material made for new media was a thornier matter. The DGA saw the need to cement its authority to govern the work of directors in the new realm in its master agreement. But the guild was wary of opening its doors to a flood of amateurs who may have shot a video that became a YouTube sensation but might never work steadily at a professional level. DGA officials did not want the burden of representing a little-trained subset of workers, nor were they eager to open the pension and health plan to people who might never make significant contributions to the funds through their employment.[4] Simply put, it could wind up costing the DGA more to take on new members than it was worth to the guild's traditional membership base.

At the same time, Roth and Cates recognized the experimental nature of the bulk of the made-for-Internet production done by AMPTP signatory companies. Internal initiatives at Disney, Warner Bros., and Sony Pictures Television, among others, to develop a portfolio of Web entertainment series were still being done on an ultra-low-budget basis with little marketing or promotional resources put behind them. The DGA sought to craft a jurisdiction solution that would ensure guild coverage for any substantial production, but would also give companies the flexibility to continue to develop material and business models internally without invoking DGA-level compensation and work terms.

Roth's guiding principle was that if the DGA tried to enforce guild terms on Internet production while it was still in its low-budget infancy, the studios would simply set up holding companies and other dodges to produce them outside of the DGA's sphere of influence. And once those shell companies were established, the DGA would have to work harder to organize the directors they employed if made-for-Internet productions prospered and demand for trained directors increased. The DGA reasoned that if the studios were able to keep the low-budget production done within their four walls, the DGA's authority would be unquestioned and it would be easier to keep track of the growth of the sector.

To address this quandary, the DGA proposed production budget thresholds that would trigger DGA contract coverage. DGA coverage kicks in if the production budget is more than fifteen thousand dollars per minute, three hundred thousand dollars per program, or five hundred thousand dollars for an entire multipart series. However, if a DGA member is hired to work on a production that falls below those thresholds, that person's employment must be covered by a DGA contract to be negotiated by the production entity with the guild.

Beyond the residuals and jurisdiction for new media, another major breakthrough in the eyes of the DGA was the commitment from the studios to give the guilds unprecedented access to documents and other information pertaining to new media business transactions. The disclosure obligation was unlike anything the major studios had agreed to in the past. It was born out of their frustration at the perception in the creative community that the studios were profiting hand over fist from new media licensing and exhibition, when in fact digital distribution seemed to have a mostly corrosive effect on traditional business models.

The studios vowed to share with guild representatives all documents related to production, distribution, advertising, licensing, marketing, sponsorship, and other activities related to their new media businesses, without redaction. They also committed to showing DGA representatives on a periodic basis all internal documents tracking the results of endeavors in new media. The sharing of these documents would be limited to only a few DGA representatives, and the guild would not be able to retain permanent copies of any of the material. But they would be able to look under the tent every six months or so. The idea was that the DGA and the studios would be able to study the development of the new media sector together, allowing the guild insight into where the money was—and was not—in a fast-changing landscape. Given the tortured history of Hollywood accounting, this point was nothing less than a monumental concession by the studios. The studios sought to make a statement that they had nothing, least of all windfall profits, to hide.

Finally, the DGA agreement included sunset provisions on all of the new media deal points, meaning that they would expire at the end of the contract's three-year term. The guild wanted to ensure that it would have to revisit the details of its residual formulas in three years' time as a protection against a highly uncertain future. In spite of all of the DGA's preparation, with studies and experts, it was impossible to predict where the film and TV industry would be in 2011. Cates's focus in the 2008 contract was, as he expressed to DGA members, "to protect our interests in the present while laying the groundwork for a future whose outlines are not yet clear."[5]

Because of the lack of contentiousness in the DGA-AMPTP relationship, the DGA was confident that the sides could work out a reasonable deal in the next go-round. There was little fear on the part of DGA leadership that it would not be able to achieve the same level of compensation in the 2011 contract. The WGA did have concerns about facing possible rollbacks in 2011 and chose not to incorporate sunset provisions into its contract.

The day before David Young's call to Alan Wertheimer, more than a dozen members of the WGA negotiating committee gathered at John Bowman's home in Santa Monica to discuss the DGA deal and the WGA's next steps. The consensus emerged that the DGA's new media terms were far better than they had expected and that the deal was a testament to the leverage the DGA had been handed by the WGA's sacrifice of going on strike.[6]

The fact that a victory seemed to be in sight emboldened a number of committee members to insist that Bowman prod Verrone and Young into hiring a seasoned entertainment lawyer to assist in the next round of talks. It was crucial, Bowman was told, that the WGA have its own Ken Ziffren–like adviser. Those people who pressed the issue knew they were putting Bowman in a tricky spot by forcing Verrone and Young to tacitly acknowledge that they needed that kind of help to seal a deal. The committee members stressed to Bowman that even the experienced DGA leaders benefited from Ziffren's counsel. The WGA had erred by not recruiting its own well-connected deal maker earlier in the negotiations process, many believed. "We made it clear to Bowman that it had to happen," said one committee member who attended the meeting.

In not so many words, the most vocal members informed Bowman that the WGA would lose the support of key negotiating-committee members if the guild did not bring in outside help for the talks with the CEOs. Bowman in turn used his diplomatic skills to persuade the WGA leadership and to get Wertheimer on board in less than forty-eight hours. This feat only enhanced the respect and admiration that negotiating-committee members had for their chairman.

The forcefulness of discussion at Bowman's house on January 19 reflected a growing concern among WGA insiders that the guild could bungle an opportunity to end the strike if Verrone and Young brought a strident tone to the meetings with Chernin and Iger. The CEOs were already wary of the WGA's president and executive director. It was important that the WGA signal its intent to make a deal by having a lawyer who could translate discussion points into potential contract language. And after months of bickering and finger-pointing, it was incumbent on the WGA that the CEOs have a familiar face in the room—someone who could not be accused of having a larger social agenda.

The move by the negotiating committee was also a sign of the frustration among many members that their influence had been usurped by the WGA West board. After the negotiations cratered on December 7, committee members kept in touch through conference calls, but they did not have much else to do beyond showing their support on picket lines. The WGA West's board of directors became the driving force in deciding the guild's strike strategy.

The complexion of the WGA West board was very different from the negotiating committee, which meant the two entities had differing perspectives on the contract negotiation. The WGA West board was dominated by veteran screenwriters, many of whom were stalwart supporters of Verrone and Young, while the negotiating committee was largely populated by prominent showrunners and younger screenwriters.

Wertheimer was a logical choice for outside counsel because of his interaction with the WGA on the Worldwide Pants interim agreement. But there was another factor that made Wertheimer the first person that Young reached out to. Wertheimer had a long friendship and professional association with screenwriter Ron Bass, who was a member of the WGA West board and an alternate on the negotiating committee. The two had once worked together at the same law firm before Bass segued from lawyering to screenwriting, penning such films as *Rain Man, The Joy Luck Club,* and *Waiting to Exhale.* Bass went from being Wertheimer's colleague to being his client.

Negotiating-committee members were aware that Young had met in December with lawyer Sam Fischer, but Fischer's connection to the Ziffren Brittenham firm (and its connections to the DGA) would make him a tough sell to some on the WGA West board, given the uneasy relations between the WGA and DGA. Wertheimer, on the other hand, came highly recommended by Bass and was well known to other board members. And as it happened, the low-key lawyer with a fondness for baseball and vintage cars was perfectly cast in the role of the WGA's consigliere.

The hiring of Alan Wertheimer was well received by the CEOs and Nick Counter as a sign that the guild was ready to cut a deal. It was seen as a bridge-building effort, one that carried more weight with the studios than another gesture made by the WGA: the withdrawal of its demand for expanded jurisdiction over reality and animation production. The proposal had been a long shot from the start, and many within the WGA regarded it as a provision that was expendable if sacrificing it would allow for headway in new media.

Still, after all the rabble-rousing on how reality programming posed a nonunionized threat to the WGA, the jurisdiction push had gained significance for the guild's most ardent supporters. Verrone was particularly invested, given his association with animation, and as such the CEOs recognized the withdrawal as a conciliatory move on his part. As Verrone and Michael Winship stated in a joint message to members on January 22, the day WGA leaders first met with Chernin and Iger, the reality and animation proposals were tabled "in order to make absolutely clear our commitment to bringing a speedy conclusion to [the] negotiations." This burst of goodwill stood in sharp contrast to the collateral damage from the AMPTP-WGA standoff that had piled up in the preceding two weeks. As the WGA continued to sign interim agreements with smaller production companies, the studios began to clean house.

By the second week of January, dozens of television writers and producers were informed by the largest studios that their exclusive long-term contracts had been canceled. The studios were able to invoke force-majeure provisions to selectively terminate some of their agreements because the strike had made it impossible for writers and creative talent to perform the duties called for in those contracts. This step, taken in varying degrees by each of the largest TV production entities, allowed the studios to instantly shave off tens of millions of dollars in annual overhead costs.

The practice of signing a large number of writers, actors, and producers to long-term exclusive contracts had become commonplace for

TV studios during the late 1980s and '90s. It was a competitive effort to ensure that the studio had a deep bench of creative talent to draw from as it developed new projects, and it was a defensive move to ensure that those creatives would not be able to deliver a big hit to a rival studio or network. For studio executives, the process became an exercise in trying to identify those writers who had the talent and the drive to come up with prime time's next big smash.

In most cases, the contracts for writers that became known as "overall deals" ran two or three years and stretched into hundreds of thousands of dollars, if not one million dollars or more over the life of the contract. In the case of well-established producers and showrunners, the deals frequently called for the studio to provide additional funds to allow them some autonomy to develop projects under their own production banner.

Television writers grew accustomed to working under the stability provided by overall deals. But by the early 2000s, the proliferation of long-term exclusive contracts had swelled to the point where the costs were untenable for even the largest studios, based on the diminishing returns in the traditional syndication market.

The major studios had begun to significantly pare their roster of overall deals years before the strike hit. They pursued a wider variety of contracts, for less money up front and shorter time frames, such as the "blind" script deal in which a studio committed to buying one or two scripts, sight unseen, from a writer. But the impetus to sign the most promising and most prominent talent to exclusive contracts persisted. When the strike hobbled television production, the studios still had plenty of creatives under long-term overall deals. The strike provided the cover for the studios to drop all but their most vital talent, those writers, producers, and actors who were part of successful shows that were ensured of returning to the air once the strike ended. Studio executives had long lamented the bottom-line burden of exclusive deals, but they resisted making wholesale cuts out of concern that such a move would make the studio less attractive to top creatives and raise questions about the parent company's commitment to TV production.

The strike provided the studios the opportunistic opening to clean the slate en masse and dramatically reduce operating costs in one fell swoop.

Even before the strike ended, top executives vowed that studios would exercise far more financial discipline in their deal making with creative talent. The changing business landscape and the wake-up call provided by the strike would force studios to be more discerning in entering into long-term exclusive commitments, or so executives envisioned.

When the strike began, contracts that writers had with AMPTP signatory companies were immediately suspended. By the time the walkout passed the eight-week mark, the force-majeure ax began to fall—primarily on TV writers, but producers and actors were affected as well. The formal notifications to agents and lawyers for those individuals who were cut came in waves during the weeks of January 7 and January 14; the first flurry hit on January 9, which became known as Black Wednesday.[7]

Word of the mass dismissals spread quickly through the strike grapevine. Everyone, it seemed, knew someone who had been cut off. The great majority of those persons affected were midlevel players—not the superstar showrunners but writers prominent enough to command an overall deal. Overnight, the legalese *force majeure*—meaning an unforeseen act caused by a "greater force" outside the control of any of the parties to the contract—suddenly became a verb in Hollywood, as in: "My deal got force majeured."

The cancellation of more than seventy long-term contracts sent a collective shudder through the creative community. The finality of having a deal terminated was a demoralizing, in some cases devastating, blow to writers who had become accustomed to the security offered by long-term studio deals. In many cases, the draconian moves by the studios only served to reinforce WGA members' determination to fight for the guild's stated contract goals. In other cases, the jolt of the force-majeure flurry spurred the first widespread sense of doubt about the WGA's stance, as striking writers faced nagging questions about whether the cause of new media residuals was worth the sacrifices that writers and others were forced to make.

The coordinated timing of the notifications was seen as the AMPTP sending a message to the WGA and its supporters that the studios still had plenty of firepower left. And that message was received: the perception on the picket line was that the force-majeure decisions were a sign of the studios digging in deeper for a long war. In fact, it would become clear in time that the studios acted when they did because executives were starting to see a light at the end of the tunnel through the negotiations with the DGA. They did not want to miss the opportunity to use the strike as the reason that would allow them to make tens of millions of dollars in contractual obligations vanish overnight.

Even before the force-majeure ax fell, there was a greater sense of combativeness among many writers once picketing resumed after the holidays. WGA members were still bitter about the December 7 blowup orchestrated by the AMPTP. There was a growing anxiousness, even among the most ardent strike supporters, that the AMPTP's focus on the DGA would ensure that writers would be out for many more weeks, if not months.

WGA leaders added to the intensity with their public battles in early January with two high-profile targets, both affiliated with NBC: the Golden Globe Awards and Jay Leno. The guild had already announced in December that it would not grant a strike waiver for the Golden Globe Awards in order to allow WGA writers to prepare material for NBC's live broadcast of the ceremony from the Beverly Hilton Hotel on January 13. The Globes, bestowed by the Hollywood Foreign Press Association, serve as Hollywood's warm-up for the Academy Awards. The gala dinner ceremony fosters a looser atmosphere than the Oscars, as champagne flows freely throughout the night at the star-studded tables. It is also a Globes tradition for several studios and HBO to throw lavish after-parties at various spots at the Hilton and in adjacent restaurants, making it easy for attendees and others to party hop until the wee hours.

By January 2, the HFPA and the production company responsible for the telecast, Dick Clark Productions (DCP), began to panic. Jorge Camara, president of the HFPA, made a public plea for the WGA to reconsider the waiver request. Leaders of the HFPA and Dick Clark Productions had privately tried to persuade the guild to grant the show a waiver as soon as the David Letterman deal was announced. Dick Clark Productions offered to sign that same interim agreement as Letterman's Worldwide Pants, which would cover not only the Golden Globe broadcast but all other TV programs produced by the company. But the WGA would not budge. The

Golden Globe Awards ceremony was an opportune target at a time when the guild needed to prove it still had muscle.

In response to Camara's January 2 statement, the WGA vowed that writers would picket outside the Hilton on the night of the Globes. The presence of WGA pickets would ensure a low turnout of stars, who were loath to be seen crossing a picket line simply for the chance of winning an award. To reinforce this sentiment among actors, SAG president Alan Rosenberg personally reached out to a number of stars who were contenders in the 2008 Golden Globes contest. The guild held a meeting at its headquarters to convince actors of the importance of honoring the WGA's picket lines—if only to enhance SAG's own bargaining power down the road. A group of publicists for top actors then sent a letter to Jeff Zucker, NBC Universal president and CEO, confirming that most of the actor nominees would not cross picket lines to attend the ceremony.

The WGA's plan amounted to a nightmare scenario for the HFPA and NBC. It would not be much of an awards show if there were no winners in the audience to accept their statuettes. And there were financial repercussions. The HFPA did not want to forfeit the six-million-dollar license fee that NBC pays each year for the TV rights to the Golden Globe ceremony. NBC faced the loss of about fifteen million dollars in premium advertising it had sold in the three-hour telecast. Zucker and other NBC executives leaned on the HFPA to postpone the Globes in an effort to wait out the labor strife. But HFPA leaders were concerned about the awards losing their stature as a predictor of the Academy Awards race.

Zucker was incensed at being in the WGA's crosshairs again with the Golden Globes, on the heels of watching *The Tonight Show* and *Late Night* struggle in their return without writers and with the difficulty of finding guests who were willing to cross WGA picket lines. Faced with a dilemma, Zucker had the brainstorm to turn the event into a live hourlong news conference where the winners would be announced. NBC would be the only TV outlet to have cameras in the room, just as if it were the traditional Globes. But the news-conference distinction was important, because it would fall under the aegis of the NBC News division, which had a separate contract in place with the WGA and presumably would not be subject to WGA pickets.

With less than a week to go, HFPA officers and Dick Clark Productions executives spoke several times with the WGA representatives, including David Young, about the news-conference plan in the hopes of getting an assurance from the guild that it would not picket the event. The WGA could still claim victory in forcing the dramatic revamp of the event.

On January 7, the HFPA and NBC alerted the media to expect a formal announcement regarding the fate of the Golden Globes ceremony at one o'clock Los Angeles time. In the morning it appeared that the sides were moving toward détente. But shortly before one, a report on the *Los Angeles Times* website detailed plans by NBC and Dick Clark Productions to produce at least two more hours of Globes-related programming to run before and after the news conference, including pretaped interviews with top nominees and clips of the nominated movies and TV shows. By multiple accounts, this report enraged David Young, who sent an e-mail to his counterparts at SAG decrying what he called "the Golden Globes scam" and vowed that the WGA would picket the event regardless. SAG officials followed up with an e-mail alert to PR firms regarding the participation of actors. By the time SAG's warning was ricocheting through Hollywood publicity circles, there was no hope of the HFPA reaching any kind of compromise with the WGA. The postshow parties were hastily canceled, and the HFPA began issuing refunds to ticket holders for the ceremony. It was a symbolic loss for many in the industry—another unavoidable sign that nothing was business as usual amid the strike—and as such it would prove to be another important win for the WGA.[8]

NBC and Dick Clark Productions wound up in a dispute a few days later over Dick Clark Production's request for a fee to cover the costs of mounting the news conference. NBC, smarting over the lost advertising revenue, refused and wound up boycotting the Globes news conference altogether, which opened the door to live coverage by other networks. Dick Clark Productions hastily arranged for six hosts of entertainment news programs— Brooke Anderson of CNN's *Showbiz Tonight*, Dayna Devon of *Extra*, Mary Hart of *Entertainment Tonight*, Jim Moret of *Inside Edition*, Guiliana Rancic of *E! News*, and Lara Spencer of *The Insider*—to announce the winners.

Because of this change, the WGA did not picket outside the Hilton. But a few dozen opportunists representing IATSE-affiliated production workers did take advantage of the assembled media and turned out with signs urging the WGA to end the strike. In the end, the Globes news conference drew limited media coverage and minuscule TV viewership.

WGA leaders were hailed by some for their strategic focus on achieving a public show of strength for the guild, while others derided them for the stridency that cost plenty of Hollywood union members the chance to be recognized and rewarded for their work. Ben Silverman, the cochairman of NBC Entertainment, caused a stir on the picket lines when he told a news program on the E! cable channel that the WGA's actions were akin to the "ugliest, nerdiest, meanest kids in the high school canceling the prom."[9] Those words would haunt Silverman, as the stewards of *United Hollywood* seized on his remarks and made plans for a stunt picket outside NBC that would be dubbed the "Ben Silverman High Winter Prom."[10] It was set for January 17, but just like the Golden Globes, it was destined to be derailed by more pressing events.

Even in these most unusual circumstances, the fate of the Globes was still most significant for what it predicted for the Oscars. With steadfast support from SAG, the WGA saw the Globes as the warm-up for the campaign to torpedo, if necessary, the gilded pillar of award season.

While the Golden Globes battle unfolded, guild leaders were also engaged in a public fight with Jay Leno. At issue was whether Leno was violating the WGA's strike rules by writing his opening monologue for *The Tonight Show*. The dispute laid bare the tension between the activism stirred in guild members who had been on a war footing for two months and the WGA's need to temper its hard-line stance at times. The uproar among some members over Leno's monologue left Patric Verrone looking disingenuous in his handling of the tricky situation.[11]

The guild's dispute with Leno began brewing on New Year's Eve. Leno and most of his *Tonight Show* writers had a meeting that day at WGA West headquarters with Verrone, David Young, and other WGA officials to discuss the show's return. Leno made it clear he was upset because he felt the guild had reneged on its earlier promise to him that there would be no interim agreement with David Letterman's company. He also told them that NBC was pressuring him to return to work, citing the "no strike" clause in the American Federation of Television and Radio Artists (AFTRA) union contract that covered Leno's services as a performer on the show. Leno further informed them that it would impossible to do the show without an opening monologue running ten minutes or so, but he planned to write the material entirely by himself, possibly even updating older jokes.

In the face of Leno's obvious irritation, Verrone was effusive in the meeting. He expressed his gratitude for the public support Leno had given the guild and explained that the change of heart on the Letterman deal was part of a larger strategy shift as relations between the WGA and AMPTP deteriorated. By multiple accounts, Verrone assured the host that there would be no repercussions from the WGA for writing his monologue, given that Leno had been a strong ally for the guild and the competitive situation he was up against with Letterman. As a former *Tonight Show* writer himself, Verrone facetiously offered to give Leno some of his old jokes for updating. It would emerge later that Young and others had concerns about the message Verrone had sent Leno in the meeting, but none of those reservations were expressed to Leno at the time.

On January 2, when Leno taped his first new episode in two months, there was a big turnout of WGA pickets outside his Burbank studio. Inside the studio, Leno delivered a monologue that immediately outraged staunch WGA supporters. Leno cited the lack of negotiations between the WGA and AMPTP as the key reason he decided to resume production. He asserted that he had to weigh the hardship caused by the shutdown for the 160 other *Tonight Show* staffers because of the strike affecting the show's 19 writers.

> I was on the strike line every day while they were talking. Then a couple of weeks ago, the talks broke off. No new talks were scheduled, so we had to come back because we essentially have 19 people putting 160 people out of work. We continue to support the guild. . . . I'm doing what I did the day I started. I write jokes and wake my wife up in the middle of the night and say "Honey, is this funny?" . . . We are not using outside guys. We are following the guild thing. . . . We can write for ourselves.[12]

Leno's admission of writing his monologue, coupled with his statement of "19 people putting 160 people out of work" raised hackles among many writers. By the following morning, guild leaders were fielding numerous complaints and calls for sanctions against *The Tonight Show*'s front man. Verrone compounded the awkwardness by telling a radio interviewer on January 3 that the guild would "have to talk to Jay" about the monologue issue.[13] Verrone called Leno later that day to inform him he could not continue to write his monologue. Leno was stunned by the reversal and aghast that within a few days he was getting calls from two veteran screenwriters asking him to appear before the guild's Strike Rules Compliance Committee.

Leno's confidence in his position was bolstered by the guidance he received from his personal lawyer, Ken Ziffren, and by executives from AFTRA. They assured him that he was free to write his own material thanks to a little-known clause that had been in the WGA's Minimum Basic Agreement since 1981. The so-called AFTRA exception gave a performer such as Leno the ability to write his own material, even in a strike situation. However, Leno, as a WGA member, could not write anything for others to perform, even if he also were part of the performance. Under the WGA's contract language, anything that Leno wrote for others to perform would be considered "literary material," whereas anything he wrote strictly for himself would not be classified as literary material. Leno ignored the calls from the strike-rules committee and continued to perform his monologue.

NBC defended its late-night star with a terse statement issued January 4: "It is unfortunate that the WGA is contemplating plans to 'investigate' Jay's authorship of his 'Tonight Show' monologue. The WGA agreement clearly permits Jay to create and perform his own monologue. The enforcement of strike rules against Jay in these circumstances would violate the federal labor laws."

On January 9, Young called Leno. He informed the host that the AFTRA exception did not apply in his case. The WGA interpreted the clause as pertaining to non-WGA performers who occasionally craft their own material for stand-up or sketch-comedy segments but do not otherwise function as writers and thus should not be required to join the WGA. Young reiterated to Leno that he was in breach of the strike rules. Leno replied that if that was the case, he might have to resign his WGA membership. Leno did not raise his voice, but he knew the weight of his words. The last thing the WGA wanted was a high-profile defection among its ranks.

Guild leaders backed off public criticism of Leno and urged members on the picket line not to "pick a fight" with Leno in an effort to maintain unity.[14] Leno's camp, meanwhile, was angered by the fact that none of the other late-night hosts who went back without writers—Conan O'Brien, Jimmy Kimmel, Jon Stewart, and Stephen Colbert—were subject to the same kind of public admonishing from the guild, though all four shows faced picket lines outside their studios. And while the volleys between the WGA and Leno petered out by mid-January, as guild leaders became preoccupied with the DGA deal and their own talks with the CEOs, the scuffle over Leno's monologue would persist long after the strike ended.

Just as it seemed the animosity between the WGA and the studios could not get worse, the first sign of warming emerged over cocktails at Peter Chernin's home in Santa Monica. John Bowman was invited into CEO turf on January 10 for a secret meeting with Chernin, Leslie Moonves, and Barry Meyer. Remarkably, the outreach to Bowman came more than a week before the guild hired Alan Wertheimer and two days before the AMPTP initiated its formal negotiation with the DGA.[15] The meeting was arranged by industry power broker Ari Emanuel, head of the Endeavor talent agency, which was known for its strong roster of film and TV writers.[16]

Like Creative Artists Agency's Bryan Lourd, Emanuel had every incentive to do whatever he could to play peacemaker between the writers and the studios. His company's clients were feeling the pain of being out of work for more than two months, which meant that Endeavor's cash flow from commissions was slowing down.

Emanuel was extremely wary of Patric Verrone and David Young and their approach to the contract negotiations. They were costing him money. And Emanuel knew firsthand that the Internet was a long way from paying off big for writers, so he questioned the wisdom of sacrificing so much in the present to secure residuals that would not be worth much in the near term.

Emanuel is known for his hard-driving style, equal parts bombast and charm, and for his skill at networking. He had called Bowman early on in the strike, more than once, to push for greater compromise in the WGA's position. He tried to cast doubt in Bowman's mind on Verrone and Young, telling him that the CEOs would never take them seriously. Bowman did not take Emanuel seriously, but he knew that the agent had valuable connections, so he urged him to convince Chernin and the others that the CEOs should get directly involved.

By early January, Emanuel arranged the gathering at Chernin's house. The invitation, however, extended to only Bowman, not Verrone or Young, which put Bowman in an awkward position. But after a month of no communication at all, the WGA could hardly turn down an invitation to break the ice. Bowman's frustration was running high, and he was being pressured by members of the negotiating committee to instigate the kind of private outreach to the other side that Emanuel had facilitated.

At the meeting, the mood was casual as the foursome sat down with drinks in the privacy of Chernin's living room. (Iger had a schedule conflict and could not attend.) Bowman had professional experience with each of the three execs, particularly Moonves. They had worked together on numerous shows over the years, and he had coached Moonves's son in Little League years before. Bowman knew Chernin from his days as head of programming at Fox, when Bowman was the showrunner on the sitcom *Martin*, starring comedian Martin Lawrence.

Surprisingly, the group had managed to keep the gathering secret, so there was little pressure to produce specific results. Bowman, who also lived in Santa Monica, had gone to Chernin's house with two seemingly divergent goals. He wanted to keep the conversation on general terms to avoid being drawn into any verbal commitments. But he also wanted to deliver one crystal-clear message about the importance of distributor's gross calculations as the basis for new media compensation formulas. It was a make-or-break point for the WGA, a philosophical issue that would keep writers out for many more months if the studios continued to refuse to accept it for new media.

Meyer listened carefully as Bowman spoke. He realized as the conversation continued that Bowman's definition of distributor's gross was not as onerous as the AMPTP had made it out to be. Bowman was focused on doing away with the home video precedent of producer's gross. He made no mention of a definition that would include the advertising revenue generated by a property in the new media realm. He was talking about the revenue that the distributor of a program would receive from the exhibitor—whether it was a website, a paid download service, or mobile phone platform—to license the content. The AMPTP for months had hammered the WGA for its irrational demand for a percentage of all new media advertising revenues. In the friendly setting of a living room, Bowman made the WGA's definition very clear.

Meyer looked around the room to make eye contact with Chernin and Moonves. The executives knew that the working group assembled to hash out the distributor's gross issue for the DGA had come up with a definition that both sides had essentially signed off on—and it was not far from what Bowman described. The mood grew more relaxed as the conversation continued.

Bowman could tell that the CEOs were gently pumping him for information on what it would take for the WGA to cut a deal. He raised the question of whether the AMPTP could be persuaded to give the WGA another shot at negotiations before it began its formal talks with the DGA. No way, Chernin was quick to respond; the WGA had its chance. All in all, the discussion during the gathering that lasted about two hours never got too specific, but Bowman left Chernin's house that evening knowing that the deep freeze in communication between the guild and the studios was over.

The next day, Bowman got a call from Chernin informing him, as a courtesy, that the AMPTP would begin its formal bargaining sessions with the DGA the following morning. By this time, the WGA's leaders were coming to grips with the fact that the DGA was negotiating the deal that would then be handed to the WGA. As such, there was an informal effort among some leaders and prominent writers, such as former WGA West president John Wells, to reach out privately to well-connected DGA members in an effort to gather intelligence on what the DGA was putting on the table.

The fact that the DGA's and WGA's fortunes were intertwined was reinforced by the gesture made by the caretakers of *United Hollywood* to table the "Ben Silverman High Winter Prom." They had gone to some lengths to organize an event that they hoped would raise money through T-shirt sales for the WGA Foundation's Industry Support Fund. But on January 15, sensing a shift in the wind, organizers presciently called off the stunt that would have been held on the same day the DGA unveiled its agreement. As explained in a post on *United Hollywood*, "Many writers believe it is important to let the DGA negotiate in an atmosphere of utmost seriousness backed up by large, forceful pickets from the WGA."[17] The WGA would have looked frivolous staging an elaborate farce on the same day the DGA touted its groundbreaking contract agreement.

The most impressive gain in the DGA agreement unveiled on January 17 was the item that took the longest to negotiate. The residual formula for paid downloads, or "electronic sell-through" in contract argot, was one area where it was crucial that the studios give a little because paid downloads represented the new media extension of the home video residual. Because the studios were adamant about retaining the basic residual formula for paid downloads, and because they would not budge on the pay rate for DVDs, the DGA had to insist that paid downloads command higher rates than traditional home video.

Given the scope of paid-download transactions, the total dollars involved would not be significant for the studios, but it would yield an important symbolic victory for the three creative guilds. The WGA in particular needed a win to justify the leadership's rallying cry of "Don't let them do to us in new media what they did in home video."

The paid-download rate was not settled until just a few hours before the deal was made public, shortly after two o'clock on the afternoon of Thursday, January 17. The broad outline of the deal had been in place weeks before, but DGA officials were all too aware that the devil was in the details, and how those details would be interpreted by the WGA's various constituencies. In the end, some of the key terms seemed tailored for maximum appeal to the WGA's single most important constituency—showrunners.

DGA negotiators dickered with their AMPTP counterparts until the last minute for every tenth of a percentage point on the download rates.

They knew it had to be a gain easily quantified for writers, not to mention their own members. "More than double" the old rate was a strong selling point, even to the most defiant on the picket lines.

About an hour before the DGA formally announced its tentative contract agreement, Peter Chernin called David Young to make the offer to begin informal discussions. Those conversations would begin the following Tuesday, January 22, with a breakfast meeting between Chernin, Bob Iger, Young, Patric Verrone, and John Bowman. The olive branch from the CEOs ensured that WGA officials would be muted in their initial response to the DGA terms. WGA leaders emphasized that they would withhold judgment until they reviewed the DGA deal in greater detail and evaluated what its key elements would mean for writers. "We are grateful for this opportunity to engage in meaningful discussion with industry leaders that we hope will lead to a contract," Patric Verrone and Michael Winship wrote in an e-mail message to members sent on the morning of January 22. "We ask that all members exercise restraint in their public statements during this critical period."[18]

But WGA members were hardly reserved in their responses. The very fact that the DGA had a deal after just six days of negotiations caused the biggest schism among writers since the strike began.

10

The Finish Line

On the day the DGA deal was unveiled, a small group of prominent writers had dinner at the Beverly Hills home of Paul Attanasio, whose résumé includes screenwriting Oscar nominations for 1994's *Quiz Show* and 1997's *Donnie Brasco.* The group included Aaron Sorkin, Gary Ross, Akiva Goldsman, and John Wells. Also joining them was Ken Ziffren.[1]

As the A-listers hashed out the deal with Ziffren, the consensus emerged that the DGA had done an impressive job with the leverage handed to them by the WGA's strike. But some at the dinner were gravely concerned about the WGA leadership and the lack of meaningful relations with the DGA or the studio CEOs. Patric Verrone and David Young were perceived to be too hunkered down in war footing to be effective in the informal talks with Peter Chernin and Bob Iger. The conclusion among the writers was that the guild desperately needed its own Ken Ziffren, a seasoned negotiator with the skills to move the sides closer to a contract. It was the same message that John Bowman would hear forcefully a few days later at his own home from members of the WGA's negotiating committee.

Wells was also very familiar with the DGA terms because he had quietly advised Ziffren and others on how to craft deal points that would be well received by writers. A dual member of the WGA and DGA, Wells had become an unofficial emissary for writers with the studio chiefs and the directors once the DGA negotiations began in earnest.

Despite his experience in contract negotiations, Wells was largely shunned by Verrone and Young during the strike. There was a strong belief among Verrone's Writers United faction that the guild had been too conciliatory toward management under Wells's leadership in the contract negotiations of 2001, when he was WGA West president, and in 2004, when he was a member of the negotiating committee.

This time around, Wells held no official post for the WGA, but he was still piped in at the highest levels. As the DGA closed in on its deal in mid-January, Wells was sought out by that guild's leaders for his insights into what issues were of most importance to writers. Wells proved an important conduit between the guilds because of the chilly relations between the WGA and DGA leadership. DGA officials barely hid their disdain for the WGA's strident tactics, and they were angered by the noncommunication from the writers' camp in the summer and fall when it was clear that events were building toward a strike that would affect all Hollywood union members. The WGA, meanwhile, was extremely wary of the DGA undercutting its leverage in negotiations if directors refused to push hard on new media.

Wells's past WGA service and the breadth of his experience as a writer, director, and producer made him perfectly suited for the role of unofficial liaison. He too was unnerved by the lack of contact between WGA and DGA leaders and how that void might be exploited by the studios.

DGA leaders were sensitive to the perception that they were willing to undercut the rest of the creative community in contract negotiations—particularly with the WGA on strike. Wells had an understanding with the DGA that he would publicly endorse the guild's contract terms if negotiators achieved certain thresholds, as advised by Wells. On January 17, the day the deal was unveiled, Wells made good on his promise. He penned a detailed analysis of the new media terms, breaking them down and putting them into context of past contract fights. He sent it as an e-mail reply to a friend who asked him what he thought of the deal—knowing that it would be instantly circulated to writer-centric blogs and websites. Wells's move was yet another example of how new media trumped the traditional news media when it came to disseminating information during the strike.

Wells was effusive, calling it "a historic deal" and crediting the WGA strike for providing the leverage. "We've won," he wrote. "As recently as a few weeks ago the companies were still saying they would 'never, ever' raise this rate. One company exec told me we were 'out of our fucking minds' if we thought we would ever get an increase in the DVD rate for EST [electronic sell-through]. This is a huge, historic victory for everyone."[2]

Wells's missive raised the ire of some of Verrone's most ardent supporters, who read it as a directive that the WGA should immediately accept the DGA terms without question and end the strike. On blogs and websites, some were quick to impugn Wells's integrity and declare it a "terrible" deal.

On the picket line outside NBC on January 18, the day after the DGA deal was announced, the prevailing sentiment was that members should wait to make a judgment until the WGA had a more thorough understanding of the deal. Some chided Wells for his instant analysis. "All we've seen is the press release," more than one picket said in response to a reporter's request for reaction to the deal. One writer likened the situation to "making a decision on a script based on an agent's cover letter." One picket wrote a timely message on her sign: "I'm not in the DGA."[3]

Outside of diehards on the picket lines, the resolve among many members was ebbing by mid-January amid the drumbeat of grim news. As rumors about the DGA reaching a deal spread, the sentiment was growing that the WGA should accept those terms for the sake of getting the industry back to work.

Even before the DGA deal was unveiled, a group of writers who became known as the "Dirty 30" quietly began to hold meetings at members' homes to discuss the state of the strike and how they could use their collective voice to effect change. The number of writers involved numbered far more than thirty, and the bulk of them were not top-tier screenwriters and showrunners but middle-class writers who proportionately suffered the biggest financial blows during the strike.

There were others who lost more in gross dollars during the fourteen-week walkout, but as a proportion of income, the heaviest toll was paid by the middle-class writers, the ones who worked regularly and could count on six-figure, but not seven-figure, annual earnings. Many of them suffered the loss of development deals as the force-majeure cuts came down.

The most vocal members of this subset considered the possibility of taking out an advertisement in the Hollywood trade papers registering their concerns. As word of this dissent spread among writers, WGA leaders hoped to neutralize the threat by having members of the negotiating committee reach out to influential voices among the Dirty 30.

On January 14, Howard Michael Gould and Robert King, alternate members of the WGA negotiating committee, met with a few dozen writers at the Beverly Hills home of showrunner Jonathan Prince. Gould was respected by WGA members for the remarks he made at the LA Convention Center membership meeting a few days before the strike began. It was a tense few hours. The writers present were "deeply unhappy with the strike and the leadership," Gould wrote in an essay published shortly after the strike ended. "These writers were hurting already, and they were afraid, and they were angry."[4]

The big fear was that the strike would persist well into the summer as the WGA waited for SAG's June 30 contract expiration. Some of the writers in Prince's living room had been informed that day that their studio deals had been terminated. These WGA members could now easily calculate how much the strike had cost them.

Over and over, Gould and King pointed to history, discussing in detail how dissent among the guild's haves and have-nots played right into management's hands and resulted in weaker contract terms. This time, they had come so far on the strength of solidarity, it would be tragic to throw it all away just as the end was drawing near. And that was not just a pep talk. It was well known that the DGA was closing in on a deal that would address the majority of the WGA's demands on new media. That was one reason the writers in the room were so nervous—they worried that if Verrone and Young were unyielding on every point, the WGA would wind up turning down a reasonable offer from the studios.

Gould and King gradually convinced the group that there was nothing to be gained by going public with their concerns at such a critical juncture. The emissaries of the negotiating committee vowed to make the group's fears and frustrations known to the WGA West board. And they promised to improve communication with members who were not as engaged with strike-related activities.

It was a remarkable feat of diplomacy. There were rampant rumors of a widespread revolt brewing by many prominent members, but the closest the guild came to an organized display of public dissent was a letter-writing campaign initiated the day after the DGA announcement by screenwriter Craig Mazin. He posted a gently worded form letter on his *Artful Writer* blog along with the e-mail addresses of Verrone, Young, Bowman, and Robert King. "Now that our combined efforts have led to a deal we can live with, I'm urging you to get the same deal for us as expeditiously as possible," read the letter that Mazin urged writers to send to WGA leaders.

The Union Blues this was not. Nor were WGA leaders deaf to the passions stirred by the DGA deal. The understanding that a large number of members were hitting a breaking point after ten weeks on strike was a crucial influence on how the WGA leadership steered the course for the remaining four weeks of the walkout. "For me, a big consideration was to leave us united as a guild. That was one of my primary goals," Bowman says. "We had to take care of ourselves for the Internet. We had to know going into the future that if the Internet takes off we'll have a mechanism in place to get an equitable amount of revenue, equal to what we've got in the past at least on a percentage basis. . . . Once we had that in hand, I knew there was no way we could go out to showrunners and screenwriters and say we need to stay on strike for more."[5]

A light rain fell on Los Angeles in the early hours of January 22, leaving dampness in the air that hinted at heavier downpours to come over the next few days. On that Tuesday morning, just before dawn, the nominations for the Eightieth Academy Awards were unveiled. Under normal circumstances, Hollywood would have been abuzz for days with talk of Oscar front runners, dark horses, and snubs. But not this year. The paralysis caused by the strike and the WGA's promise that it would picket outside the ceremony had sapped the excitement and the sport out of the race.

Industry insiders knew that something even more important than the Oscar nominations was taking place that morning. Verrone, Young, and Bowman met with Peter Chernin and Bob Iger for breakfast at a secret location that turned out to be the Luxe hotel in Brentwood, just west of the UCLA campus.[6] The agenda for the morning was mostly to clear the air and prepare for the roll-up-the-sleeves work to begin the following day. But the CEOs made it clear that the DGA deal was the basic template that the AMPTP negotiators would start with, albeit with some tailoring to writer-specific needs. They were unequivocal that no side issues be allowed to divert the focus of the talks. The WGA's demands regarding reality and animation had to come off the table.

WGA leaders, meanwhile, pressed the CEOs on the DGA's definition of distributor's gross and the details of the jurisdiction agreement. Chernin and Iger told them that those details would be left to the lawyers, and they praised the guild's decision to retain Alan Wertheimer. The meeting that morning was about handshakes and about looking one another in the eye and making a commitment to getting a deal done that would get the industry off its knees.

Peter Chernin and Bob Iger brought a sense of gravitas and urgency to the room when the contract discussions began in earnest at the Luxe the day after the breakfast meeting. Nick Counter and studio labor executives were preconditioned to say no in guild contract talks. Their job performance was evaluated on how effectively they were able to hold the line on union demands. The CEOs, on the other hand, had the authority to say yes. And they had every incentive to work toward a consensus and move the process along as quickly as possible. Chernin and Iger had plenty of other responsibilities to attend to at their conglomerates beyond haggling with the WGA. In the interest of settling the strike that was creating so many problems for their core businesses, the CEOs were inclined to give more on issues that the AMPTP negotiators had identified as deal breakers, like distributor's gross. "As soon as the CEOs entered the room it was obvious that an end was in sight," Bowman says. "We quickly focused on the crucial Internet issues and found an economic way to define 'reuse.' Once we got to (Internet) jurisdiction, we knew we had a deal in sight."[7]

For the WGA, the face time with the CEOs also amounted to a matter of respect. The DGA had been given the benefit of the attention from the top on their deal; it was only fair, in the WGA's view, that writers be afforded the same courtesy. Chernin and Iger steadfastly stayed out of the discussions of percentages for residual formulas and other monetary questions, as they had in the negotiations with the DGA. They were there to provide the moral authority, to convince the WGA that they were being heard at the highest level. And they also consistently hammered the message that the studios were not open to discussing wholesale modifications to the DGA template. It was essentially a take-it-or-leave-it offer for the WGA, though neither the CEOs nor the AMPTP's Counter and Lombardini were so impolitic as to be that blunt. In many ways, the stature that Chernin and Iger brought to the meeting rooms at the Luxe made it easier for WGA leaders to accept no. "We went in (with the WGA) and just told them that the DGA's template is the template and we're not backing off of it," Chernin says. "We'll adjust things that are specific to writers, but that's it. And from there it was just about working through those things."[8]

Chernin and Iger divided up the list of their fellow CEOs and would keep them updated by phone. They encountered little resistance from Leslie Moonves, Jeff Zucker, Sony Pictures Entertainment's Michael Lynton, Viacom's Philippe Dauman, and MGM's Harry Sloan. By this time the CEOs simply wanted Hollywood back to work.

The talks on Wednesday, January 23, lasted most of the day and went smoothly. Young and Bowman pressed for details on the DGA deal terms, particularly on parameters for guild jurisdiction over made-for-Internet productions.

Two days later, more progress was made during a lengthy session at Alan Wertheimer's home in Brentwood. While a steady rain poured outside, Bowman, Young, and Wertheimer sat around a table with Chernin, Iger, and Nick Counter, eating sandwiches and talking over the thorniest remaining issues, including the compensation for Web streaming. It was, at long last, a conversation, with each side listening to the other's reasoning and objections. Wertheimer would later take the discussion points and translate them into legalese that was exchanged with AMPTP lawyers. The ability for the WGA to quickly respond in a legal framework with paperwork that could be reviewed by both sides was essential to moving the process along and giving both sides the feeling of momentum toward a resolution.

On the evening of Friday, January 25, after a day of substantial progress at Wertheimer's house, another breakthrough in relations occurred that would have been unthinkable just a few weeks before. Leslie Moonves and CBS's top labor executive, Harry Isaacs, met Patric Verrone and David Young for dinner in a private dining room at the Four Seasons hotel in Beverly Hills.[9] The invitation came from Moonves, as a goodwill gesture aimed at establishing, at long last, the personal connections that could help smooth out any bumps that might emerge as the sides zeroed in on a deal. Moonves is well known for his persuasive charm, and as a conversationalist he was well-matched by Verrone. By multiple accounts the dinner lasted several hours and was a friendly affair. And it only took hours for word of the bread breaking to spread in industry circles. It was viewed as more welcome evidence that the strike's days were numbered.

The following Monday morning, the WGA announced it would grant a production waiver for CBS's telecast of the Fiftieth Grammy Awards on February 10. There would be no WGA pickets to deter artists from participating in the ceremony at the Staples Center in downtown Los Angeles. The WGA cited as its reasoning the fact that "professional musicians face many of the same issues that we do concerning fair compensation for the use of their work in new media." But the industry read it as the WGA rewarding Moonves for his attempts at peacemaking.

All of these signs of warming only magnified the surprise when reports surfaced that the WGA had invited a group of Wall Street research analysts to a presentation in New York designed to put pressure on CBS's stock price. The February 5 gathering at the Cornell Club in midtown Manhattan aimed to convince analysts to lower their investment rating on CBS's stock in light of the disruptions caused by the strike. CBS was singled out because of its vulnerability as the AMPTP conglomerate most dependent on network television for its earnings, and because Moonves was known to be more inclined than the other CEOs to push for compromise. The letter from David Young told analysts and key institutional investors that the presentation would include speeches from Patric Verrone, Michael Winship, SAG president Alan Rosenberg, and actors and writers from CBS programs.[10] "An extended strike will affect the pilot season for fall television series, the customary upfront ad purchasing season in early May, the ability of networks to meet the required ratings performance for ad revenue already received, and important ancillary revenues on the sale of series to secondary markets," Young wrote. The invitation was sent two days after Young and Verrone had dinner with Moonves and Isaacs.

Multiple members of the WGA's negotiating committee were incensed when they heard of the plan for the meeting. They saw it as a provocative move that was nonsensical at a moment when the sides were finally communicating again. Some were outraged at the lack of common courtesy it demonstrated, coming on the heels of the personal outreach by Chernin, Iger, and Moonves.

Still more fears were stirred on January 29 when Rosenberg and SAG executive director Doug Allen issued a lengthy message to SAG members, criticizing aspects of the DGA deal—even accusing the DGA of agreeing to "rollbacks" in the new media residual formulas. SAG's missive immediately raised suspicions that it had been orchestrated to allow SAG to serve as a proxy for the WGA, which could not afford to speak so plainly while it was in the midst of negotiations with the CEOs. The DGA responded quickly, calling SAG's analysis "specious." The DGA's heated statement expressed the fears of many WGA members who were weary of the strike grind. "Their letter has one purpose and one purpose only: to interfere with the informal talks currently underway between the WGA and the studios," the statement from DGA president Michael Apted said.[11]

Bowman, Verrone, and Young fielded vociferous complaints from negotiating-committee members and others about the danger of strident rhetoric and tactics at such a delicate moment in the negotiations. The plan for the Wall Street presentation was scrapped on January 30. The anger stirred by the plans for that meeting was fortuitous, because by February 5 guild leaders on both coasts would be preoccupied with arranging an entirely different gathering—a membership meeting to review the details of a tentative contract agreement. The speed with which the sides moved to consensus was a testament to the authority and the urgency that the presence of Chernin and Iger brought to the room. "They were here to get this done. They were ready to deal," says WGA East president Michael Winship, who was in Los Angeles for most of the sessions with the CEOs. "I think they were frustrated that it had gone on as long as it had and were ready to come to some kind of an agreement."[12]

On Saturday, February 2, Patric Verrone, John Bowman, and numerous WGA members were among those individuals who attended a party for *Harvard Lampoon* alumni at Hollywood's famed Magic Castle. The chatter among partygoers in a wood-paneled room at the private club revolved around predictions of the imminent end of the strike. A rumor spread that Verrone would break the news that night to his fellow Crimson graduates.[13]

Verrone eventually approached the microphone set up in the room and with a dour expression did his best to temper expectations. The talks with the CEOs appear to be promising, Verrone told the crowd, but the WGA wanted to be careful about getting members' hopes up too soon. Verrone continued for a few more minutes and handed the mic to Bowman.

Bowman smiled broadly at Verrone, took a dramatic swig of his drink, and declared: "Don't listen to that guy. The strike is done." The roar of applause, laughter, and cheering kept the room abuzz for the rest of the night. Bowman was, of course, exaggerating, but most people there knew he never would have made such a statement unless he was feeling extremely confident. And there was good reason for his optimism.

Friday, February 1, had been an arduous day of talks at the Luxe hotel for the WGA leaders and the CEOs. The sides went back and forth over compensation terms for Web streaming. They went over and over the specifics of the Internet jurisdiction terms in an effort by the WGA to ensure that there were no surprises later. As intense as the discussions were, it was clear to both sides that numerous other issues had been settled. There was really only one thing standing in the way of a handshake deal.

The sides had been talking on and off for hours about Web streaming. The WGA was unhappy with the fixed residual formula; the CEOs reiterated there were not going to be major changes to the basic DGA template. Bowman and Young pressed hard on a proposal developed by Chuck Slocum, the WGA's assistant executive director. Slocum is the guild's longtime statistician and analyst of industry financial data as it pertains to WGA members. He has an encyclopedic knowledge of the WGA master contract and the myriad formulas that determine writers' compensation.

Slocum knew how important it was for the WGA to achieve a residual formula for Web streaming based on a percentage of distributor's gross rather than a flat fee. In preparing for the informal negotiations with the CEOs, Slocum studied the DGA template and suggested that the studios might bend on the idea of shifting the Web-streaming formula to 2 percent of distributor's gross in the third year of the contract. And he had a fail-safe in mind if that idea did not fly with the CEOs. The WGA would agree to impute, or predetermine at the time of the contract signing, the dollar value of that 2 percent as being twenty thousand dollars for a half-hour program over a twenty-six-week period and forty thousand dollars for an hourlong program. The imputed-value clause would ensure that distributors would face predictable residual payments in that year, but it would also allow the guild to claim victory in Web streaming.

The WGA's persistence wore down Chernin and Iger's inclination to resist changes to the DGA template. In the spirit of compromise, the executives agreed to the third-year shift in the midafternoon of February 1. Chernin and Iger understood the WGA's need for selling points to its membership, and they knew it was not such a significant concession that the other CEOs would balk. There was some further discussion about the finer legal points of the third-year formula change, but after the CEOs gave their verbal commitment, the sides went back to their separate rooms for private discussions.

Soon, Chernin was thinking about how nice it would be to attend the Super Bowl in Phoenix that Sunday without nagging worries about the state of the strike. By five o'clock, Chernin and Iger were getting ready to wrap up for the day. They were looking for a handshake and a commitment from guild leaders that the deal would be recommended for approval by the governing bodies of WGA West and WGA East. But the duo was met in the hallway between the meeting rooms by Bowman, Verrone, and Young, who informed the CEOs that they were still unsatisfied with aspects of the deal and wanted another day at the bargaining table. Specifically, they were unhappy with the length of the free promotional window for Web streaming before residual payments kicked in. Chernin could not contain his exasperation. "We're done," he snapped. After a beat,

Chernin declared that he was "not a professional nitpicker" and walked with Iger back into the CEOs' room.[14]

Bowman, Verrone, and Young returned to their room. Wertheimer had observed some of the hallway exchange, and he flatly warned the trio that the other side's patience was running out. The seasoned lawyer had seen that kind of visceral reaction in plenty of senior executives when they felt that negotiations were going out of bounds. He advised the WGA trio that it would be a mistake to push for more on the heels of the third-year concession on Web streaming.

After months of sparring and strategizing, the WGA leaders were inclined to keep fighting against a provision that they felt was deeply unfair to writers. But there was no question that fatigue was setting in to the WGA camp as well. Wertheimer was unequivocal in his counsel, and it did not take long for Young and the others to acknowledge that he was right.

But there was yet one more point that the WGA wanted to put before the CEOs. It was unlikely to be a deal breaker for either side, but the guild leaders felt obligated to try while they had the CEOs' attention. The WGA wanted a commitment from the studios that writers terminated because of the strike would be reinstated at their prestrike salary and position. Ideally, the guild would like to have seen all writer contracts terminated during the strike restored, but such a demand clearly would have been a deal breaker for the studios. So the guild pushed for the return of all writers on TV series that resumed production after the strike. Writers who had been under overall deals but were not actively working on a series at the time of the strike would be out of luck. But the WGA could ensure that the studios would be obligated to reinstate a large group of established writers and influential WGA members.

When the WGA put this point on the table in the joint meeting room, not a half hour after Chernin shot down the request for another day of talks, the CEOs barely hesitated. They realized it would be another important selling point to the membership, and they knew that the studios would have no choice but to hire most of those writers back anyway. It would take experienced hands to restart series that had been shuttered for more than three months. Studios could not afford to take the time to recruit new writers if they hoped to get their existing shows back on the air before the end of the TV season in late May.

By the time the WGA got the response they had hoped for, it was around six o'clock. With no fanfare, the agreement that had seemed impossibly out of reach only weeks before came to pass over a conference-room table at the Luxe. Bowman, Verrone, and Young shook hands with Chernin and Iger. The discussions and exchange of paperwork between the WGA and AMPTP camps would continue nonstop for another ten days, but for all intents and purposes, the strike was over.

As word spread of the breakthrough, WGA leaders had the delicate task of managing expectations and keeping the picket lines well stocked. The guild wanted to make sure it had as much leverage as possible through the bitter end. And to the surprise of many in the industry, the guild's center held, even as the strike entered its fourth month. The guild's official and unofficial outreach to restless clusters of screenwriters and showrunners had been very effective. There were no significant public displays of dissent even with the alarm stirred by the DGA deal.

On the morning of Monday, February 4, the crowd was more than one hundred strong outside of 20th Century Fox's main gate as gusty winds buffeted picket signs and sprayed water from a wall fountain onto writers' legs as they made their loop. No less of a star showrunner than Joss Whedon, creator of *Buffy the Vampire Slayer*, arrived at the studio at six o'clock to help set up for the day. "I wanted to be sure someone was out here early with one of these," Whedon told a reporter as he defied the wind to hoist his sign high in the air.[15]

WGA West board members and negotiating-committee members fanned out to the eight primary picket sites that morning to reinforce the two-pronged message that top leaders sent in an e-mail dispatch to members that morning. Yes, the WGA and studios were closing in on a deal—the guild wanted to allay worries that stridency would keep them out for many more months—but they were not at the point of a signed agreement, which meant that members had to remain vigilant with feet on the street. There was no doubt that picket participation dwindled in the last two weeks of the strike, but not by so much that it indicated the rank and file had given up the fight. And those pickets who did turn out were quick to absorb the spirit of the leaders' message, and they relayed that to reporters looking for reaction to reports that a settlement was near. "When Patric Verrone tells me to go back to work, then I'll get excited," said one writer making the rounds outside 20th Century Fox.

Behind the scenes, Wertheimer and his AMPTP counterparts were working feverishly on the contract language and documents to be presented to both sides for approval. The week of February 3 was a blur of conference calls, e-mail and fax exchanges, and, toward the end of the week, face-to-face meetings at AMPTP headquarters. On Tuesday, February 5, the WGA was confident enough to announce that membership meetings would be held that Saturday, February 9, in Los Angeles and New York, to present the terms of the proposed deal and get "input" from members. The meetings would allow WGA leaders to take the temperature of the members and avoid the embarrassment of having a deal recommended by the boards of the WGA West and East rejected in the final ratification vote by members. It also adhered to the "we are all in this together" theme, as Verrone and Winship wrote in their message to members.[16] "We have gotten to this point in our negotiation as the direct result of the power of this strike, which each of you has generated. Neither the Negotiating Committee, nor the West Board or the East Council, will take action on any contract until after the membership meetings are held and your voices have been heard," the presidents wrote.

The sense of relief among writers was palpable after the meetings were set and the evidence mounted that a deal was nearly in hand. By Wednesday, the guild called for a central picketing site at Disney to guard against the crowds at the other LA-area picket sites getting too thin. The guild had already tabled the picketing at one studio, Sony Pictures Entertainment in Culver City, in order to concentrate its firepower on the more heavily trafficked sites like 20th Century Fox, Disney, Warner Bros., NBC, and Paramount.

As soon as the strike stretched into February, there was an additional force driving the sides to a resolution: the Oscars. The annual Academy

Awards ceremony was set for February 24 at the Kodak Theater in Hollywood. The threat of WGA pickets disrupting the Oscars' grandeur was a leverage point for the guilds. The CEOs wanted to avoid a replay of the Golden Globe Awards debacle. To have to cancel or modify the Oscar telecast would be the ultimate admission of defeat, a sign of the failure of leadership in Hollywood that the general public would surely notice.

If that was not reason enough, the Academy Awards deadline took on added significance because Gil Cates was at the helm as executive producer of the live telecast carried by ABC. The CEOs felt a debt of gratitude to Cates for helping to forge the new media residual template in his role as head of the DGA negotiating committee. They were motivated to remove the black cloud of potential WGA pickets and no-shows by top stars. Although it seemed superficial to many on the picket lines, February 24 was seen by both sides as a point of no return. There was a feeling that if the strike stretched past the Academy Awards telecast, it would go all the way into the summer, when WGA members could link arms with 120,000-plus members of the Screen Actors Guild.

But just a few days into February, worries about the Oscars abated as the sides were clearly making progress. Cates and officials at the Academy of Motion Picture Arts and Sciences (AMPAS) vowed to go ahead with the ceremony no matter what. AMPAS officials kept pressing the WGA for a waiver to ease the concerns of major stars, but the guild would not budge. "I'm nervous. We're getting down to the final moments; we need to make plans," AMPAS president Sid Ganis told *Daily Variety*.[17] But Ganis was fretting out of an abundance of caution. On the day that he made that statement, the movement toward a settlement of the strike was unstoppable.

The turnout for the February 7 mass picket outside Disney's whimsical main gate in Burbank was several hundred strong, but the mood was unmistakably different from previous rallies. The strike was starting to be referred to in the past tense, and pickets were indulging in a little nostalgia for their time on the lines. People who had spent weeks pounding the pavement together were now exchanging telephone numbers and e-mail addresses. Group photos were taken for posterity. As one veteran comedy writer observed, "It's like Labor Day in the Catskills."[18] Strike captain

Michael Tabb, who put in his time on the picket line outside Disney with an orthopedic walking boot on his left foot because of an injury, made the rounds with a picket sign covered with hundreds of signatures of fellow strikers. "I want to be able to show my grandchildren that I actually did stand up for something," Tabb said.

The following day, the West Coast strike captains held their regular Friday meeting. The WGA East staged a rally with more than three hundred pickets outside the opulent Time Warner Center at Columbus Circle in Manhattan. The WGA East even sent out a message to members planning for a Wednesday rally outside Viacom's headquarters in midtown. But even the most diehard strike supporters were preparing to lay down their signs for good. The focus on both coasts was firmly on Saturday's membership meetings.

Behind closed doors, AMPTP and WGA staffers worked nonstop to finish off the final paperwork. After so much time and angst, both sides were wary of making a mistake due to fatigue or the eagerness to conclude a deal. Terms and contract language were checked and triple-checked. Tempers flared suddenly, but briefly, on the day before the meetings when the WGA questioned some details of the distributor's gross definition—questions that the AMPTP representatives took as an accusation that the studios were already planning to be duplicitous in their calculation of the formula. A few phone calls were made to the group of executives who hammered out the original terms with the DGA, and the flare-up was quickly doused.

Also on that Friday, as exhausted WGA and AMPTP staffers could see the end in sight, AMPTP's Carol Lombardini posed an important question to Patric Verrone. NBC Universal executives wanted an assurance that there would be no poststrike recriminations for *Tonight Show* host Jay Leno. Verrone, according to a later WGA investigation, said there would not be.

After more exchanges of paperwork and telephone calls, guild officials huddled late into the night reviewing the finished documents. Winship, who had been in Los Angeles for the final days of negotiations, caught a late flight back to New York so he could attend Saturday's membership meeting.

Shortly before three o'clock Los Angeles time on the morning of Saturday, February 9, WGA West and East sent an e-mail message to members from Verrone and Winship. "We have a tentative deal," the letter began.[19]

"I believe it is a good deal," Michael Winship told the reporters who waited for him outside the Crowne Plaza Hotel in Times Square on Saturday afternoon. Winship made a few brief remarks before he went inside to preside over the WGA East's membership meeting, which drew more than one hundred members and ran more than two hours. There were pointed questions put to Winship and other members of the negotiating team, but the mood was overwhelmingly positive and prideful that the collective sacrifice had been worth it in the long run. Irish filmmaker Terry George, a negotiating-committee member, roused the room by positing that the WGA had "defeated a tradition of rollbacks" for union workers that began with President Ronald Reagan's firing of striking air-traffic controllers in 1981.[20] Michael Moore, the firebrand auteur of feature documentaries such as *Bowling for Columbine* and *Fahrenheit 9/11*, noted the irony that the first landmark labor action of the twenty-first century came from writers. "I would have thought it'd be autoworkers or ironworkers getting this victory but instead it's the people who got beat up in school for writing in their journals," Moore, a WGA member, told a reporter as he left the meeting.

On the West Coast, more than one thousand writers gathered at Los Angeles's Shrine Auditorium for the 7:00 p.m. meeting, which ran nearly three hours.[21] Negotiating-committee members received an extended standing ovation as they filed onto the dais on the stage. David Young earned renewed respect from many members with his candid, point-by-point discussion of the major deal points. Young, Verrone, and Bowman offered a detailed analysis of where the guild won big and where it had to give in, and why. As was the case for the WGA East, many in the crowd were critical of the length of the promotional window for Web streaming and other points.

In the main, however, the WGA leaders were hailed as conquering heroes. Members felt a sense of relief mixed with the euphoria of victory after taking a principled stand at great personal cost to many. "People have crapped on this union as being about rich people trying to get richer," Matt Selman, a longtime writer on Fox's *The Simpsons*, said outside the Shrine Auditorium as the meeting broke up. "A lot of rich people, and medium-successful writers, of which I would count myself, gave up a huge amount of money so that writers who haven't even been born yet can make a decent wage."

By the time of the Shrine meeting, Mike Scully, the showrunner who made the picket rounds outside Fox on crutches during the first two months of the strike, was walking on air. "I've never been more proud to be a member of this guild. I've never felt more like I was a member of a real union," Scully enthused. "Anyone who would say, 'Well, we didn't get everything we asked for' doesn't know what a labor negotiation is. This is a very good deal for us."

There was some expectation that the strike would be called off that night as the exclamation point to the meeting. But Verrone adhered to the "we are all in this together" ethos by announcing that the guild would hold a vote the following Tuesday, February 12, to determine whether the strike would end before the formal contract ratification vote, which would take another two weeks to complete. The WGA East council and WGA West board were set to vote Sunday on the contract, based on the feedback from the meetings, but guild leaders wanted to give members a say on how to handle the end of the strike. There was more than a little posturing in this move in light of the overwhelming evidence that writers were satisfied with the contract terms and chomping at the bit to return to work.

By Sunday morning, after the negotiating committee, the WGA East council, and the WGA West board each voted unanimously to endorse the contract and send it to members for ratification, guild leaders were confident enough to call off picketing for Monday and Tuesday. And in a nod to its most influential constituency, the guild gave its blessing for showrunners and others with producing responsibilities to return to their offices on Monday to do nonwriting work. For showrunners with active series, it meant starting the process of picking up where they left off on the night of November 4.

On the afternoon of Tuesday, February 12, thousands of WGA members streamed into the lobby of the Writers Guild Theater in Beverly Hills to cast their votes on ending the strike. Minutes after the polls opened at 2:00 p.m., it was clear that counting the votes would merely be a formality. The mood as writers lined up to drop their votes into the white ballot boxes was jubilant. Some brought their children along to mark the occasion.

The polling ended at 6:00 p.m., and within an hour Patric Verrone was presiding alone over the last press conference of the strike. The final tally was 3,492 votes in favor of ending the strike to 283 against. "The strike is over," Verrone began. He spoke with gravitas that yielded to a wide smile after one man among the two dozen or so journalists, photographers, and camera operators in the theater interrupted Verrone's opening words with a loud "Yea!"[22]

After about ten minutes, Verrone brought the questioning to an end. As he walked away from the podium, the WGA West's indefatigable leader received a spontaneous round of applause.

11

The Bloodletting

Was it worth it? Were the contractual gains achieved amid the pressure of the WGA strike worth the sacrifice in immediate earnings for writers and others in the creative community?

Those questions are sure to remain a subject of intense debate in Hollywood for years to come. In contrast to the unity displayed during the heat of the battle, industry insiders have divergent perspectives on the strike and its long-term impact.

There is no denying that writers collectively lost more than $100 million on TV episodes that were never produced because of the strike and production deals that were terminated. Feature film writers suffered with screenplays that were never written, or polished, or those completed drafts that were derailed out of the production track by belt-tightening at the studios. There is also the opportunity cost, much harder to quantify, of projects and deals that might have come to fruition had it been business as usual during those one hundred days.

In the years since the WGA's hard-fought contract went into effect on February 13, 2008, the upside to writers, directors, and actors from new media residuals and jurisdictional gains has not come close to offsetting the losses incurred in the three-and-a-half-month work stoppage. For the WGA West's 2009 fiscal year (ending March 31, 2010), new media residuals for guild members amounted to about $2.8 million–$2.11 million generated by the reuse of TV programs and $690,000 from feature films.[1]

In assessing the legacy of the strike, much of the creative community divides along the lines of the split between the WGA and DGA in their approach to the 2007–8 contract negotiations. The WGA set an antagonistic tone for the 2007 negotiations with its early rhetoric. After the debacle of the recoupment proposal, Nick Counter dug his heels in and sought to wear down the other side. Counter sought to call the WGA's bluff, in the hope that the prospect of actually having to pull off a strike, or the threat of the DGA making a deal, would pressure the WGA leadership into backing down. The DGA, meanwhile, had the research to demonstrate that new media was not a major source of income for the studios and would not be in the foreseeable future. To DGA leaders, those forecasts meant that 2007 was not the moment to go to the mat over new media residuals.

The WGA set off on its quest with inflated estimates of the value of new media—some based on the conglomerates' own rosy predictions to Wall Street. But in the end, it did not matter if the revenue was a trickle or a windfall. WGA leaders were adamant that writers could not afford to wait, based on the studios' history of intransigence on residuals for new formats. "Fool me once, shame on you; fool me twice, shame on me. When (the studios) came back and said, 'Well let's have a study,' there was this instant feeling of, 'Oh come on, we've been down this trail before,'" Michael Winship says. "It's a stalling tactic. We just were fed up with it. . . . The whole argument about, 'Well, we don't have business models for this sort of thing'—that's what they said about the DVD, and before that about home video. We'd reached the point where people were just not going to take it anymore."[2] And the WGA had done its fieldwork with its membership, which resulted in the bedrock support that facilitated the most expansive, most aggressive labor action since the guild's formation in the 1930s.

At the outset, the leadership of the major studios was just as determined, if not as organized as the writers, to resist the WGA's demands. There was already great frustration with the existing residual system. The last thing Hollywood's largest employers wanted to do was add to their obligations in a marketplace under siege from the disruptive effects of new media. "The strike was about (the WGA) saying, 'We're going to add various things in new media on top of what we already have,'" Peter Chernin says, "and the companies were basically telling them that we're not going to saddle ourselves with things that preclude our ability to develop these new platforms as a business."[3]

History will judge the merits of the decisions made and tactics employed by the WGA, DGA, and studio leaders during a transformative period for the entertainment industry. What is indisputable at this vantage point, however, is that the strike was a part of a confluence of events that accelerated the changes that have exacted a heavy toll on the earning power of all but the top echelon of the creative community in Hollywood.

The end of the strike dovetailed with the start of the global economic downturn sparked largely by the crisis in the US mortgage-loan market. The sudden and sharp drop in consumer spending, amid a wave of home foreclosures and layoffs, sent a panic through Hollywood's largest employers. The fear stoked by the economic turmoil ran deeper and spurred more draconian cuts by studio management than even their response to the strike. The conglomerates implemented austerity programs that ranged from curtailing magazine subscriptions and first-class travel privileges to mass layoffs of more than one thousand staffers combined by the Walt Disney Company, Time Warner, Viacom, Sony Pictures Entertainment, and other entertainment companies.

For many writers, the end of the strike did not mean an immediate return to work, even for television writers who were employed at the time the guild went out. Most of the highly rated prime-time shows rushed back into production to salvage what was left of the season. But a number of newer shows were kept on production hiatus for another four or five months, as the networks decided it was better to reintroduce the shows in the fall rather than spend the money and marketing resources it would take to quickly resume production. That decision was hard on working writers who had already lost three months of prime earning potential. Some writers felt it was payback from the conglomerates for having gone on strike. In fact, these were strategic decisions made at a time when network execs were getting nervous about the state of the economy.

In the eighteen months that followed the end of the strike, the major studios systematically cut the salary structure for established TV and film writers almost by half. Amid the panic induced by the sharp acceleration of the recession in the second half of 2008 and 2009, studios became incredibly selective on the projects pursued and the prices paid to writers in particular. It was an additional blow to the working writers who had borne the brunt of the losses during the strike. But it was particularly bad for the WGA's upper middle class. Writers who were accustomed to getting their "quote" of $250,000–$300,000 per screenplay were facing take-it-or-leave-it offers of $150,000 or less. The pool of writers looking for work was so big that studio executives had no shortage of alternatives to draw on for assignments. Writers who were able to successfully pitch prospective ideas to studios were offered far less initial compensation than they were accustomed to, especially for established name writers. The shrinking of the pay scale was consistent across all job categories, from rewrites to polishes to adaptations of existing literary works like novels and magazine articles.

For television's creative community, the worst of the bloodletting came in the spring of 2009, as the broadcast networks were making decisions on the programs that would be ordered for the 2009–10 season beginning in September. Showrunners on even top prime-time hits were told by their studios that production budgets for the coming season had to be cut by as much as 15 percent to 20 percent. A good portion of those savings had to come out of the budget for the writing staff, which meant cutting staff positions and cutting salaries. New shows had to assemble their writing staff and make casting decisions based on smaller budgets.

The cost-cutting mandate was the same at every major studio in the face of the economic uncertainty. The drop in advertising spending was so great that network executives were worried about having enough cash flow coming in to cover their license-fee obligations. Studios worried about investing too much in deficit spending on shows if the syndication market was also going to be compromised by the advertising downturn at the TV stations and cable networks that buy off-network programs. The domino effect was felt throughout the creative community. In some instances, actors and writers had to forgo raises that were already written into their contracts as a condition of a pilot getting picked up or a show getting renewed. Plans for elaborate location shoots were rewritten as scenes that could be shot on a soundstage. Expenditures on everything from craft services to promotional campaigns were reined in.

The broader economic downturn came at a time when the studios and networks had already been scrutinizing every aspect of the cost structure of scripted programming because of the strike. Hollywood's largest employers had made the decision to scale back expenditures on TV development and production wherever possible, starting with the force-majeure terminations of so many long-term deals with writers, producers, and actors. When the economy tumbled, the conglomerates were well prepared to act swiftly and take advantage of the weak job market for writers that persisted in the months after the strike.

In the tumult of the strike period, there were numerous pronouncements from high-ranking Hollywood executives that the television industry would never be the same in the wake of the strike. Many predicted the networks would rely ever more on less expensive unscripted series and imported programs from the United Kingdom, Canada, and other territories. The most dramatic declaration came from Jeff Zucker, NBC Universal president and CEO. On January 29, 2008, Zucker used the forum of his keynote address at the annual National Association of Television Program Executives (NATPE) conference in Las Vegas to announce a number of dramatic changes in NBC Universal's business practices. "We are in the middle of a wrenching analog-to-digital transition marked by game-changing technological developments and profound shifts in consumer behavior, all of which demands a re-engineering of our businesses from top to bottom," Zucker told the crowd. "We've needed to do this for quite a few years now, but there was no real sense of urgency behind it. Inertia kept things moving in the same direction, a gentle downward slide disguised by a strong economy and robust ad market."[4]

Zucker vowed that NBC would try to forgo the traditional process of producing pilots before deciding whether to order a project to series. Eliminating the expense of producing pilots that do not make the cut for series orders would save NBC tens of millions of dollars a year. The fact that the traditional January–April timetable for pilot production had been upended by the strike made it easier for NBC to change its practice going forward.

Zucker likened the pilot season's disruption by the strike to a forest fire for the entertainment business. While acknowledging the "devastating consequences" the strike had throughout the industry, he also noted that "fires fertilize the soil with new ash and clear the ground, often setting the stage for robust growth."

NBC adhered to Zucker's dictum in the truncated pilot season that followed the end of the strike. But each of the shows the network ordered to series on the strength of scripts, rather than a produced pilot, were on-air flops: the comedy *Kath and Kim* and dramas *My Own Worst Enemy*, *Robinson Crusoe*, *The Philanthropist*, and *The Listener*. NBC's rivals were highly critical of the idea of giving up on pilots, with one executive likening it to putting a new model of a car into mass production without first creating a prototype.

Zucker's focus on reengineering NBC's prime-time operation led to the network's bold experiment in the first half of the 2009–10 season with *The Jay Leno Show* talk and variety hour running Monday–Friday in the 10:00 p.m. hour—the time slots usually reserved largely for scripted drama series. *Jay Leno* is destined to be remembered as one of prime time's biggest flops.

Within two years of Zucker's NATPE speech, NBC was squarely back in the business of producing expensive pilots with high-priced writers and producers as the network struggled to rebuild its prime-time lineup. At the same time, Zucker wasn't all wrong. The US television industry since the strike has increasingly embraced alternative models for producing and financing scripted programming, some of which call for skipping the pilot process in favor of multiple episode orders.

As disruptive as it was, the strike helped burnish Hollywood's corporate earnings in the months that followed the end of the strike. Disney, News Corporation, CBS Corporation, and NBC Universal saw positive earnings benefits from the immediate drop in spending on production and marketing expenses. The loss of advertising revenue from lower-rated repeats and replacement programming was not recorded as quickly on the conglomerates' books.

But the short-term boost was no cause for celebration among the CEOs. The damage done by the strike was evident in the ratings for hit shows after they returned with new episodes in March and April. CBS, not surprisingly, was the most aggressive in pushing producers to get fresh episodes on the air as quickly as possible. The network's highly rated Monday comedies—anchored by prime time's most-watched sitcom, *Two and a Half Men*—were the first shows to come back after the strike, on March 17. CBS's half-hours held up pretty well, but dramas including *CSI*, *CSI: Miami*, *Grey's Anatomy*, and *Desperate Housewives* returned with ratings that were 10 percent to 20 percent lower than viewing levels before the strike. Those lost ratings cost the conglomerates far more over the long haul than they saved with the unexpected shutdown of production.

Once viewers were abruptly broken from the habit of keeping up with favorite shows during the September–May season, no amount of on-air promotion was effective enough to alert the audience that prime-time TV was back to business as usual in the late spring. The Big Three networks registered similar audience erosion in the wake of the 1988 strike, which delayed the start of the 1988–89 season until October and November and later, for some shows. In 2007 viewers had many more alternatives to choose from—on the TV dial as well as online—in lieu of their ingrained habit of tuning in for NBC's *The Office* on Thursday at 9:00 or *CSI: Miami* on Monday at 10:00. Even two years after the strike, ratings for most prime-time hits had not fully rebounded to prestrike levels. Some of it can be chalked up to the continued fragmentation of the audience across dozens of cable channels, online sources, and video games. But the strike interruption certainly did not help.

The fallout of the ratings drop has fueled lingering bitterness about the strike from all who were affected. From the perspective of many show-runners, the CEOs and their proxies at the AMPTP had an obligation as leaders to make sure that the industry did not suffer another strike. If the studios had responded to the WGA's new media demands in a serious way, the walkout would never have happened. From the perspective of many CEOs, and even some on the creative side of the fence, the strike amounted to a self-inflicted wound by WGA members, who returned to work to find a much tighter job market, lower pay, and a tougher environment in which to field a successful TV series or feature screenplay.

The WGA West's annual earnings reports tell a mixed tale. Earnings in 2009, the first fiscal year after the end of the strike, were up sharply for

TV writers, but total employment was still lagging the peak years before the strike. WGA research indicates the earnings gap between the top echelon of TV and film writers—the top 5 percent of guild earnings—and the rest of the membership is steadily widening. In this sense, employment in Hollywood mirrors the national trend of great disparity between the top and the vanishing of middle-class earners.[5]

For fiscal year 2007, the WGA West had 4,657 members generating a total of $982.9 million in earnings from film, TV, and radio work, which marked an 8 percent gain in earnings over the previous fiscal year. Those figures reflected the prestrike stockpiling of material by the studios, particularly on the feature-film side. The peak year of employment for WGA West's Hollywood writers remains 2000, when 4,680 members reported income.[6] For fiscal year 2008, which bore the brunt of the strike losses, WGA West member earnings fell 15.4 percent, to $831.3 million, and the number of working writers dropped to 4,339.[7] In 2009 total earnings rebounded 12 percent from 2008 to $931.9 million from 4,328 writers. Those gains were driven largely by TV writers, who generated a record $502.4 million in earnings, a 10 percent gain from 2008, from 3,094 writers. The growth reflects the swift expansion of original scripted programming on cable networks in recent years. Total TV writer employment remained lower than its peak years in 2000 (3,564) and 2001 (3,480).[8]

Residual payments, which are counted separately from the WGA's general writer-income statements, continue to decline in the most lucrative categories for writers, namely, broadcast TV reuse. Basic and pay cable's expansion of rerun use has helped offset the declines, albeit at lower residual rates, for a wider group of recipients.

In fiscal year 2009, WGA West members earned a total of $286 million in residuals, down slightly from 2008 ($287.9 million). Residuals from broadcast network reruns of TV programs, the most valuable to writers, dropped 7.3 percent from 2008 to $23.96 million. Domestic broadcast syndication fell 13.2 percent to $18.88 million. The two major basic-cable residual categories posted big gains in 2009, as the volume of repeats shifted inevitably away from broadcast networks to the plethora of cable channels. For basic-cable reruns of shows made for network TV (ABC, CBS, NBC, Fox, CW) or pay TV (HBO, Showtime, Starz), residuals gained 7.6

percent to $28.87 million. Cable reruns of made-for-basic-cable shows (that is, a cable network rerunning its own programming) spiked 23.8 percent to $15.71 million.

Residuals from home video sales of television programming continue to grow, as TV aficionados grow accustoming to buying DVD box sets of their favorite shows. But feature-film residuals are down sharply, reflecting their higher benchmark of earnings and the overall slump in home video sales. TV home video residuals climbed 21.6 percent to $11.56 million in fiscal year 2009. Feature-film residuals slumped 13.3 percent to $41.40 million.[9]

Beyond the immediate pre- and poststrike years, the WGA's research has found that the employment picture for TV writers has tightened during the past decade. According to the WGA West–commissioned *Hollywood Writers Report* for 2009 by UCLA professor Darnell Hunt, WGA West membership declined 1.7 percent from 2003 to 2007 to 8,131. (WGA West's membership peak stands at 9,056 in 2000.) Overall employment of writers in television dropped 6.2 percent from 2001 to 2007, while film employment grew 1.5 percent during the same period. The number of staff writer-producer jobs on TV series declined 13.7 percent between the 2001–2 season and 2007–8, when about 1,500 writers held staff positions on ongoing series. Most of the jobs lost were at the rank of supervising producer or above.

The median earnings mark for all writers climbed from $90,516 in 2001 to $104,857 in 2007. But median earnings for younger writers, ages thirty-one to forty, dropped 6.4 percent to $87,500 from $93,500. Before 2005 writers in that age bracket were the WGA's highest-earning age group. Now the guild's highest-earning group is in the age range of forty-one to fifty.[10]

The WGA maintains that over a five-year span, given the inevitable periods of unemployment for TV and film writers, the average income for guild members levels out at about $62,000 a year. However, given the wide variations in earnings for members at the bottom and top rungs of the income scale, such averages are hardly representative. According to the *Hollywood Writers Report*, one-quarter of WGA West members made less than $37,700 a year during the study period, while half of the membership made less than $105,000 a year. "The people I feel most sorry for after this strike are the writers who have been in the business for 10 to 12 years, have just gotten their first full producing credit and were making $18,000 to $20,000 an episode (before the strike). Those jobs are gone. And they ain't coming back," says Dick Wolf, the creator and executive producer of *Law and Order* and its offshoots.[11] Wolf, who ranks among the most successful TV writer-producers of all time, was an outspoken critic of WGA leaders during the strike. He was among the few writers who publicly warned that the fallout from a work stoppage would cost WGA members in the long run. "People say, 'God, it's going to take years to make up the income lost in the strike.' This is income that will never return," Wolf says. "This was an ego-driven exercise that got (writers) less than nothing."

Although there has been revisionist thinking on the strike among some in the creative community, Wolf is still in the minority with his extremely negative assessment. Because the WGA leadership effectively cast the 2007 negotiations as a do-or-die moment for new media, many writers generally feel it was a necessary sacrifice, albeit one that went on four to six weeks longer than need be. "Every writer knew we had to get (new media residuals). We had to get it and we were all going to take a hit for it. Different people took bigger hits than other people did," John Bowman says. "But we did know that writers have sacrificed for us in the past and we had to do something, right now, to protect writers in the future. We don't have a pension and health plan because people didn't sacrifice."[12]

From the start of the walkout, many in the creative community believed the AMPTP did everything it could to prod the WGA into striking in order to allow the studios to slash their overhead costs and downsize the upper reaches of the pay scale for writers. An even more conspiratorial viewpoint posits that the AMPTP was betting that the strike would splinter the guild once and for all, giving studios the upper hand in deal making once writers were no longer represented by a single bargaining agent. "The strike was ridiculous. They backed us into a corner," says Steve Levitan. "If, on that last Sunday, they had made even a slightly acceptable offer, we wouldn't have gone on strike. But they really left us no choice."[13]

On the management side, there are many who believe that the WGA was determined to go out no matter what the AMPTP put on the table.

Conspiracy theorists in this camp believe the WGA desperately wanted to strike in order to inflate the importance of the guild in the eyes of members, after the leadership stumbles of Patric Verrone's immediate predecessors. There is also a deep-seated belief, even among some who were supportive of the strike, that a group of veteran WGA members had been agitating for a strike simply because it had been so many years since the 1988 walkout and because new media was such a natural rallying cry. One prominent writer-producer likened this group to "mad dogs in the basement clawing to get out."

In fact, the circumstances that led to the one-hundred-day walkout defy easy explanation, or easy categorization of the sides as heroes or villains. "Bottom line—did the writers do some things wrong? Yes. We should have focused more on the Internet" from the start, WGA negotiating committee member Neal Baer says. "Did the AMPTP cause major problems? Yes. Should the AMPTP have negotiated in good faith? Yes. Did they? No. . . . I feel the story isn't going to be over until we see those (studio) books over the next three years and see what happens."[14]

The notion that the AMPTP plotted to goad the WGA into striking gives the studios too much credit for being well organized, which they were not, as underscored by the debacle of the recoupment proposal. Although none of the CEOs wanted to see the traditional residual system implemented in new media, the fissures among the largest AMPTP members only grew as the strike wore on. "We naively thought it was going to take years for (new media) to develop as a business," said Warner Bros.' Barry Meyer. "So where we started with this negotiation was: 'Let's analyze it, let's look at it together with all of the guilds.' Let's see where it's going and we can make a decision in a year or two or three.'"[15]

The attitude among the CEOs of the AMPTP board-member companies depended on how badly their core businesses were getting walloped by the work stoppage. The conglomerates that had no direct exposure to a broadcast network—Sony Pictures Entertainment, Viacom, and Warner Bros.—were ready to fight it out. News Corporation, Disney, and NBC Universal felt more urgency but were cushioned in the loss of original programming for their networks by heavily diversified operations. CBS Corporation, with the CBS network as its cornerstone, was more vulnerable the longer the strike went on. That naturally made CBS's chief executive, Leslie Moonves, more inclined to compromise for the sake of getting fresh scripted programming back on the air. CBS's push for resuming negotiations after the strike began and other behind-the-scenes maneuvers led to some tension among Moonves and his fellow CEOs. Nick Counter's role in the past had been to help the members work through divisive issues in order to present a united front to the guilds. This time around, though, achieving unity among the AMPTP board members was much more of a struggle. With the consolidation of ownership over fifteen years and the complexity of the new media compensation issues, the studios are increasingly divided on policy and industry issues. The schism among the companies with different business priorities was evident at the AMPTP's negotiating table.

In the end, Chernin and Iger focused almost as much on keeping the studios unified under the AMPTP umbrella as they did on making peace with the WGA. Both believed it was vital to keep the AMPTP coalition together amid strike conditions and beyond. Hollywood history had shown that if the largest studios were not aligned under a single bargaining unit, unions would seek out the weakest member and try to force the most advantageous deal possible and demand that others match it.

Although the involvement of Chernin and Iger was crucial to breaking the impasse, executives who were close to the process warned that relying on CEOs to broker industry-wide labor contracts is not a workable solution for the long term. First and foremost, CEOs already have full-time jobs. That fact inevitably makes them impatient at the bargaining table. They are eager to move on after the broad strokes of a deal are agreed on, leaving important details hanging in such a way as to provoke disputes of interpretation down the road. Both sides are better served if dedicated labor negotiators oversee the bargaining—so long as the atmosphere in the room is conducive to constructive dialogue, something that was sorely lacking between the AMPTP and WGA representatives.

Meanwhile, the idea that the WGA was hell bent to hit the streets does not square with the motivations of the working showrunners and screenwriters on the negotiating committee who had so much to lose if a strike came to pass. John Bowman had as much at stake as anyone, having walked away from a new late-night sketch-comedy series, *Frank TV,* that premiered on cable channel TBS two weeks after the strike began. "I don't know if (the AMPTP) forced a strike, but they certainly didn't do everything they could to prevent it from happening," Bowman says. "If they wanted to stop it, they wouldn't have walked away from the negotiating table twice."[16]

As recounted in the preceding chapters, fear was both the spark and the kindling of the strike. Both sides shared great fear of the uncertain future for entertainment-industry economics as digital technologies and new distribution platforms threaten to erode the foundations of Hollywood's traditional major profit centers: advertising, syndication, home video sales, and theatrical exhibition. The WGA went into the negotiations demanding that these new platforms be addressed in the 2007 contract negotiations in order to ensure that writers would be compensated when their work was reused in new media. The WGA's campaign to persuade members that new media was a strike-worthy issue was driven in large part by the specter of the network-studio conglomerates conspiring to eliminate residuals altogether by shifting all TV programming to Internet-based platforms, where they had no obligation to pay for reuse. Studio leaders exacerbated the problem by failing to address compensation terms with the guilds until long after new technologies like paid iTunes downloads and advertising-supported Web streaming were in place.

Because the battle lines were sharply drawn and the suspicion high on both sides, the larger question of how the traditional network TV business model will adapt to changing times was never discussed in a meaningful way. The AMPTP went on the offensive with its recoupment proposal that was as radical as anything the WGA proposed. WGA leaders deftly rallied the troops by painting a picture of residuals under attack, but the attack is being waged by television viewers rather than greedy executives. The volume of traditional network residuals paid to TV writers—the most lucrative rerun compensation—is dwindling because the networks simply are not airing as many reruns as they once did, particularly during the summer months. Viewers will not sit still for them. Not only do they have more channels to choose from, but there are more ways to watch encore episodes on their own timetables (through DVRs, Web streaming, paid downloads) than ever before.

Networks have had little choice but to become more selective about the shows that get on-air reruns to remain competitive—a trend that was accelerating before shows were routinely available via online sources. Dramas with close-ended story formats such as *Law and Order* and *CSI* tend to perform better in repeat telecasts than shows with heavily serialized story lines like *Desperate Housewives* and *Lost.* Half-hour comedies tend to fare better than dramas, but in the past decade the number of prime-time comedies has dwindled sharply from the late-1990s peak. "You're seeing a real fractionalization of the audience," says Warner Bros.' Meyer. "The whole idea of running a show at a set time and forcing everybody to see it then or wait for the summer rerun is over. Technology gives you the ability to put it in a lot of different places."[17]

This shift in audience behavior has created a quandary for networks, which used to count on amortizing their programming costs through repeat telecasts. But if the ratings for those repeats turn out to be negligible, it can wind up costing more in residuals and other rights-fee obligations than the repeat takes in through advertising. Networks increasingly turn to lower-cost unscripted programming as an alternative to repeats, particularly during the summer months. But that still does not solve the amortization problem for high-cost scripted programming—a dilemma that helps to explain the AMPTP's intransigence on Internet residuals. "You can't force consumers to behave the way you want them to. The marketplace is making those changes," Peter Chernin says. "Writers are so upset that (traditional TV) reruns are going away. Well, they just are. No one wants reruns to go away less than the networks. But they are."[18]

As the number of digital distribution outlets for movie and TV content—from Hulu to Netflix to burgeoning mobile TV services—the volume of traditional network TV reruns is only going to decrease in the coming years. In that sense, the WGA's approach was rational. The guild had an obligation to its members to establish a toehold with new media residuals as the business entered a period of dramatic change and uncertainty. But the rallying cry of getting "screwed" by studio overlords shaded the reality that the conglomerates were earning negligible revenue from new media. What was missing from the negotiations that led to up to the November 5 walkout was a frank discussion of how the industry's economics are shifting for all stakeholders.

The biggest adjustment that studios, as the bankrollers of a large volume of prime-time series, face is the pressure to manage their resources in a more deliberate and efficient manner than in decades past. In short, the hits do not pay for the misses like they used to. The television production business has long supported profligate spending on development deals, talent contracts, and pilot production because the shows that made it to syndication delivered such huge returns. And the largest studios could also count on the cushion of the steady cash flow generated from worldwide licensing of library programs.

Now, the profit margins from new and library product sales are shrinking, and the syndication business model is under extreme pressure from the explosion of on-demand options. Although international licensing and home video sales have grown in the past decade, the long-term impact of digital distribution remains murky—which gives CEOs pause. "The deficits that companies take today on prime-time programming are greater than they've ever been before," says Meyer. "There's a strong and healthy international market, and there's a strong and healthy video market for some shows. There is a growing market for on demand downloads and web streaming. Some of it makes money through advertising, and some of it is paid by the consumer. Those markets continue to grow, but they are not even close to compensating (networks and studios) for what is being lost in the primary markets."[19]

Some in the entertainment industry view the writers' strike as the tip of the iceberg in terms of the upheaval that Hollywood will undergo in the coming years. And the hardest-hit sector in the near term will be that which one CEO described as "the vast middle"—the writers, directors, actors, executives, agents, publicists, and others who have not attained superstar status but have been able to make a good living nonetheless. "The scary thing about the Internet for almost everybody is that the old gatekeepers are gone. The gatekeepers are dead," says John Bowman.

"We've all benefited from the gatekeepers. We've certainly benefited from a near-monopoly of broadcast TV on entertainment, because it meant that advertisers only had one place to go. It's been good for everybody who's on the inside."[20]

In an on-demand, multiplatform world, hit shows are more valuable than ever, because there are more ways to exploit the program (iTunes, Hulu, DVD sales, and so on) and the following it engenders (licensing and merchandising, webisodes, spin-offs). Network TV has always been fueled by hits, since the days of *Texaco Star Theater* and *I Love Lucy*. But the traditional approach to prime-time programming also allowed for less successful programs to stay on the air. In the industry they are known as "satellite shows," and they often air adjacent to anchor shows or in low-priority time slots like Friday night. Before DVRs, downloads, and Web streaming, a network needed a handful of satellite shows just to fill out its schedule. Networks and studios could abide mediocrity in quality or quantity of viewers because it was impossible to expect every program in the lineup to be a blockbuster. Now, with viewers increasingly watching TV on their own timetables, it is becoming harder to funnel viewers into satellite shows. Those satellite time slots in many cases are being filled by low-cost reality shows or newsmagazines, which come at a cost of jobs for actors, writers, and directors.

Moreover, viewers have exponentially more options to choose from thanks to the explosion of niche cable and Internet outlets that collectively nibble at the heel of what was once the Big Four's dominant market share. That niche programming typically is produced on a much smaller budget than traditional scripted network TV series, which means lower salaries and less back-end potential for creatives. Network executives insist that their business model is choking on the competition from lower-cost alternative programmers who do not shoulder the same obligations for residuals and royalties for programs that ABC, CBS, NBC, and Fox do. And all of that boils down to a strain on middle-class wages in television that is having a ripple effect throughout the industry. "Every major new piece of technology has impact in two ways: It gives people more choice, and it gives people more control. And those are negatives for the economics of this business, by definition," Chernin says. "More choice means that you're spreading those dollars among many more different pieces. . . . We can't force people to watch shows anymore by how we schedule things. Viewers can go find whatever they want when they want. Those are all fundamentally positive trends that are good for consumers, but they're big challenges to the economics of the business. We can whine about it all we want, but no one can control it."[21]

With the issues so complex, and the divide between the sides so deep, what finally turned the tide? After three months, fatigue played a significant part in bringing the sides together. Writers had demonstrated admirable resolve and solidarity in the face of lost wages, lost deals, and the general turmoil in the marketplace. But that unity was starting to crack among influential members—and nobody was more keenly aware of the slow but steady erosion of support than David Young, by multiple accounts. Young had a strong sense of the mood swings among various subsets of the membership.

People who worked closely with Young said he was always clear-eyed in his analysis of the guild's vulnerabilities in the late January–early February period, after the DGA reached its agreement. He was never blinded by the intense loyalty demonstrated by the cadre of strike captains and picket-line mainstays. He knew exactly when the guild was in serious danger of losing its most important constituencies. And through his broad experience with strikes, he knew when the moment came to shift from war footing to diplomacy. This understanding came as a surprise to some of the CEOs who had come to see Young as a reckless ideologue. Young's ability to pivot into deal-making mode won him high marks with Peter Chernin and Bob Iger, by many accounts. "There comes a time in any strike where it's time to settle. And that time is when the pressure is greatest on both sides," Young said at the news conference held at WGA West headquarters on February 10, 2008, the day after the membership meetings in Los Angeles and New York. "It was going to be a huge issue for the industry to lose the Oscars, to lose (the 2007–8) television season (and) to lose potentially the next television season. Obviously, those were huge issues for our membership as well because if those things are lost, member income is lost for months. That's what creates the pressures on both sides to make a deal," Young said.[22]

Young disputed that the restlessness of many showrunners and other key members drove the WGA to make its final compromises. "We got stronger as this strike went on. Usually your power peaks at the beginning and then you go into attrition mode. I think this deal finally came because our power was greatest in the last couple of weeks when we made the deal," Young said.

The importance of John Bowman's role in that period cannot be overstated, WGA members say. Bowman was the liaison who began the thaw with the CEOs and remained a respected figure among both the hard-line strike supporters and his fellow showrunners. "His personality and ability to negotiate is what helped get us through," Baer says. "He had to walk a tough, tough, tough tightrope, not just between the CEOs and the writers, but between Patric and David and the negotiating committee. And the (WGA West) board."[23]

Ever the pragmatist, Bowman knew there was nothing to be gained by pushing the membership once key contract demands had been addressed in the DGA template.

Mike Scully, the showrunner who made the picket rounds with a cast on his foot for the first few weeks of the strike, says the triumvirate of Verrone, Young, and Bowman was highly effective in leading the guild through trying times because each brought different skills to the task. "Patric and David did an amazing job under incredibly stressful circumstances, but I think the membership felt the strongest attachment to John. The three of them made a great team," Scully says. "John always comes across as a no-bullshit guy. He just tells you the way things are, even if you don't want to hear it. In a labor dispute, particularly in a long labor dispute, you really want to feel the information you're being given is accurate," he says. "Digging your heels in and fighting to the last man is a great unifying feeling, but sometimes you just need somebody to say, 'I don't think this is fair, but it's the best we're going to do right now and we'll try to do better in the future.'"[24]

And just as writers grew tired of the fight, so did management. The sustained support for the strike from working writers had been a jolt to executives and the broader creative community after so many years of labor peace in Hollywood. The strike underscored the pervasive unease among Hollywood's hired hands after more than a decade of consolidation in the entertainment industry and the promise of even greater transitions to come. "Our public meetings were all turning points" during the strike, Bowman says. "At each one, our solidarity was overwhelming. I believe this is what finally drove the CEOs to the table. It was clear that this time, we weren't going to fold."[25]

The calendar also played a big part in nudging the sides to compromise. The February 24 Academy Awards telecast became a psychological deadline that carried weight with both sides. Any significant disruption to Hollywood's Oscar pageantry would have been a black eye for the industry, particularly its executive leadership. And after the Golden Globe Awards debacle, there was no question that the WGA's pickets were a threat to the Oscars.

Another important factor was the creeping realization that if the strike ran past February, it would be virtually impossible for the major networks to produce pilots in time for the traditional mid-May announcement of programming for the upcoming September–May television season. "We had effectively scrubbed the Golden Globes down to next to nothing. We certainly were making plans for a full court press to do the same to the Oscars," Michael Winship says. "And I think it was (also) the studios and the networks looking and realizing that this (TV) season is almost totally shot to hell, and pretty soon the pilot season's going to be shot to hell for next year. And we were getting into a position now where it was affecting motion pictures. Then I think the Oscar date took on this iconic aspect—they didn't want it to get past the Oscars."[26]

Bowman emphasizes the important role that the Internet, e-mail, and other new communication tools played in organizing guild members and heaping pressure on the AMPTP conglomerates. "We used the Internet to (disclose) our negotiating strategy. The CEOs just couldn't dictate the story," Bowman says. "And once everybody could decide on their own whether we were reasonable or not, then the (AMPTP) actually had to show signs of being reasonable in order to get our membership to say, 'OK, it's time to settle.'"[27]

What did the WGA get for its hard-fought contract? That is even harder to answer than the question of who was right and who was wrong in the run-up to the walkout. The potential for earnings in new media will swing wildly depending on whether a critical mass of consumers embrace new forms of distribution. Even as the WGA prepared to negotiate the successor to the contract forged by the strike, there was no clear consensus in the entertainment industry on the most lucrative business models or optimum distribution systems. The landscape has become only more crowded with contenders in the years since the WGA strike ended.

Although guild officials and entertainment-industry lawyers have eagerly parsed every fraction of a percentage in the 2008 WGA contract, such scrutiny of individual items misses the forest for the trees, according to Peter Chernin. "The hard part of these deals is that if you look at any of those guild (master) contracts there are 100 different points in them. Taken individually, any one of these points can appear unfair to one side or the other," Chernin says. "Remember, you have all sorts of things that have been in those contracts since the '50s and '60s, when in fact the business has changed tremendously. The point is that any time you approach a contract negotiation, you can't look at each point on its own. You have to look at the contract as a whole."[28]

Patric Verrone did not hesitate to declare the final contract a major victory for writers. "This is the best deal this guild has bargained for in 30 years after the most successful strike this guild has waged in 35 years," Verrone said at the news conference held at WGA West headquarters on February 10, 2008, the day after the membership meetings in Los Angeles and New York. "It was arguably the most successful strike in the American labor movement in a decade—certainly the most important of this young century," Verrone said. "Unlike contracts past and new technologies past where we were simply told 'Here's the deal' and then stuck with it for a generation, I think this time we have a deal that we like to begin with and that we can improve upon as the technology advances and as the business models evolve."[29]

Over time it has become clear that the area in which the DGA deal template yielded its greatest gains in residual fees—the formula for download-to-own (a.k.a. electronic sell-through) sales of movies and TV programs—has largely been usurped by the popularity of Web-streaming services such as Hulu, Netflix, and YouTube. The dawn of Hulu as a major player in legal digital distribution dovetailed with the end of the strike. The Internet video venture was established in early 2007 as a joint venture of NBC Universal and News Corporation, with funding from the blue-chip Providence Equity Partners media investment firm. It was designed to be a "YouTube killer," or a legal alternative to the many pirated clips and full episodes of new and vintage TV programs easily found on the Google-owned streaming behemoth.

Because it had a wealth of contemporary TV content and an easy-to-use interface, Hulu quickly outpaced iTunes and NBC and Fox's network websites as the destination for viewers seeking online replays of network TV shows. Hulu's Web-streaming service also offered more truly instant on-demand access than iTunes, which requires download time that varies according to the user's broadband capability and the length of the pro-gram sought. Hulu opened its doors to the public (after about six months in beta-test mode) on March 12, 2008, one month to the day after the end of the strike. Hulu became so popular, which is not to say profitable, so quickly that by the summer of 2009, the Walt Disney Company bought a stake in the venture and contributed its popular programs to the Hulu lineup.

Cynics would say the studio negotiators knew the download-to-own market had plateaued, and thus they granted concessions in that formula to get off cheap. Web-streaming residuals are not as generous as down-load to own, and they are encumbered by the seventeen- and twenty-four-day free window for TV programs.

But executives who were intimately involved in crafting the new media agreement say that scenario gives the studios too much credit for being able to predict the future. The most unnerving thing about the explosion in new media is the uncertainty of predicting how new markets will grow and how consumers will embrace or ignore new platforms. The advent of Apple's iPad in 2010 added a new level of angst in Hollywood, as the larger screen makes it much more functional and palatable to many viewers than watching on a tiny iPod or iPhone screen.

In response to the growing availability of broadcast programming online, cable programmers have felt the pressure of consumer demand to make more of their programming available via broadband on an on-demand basis. But this is another area where technology threatens to undermine a crucial source of revenue and profits for the major media conglomerates that depend on cable- and satellite-TV providers to pay high carriage fees for the most popular cable channels, such as USA Network, ESPN, TNT, and TBS, as well as pay-TV channels HBO, Showtime, and Starz. If cable programs are made available for free online, consumers would have less incentive to continue to pay the monthly bill for a bundle of channels. Giving consumers the flexibility to cherry-pick the shows they want to watch online disrupts the fundamentals of the cable-programming and distribution business, which is rooted in selling channel packages. Cable programming services have been the most significant driver of corporate profits for Time Warner, Disney, News Corporation, and NBC Universal for more than a decade.

The subscription-TV industry's response to the growth of Hulu and Netflix has been to develop proprietary online services that offer a limited menu of shows via broadband, but only to viewers who maintain a monthly subscription to a traditional cable or satellite provider. The initiative has been primarily championed by Time Warner chief executive Jeffrey Bewkes, who branded the concept "TV Everywhere," recognizing that broadband access offers viewers the option of watching programs on mobile devices. Unlike the centralized distribution of Hulu, each cable and satellite operator has developed its own interface and brand name for its video-on-demand and broadband services. The viability of this effort hinges on complex "authentication" technology to enforce its subscribers-only model, which has proven vexing in trial runs even for leading-edge cable provider Comcast Corporation. Just like satellite providers DirecTV and EchoStar Communications' Dish Network, telephone giants AT&T and Verizon have joined the subscription-TV service fray in recent years, offering channel packages that compete with cable and satellite. And they too are implementing TV Everywhere–style broadband services.

But technology has moved much faster than the business side of Hollywood ever could. That is not a contract-negotiating subterfuge; it is a fact. News Corporation and NBC Universal took the plunge with Hulu with the understanding that some of their traditional TV audience might be cannibalized by the online availability of shows. Despite the popularity of the service, Hulu had yet to turn a significant profit after five years of operations because of the vast differences in the volume and pricing of advertising on the Internet and TV—so much so that the company in 2010 launched the Hulu Plus subscription service in an effort to better monetize its content. As with TV Everywhere services, the highest hurdles to clear are the challenges of accurately measuring the online audience and convincing Madison Avenue to accept combined ratings from TV and online viewing as the basis for advertising sales. In 2010 Netflix surprised Hollywood by spending big to license top-tier film and TV shows for its growing Web-streaming service. Seemingly overnight, the company that started as a DVD-by-mail service began to transform itself into an Internet video distributor with an ambitious plan to compete with the established cable and broadcast TV players by establishing a new subscripted video-on-demand window for the reuse of movies and TV shows.

The logistical issues surrounding the need to update arcane audience-measurement systems for a multiplatform world are arguably more vexing than the development of Web-streaming technology itself. And it will be even tougher to change the cultural mind-set of traditional television and advertising executives, who have been schooled to value audiences drawn by live TV viewing on a mass-market basis above all else. These changes are generational shifts that will not come quickly or easily for the industry's contemporary leaders. Where so much power, influence, and profit are at stake, change of the scale that television has experienced in the past decade inevitably sparks fear and retrenchment before an industry is transformed, in fits and starts, to meet the needs of a new business paradigm.

Hollywood's CEOs were not lying when they asserted that the business models to support the marriage of old and new media had not been formulated, not by a long shot. But they were tone-deaf when much of the creative community stood up to demand a form of protection for their livelihoods at such an uncertain moment. Judging by past precedent, the WGA was right to demand that new media compensation be addressed sooner rather than later.

The combative tone set by Patric Verrone and David Young put the CEOs on edge, making it harder for either side to reach out with the behind-the-scenes deal making that had long been the salve for Hollywood's labor pains. The void in industry-wide leadership, created by the disparities and conflicting agendas of media and entertainment conglomerates, made such outreach impossible until it was too late to stop the picket lines from forming.

But there were other factors that fueled the strike that were tied in to a much larger shift in America's sociopolitical and economic landscape. It is no coincidence that Hollywood writers took to the streets one year almost to the day before Barack Obama was elected president of the United States. The groundswell of support for Obama's underdog presidential campaign tapped in to the same vein of idealism—pent up after the trauma of September 11 and spurred by disdain for the Bush administration and the Iraq War—that WGA leaders expertly invoked to move writers to action on an issue cast as a once-in-a-generation battle for the future.

In Hollywood the suspicion of institutions was compounded by the dramatic consolidation of major employers over the preceding fifteen years. Writers who increasingly felt intimidated by working for multinational network-studio conglomerates suddenly had an outlet for their frustration. And overnight there was a feeling of being enveloped in a community with shared priorities and shared sacrifice for the greater good. Against this powerful dynamic, economic arguments about the earnings potential from new media were fruitless. "There are a lot of people who lost more in the first two weeks of the strike than they'll make in their entire careers from new media," says Steve Levitan.

Levitan and his writing partner, Christopher Lloyd, were among the showrunners and producers who struggled to relaunch fledgling shows after the strike ended. The pair's Fox sitcom *Back to You*, which premiered six weeks before the strike began, aired four more times in the spring of 2008 before it was canceled. Levitan and Lloyd rebounded in a big way the following year with a show destined to become a critical and commercial smash, ABC's *Modern Family*. Long before he knew *Modern Family*'s fate, however, Levitan was unequivocal in asserting that the long-term gains from the strike outweighed the short-term sacrifices. "What really filled me with hope and good feelings about this community is that there were so many people willing to say, 'This isn't about me.' This is about the future generations," Levitan said in 2008. "We're a generation that has been entitled; so many things have been handed to us. It just felt good to do something that was in some way selfless and that was going to benefit people long after we're gone. I wanted to be part of something where we showed some backbone."[30]

Epilogue

Like the rest of the world economy, the entertainment marketplace was unpredictable during the three-year period covered by the WGA's 2008 master contract. The new media landscape evolved and expanded in ways that no one saw coming in early 2008.

Netflix transformed itself in 2009 and 2010 from a mail-order DVD service to a subscription-based streaming-media hub that is aggressively chasing content deals, in Hollywood and elsewhere. Facebook, Twitter, and other social media were barely on the industry's radar at the time the strike was settled. Hulu's swift rise into an Internet video behemoth began with its official launch on March 12, 2008, one month to the day after the end of the strike. The timing was coincidental, as it came after nearly five months of beta testing of the service. But it was telling nonetheless.

Nobody was thinking of Facebook as a future rental platform for blockbuster movies, or Twitter as a vital promotional tool to drive consumer awareness of movies and TV shows. The availability of numerous forms of video-on-demand services was greatly expanded through content-licensing agreements between Hollywood studios and cable-system operators, satellite, and telco TV providers. Amid this expansion of content licensing on multiple fronts, there has been no uniformity among Hollywood's largest conglomerates. Decisions on the type of programming licensed and release windows have varied widely from shop to shop, which has tested the mettle of a legion of business-affairs executives accustomed to working within a set of long-established templates.

Even the nature of the uncertainty about where the industry is headed has changed. In the prestrike era, the pervasive mood was one of near panic about the prospect of digital distribution and piracy devastating film and television, just as it did to the music industry. In the months after the strike, the recession allowed the major studios to flex their muscle to downscale the creative community's pay scale virtually across the board. In this way, Hollywood mimicked many other large corporations in pre-emptively cutting jobs and costs as an insurance policy to protect profits.

At the same time, the studios, in varying degrees, displayed a greater willingness to open their vaults to the digital and video-on-demand realm. In the years following the strike, Hollywood took its first steps toward carving out new release windows for films and TV shows to take advantage of the ability to charge a premium for allowing viewers to access first-run programming on an on-demand basis. The concerns about the extra exposure eroding the traditional home video and syndication profit centers were still prevalent, but the studios could not ignore the highly competitive marketplace for content licensing that emerged in 2011, as Netflix, Hulu, Amazon, Microsoft's Xbox, and others sought to build up their streaming-media platforms. Otherwise, Hollywood would have left money on the table. By 2011 the major entertainment conglomerates were touting the growth of new media content-licensing revenue, in the United States and foreign markets, in quarterly earnings announcements.

The expansion of what became known as "over-the-top" outlets (distributors that rely on Internet distribution rather than cable or telephone wires or satellite dishes to reach subscribers) had a side benefit for the major networks and studios in setting benchmarks for the value of on-demand rights to top TV shows and new-release movies. It also added a new layer of complexity to contracts between traditional multichannel video providers—a.k.a. cable, satellite, and telco providers like Comcast, DirecTV, and Verizon Fios—and the major broadcast and cable networks.

As Netflix and other new entrants began offering viewers on-demand access to programming, traditional subscription TV providers were forced to respond with services of their own. But top cable channels like HBO, TNT, USA Network, FX, and others had generally been wary of making their shows available online for fear of encouraging consumers to drop their monthly subscription services. Those channels depend on the operators to pay the carriage fees that make up more than half of their revenue base. It is those carriage fees that make cable programming a more attractive business from a profit perspective than the free-to-air Big Four broadcast networks that rely almost exclusively on advertising sales for profits.

One attempt to solve this dilemma was a system that became known as "authentication." It allowed cable channels to make selected programs available for Web streaming, but only if the user was already a subscriber to a cable, satellite, or telco TV service. Users would be "authenticated" to access Web streaming through a range of platforms (including Hulu) via a password or embedded code provided by their operator. The plan was initially championed by two titans of the industry with much at stake in protecting the status quo: Time Warner chairman and CEO Jeffrey Bewkes and Comcast Corporation chairman and CEO Brian Roberts. Not only is Time Warner Hollywood's largest cable programmer, as the home of HBO, TNT, TBS, CNN, and the Cartoon Network, but its Warner Bros. unit is also the largest producer of films and TV shows. Comcast is the nation's largest cable operator and, as of 2011, the parent company of NBC Universal, home to USA Network, Syfy, E! Entertainment Television, Oxygen, MSNBC, and many other channels. Although the authentication process was technically complex and slow to roll out to consumers, online and on-demand rights to programming became an important bargaining chip for entertainment conglomerates in negotiating carriage agreements for their cable channels.

The same was true for broadcast TV station owners. The largest station groups, particularly the major-market stations owned by Fox, CBS, ABC, and NBC, began demanding significant carriage fees from cable and satellite operators. Broadcasters leveraged a nearly twenty-year-old Federal Communications Commission rule known as "retransmission consent" to force operators to pay monthly fees for the right to carry their stations. That requirement marked a strategy shift for station owners, and it led to a series of high-profile showdowns in which local stations were dropped, or threatened to be dropped, by operators.

The fact that broadcasters began focusing in the 2008–9 period on extracting big money from retransmission-consent rights underscored the volatility in the traditional TV marketplace and the recession-driven downturn in advertising sales. In exchange for the new fees, broadcast stations and the networks frequently granted operators expanded video-on-demand and Web-streaming rights, often with provisos that the same programming could not be made available to Netflix and other alternative platforms for days or even months. The accelerated growth of Web streaming was just one of many significant changes in the entertainment industry that occurred during the years that followed the end of the strike.

By the time WGA and AMPTP representatives sat down in February 2011 to negotiate the successor to the contract forged out of the strike, the outlook for the traditional business of Hollywood was at once more unknown and more promising than it was in 2008. The producer who lamented "there is no longer a way to make money in series television" shortly after the strike ended remained skeptical three years later, but was more optimistic after Netflix, Amazon, et al. began writing bigger checks to the studios for content-licensing deals.

In the immediate aftermath of the strike, there was much talk among writers of the Internet as a democratizing force that would allow content creators to bypass networks and studios in distributing their material to viewers. A handful of Internet-content ventures were assembled, some with high-profile WGA members as participants and investors. The most successful of these endeavors came from Joss Whedon, who spearheaded the production of *Dr. Horrible' s Sing-Along Blog*. The satirical forty-minute "supervillain musical" was released via Web streaming and Apple's iTunes in segments over three days in July 2008. The project benefited from a flood of media coverage, and the built-in audience appeal of stars Neil Patrick Harris and Nathan Fillion, not to mention Whedon's sizable following of *Buffy the Vampire Slayer* devotees. But even after *Dr. Horrible* made a splash, few Hollywood writers followed its cue with notable made-for-Internet productions. Whedon and the rest of the *Dr. Horrible* creative team returned to working on traditional TV and movie productions.

The studio chiefs were right when they warned in the summer of 2007 that the new media market for Hollywood content would evolve quickly in unforeseen ways. But events proved that the WGA was equally right to demand that the foundation for compensation be established. A three-year study would only have been inconclusive at best and out of date the moment it was finished.

The circumstances surrounding the negotiation of the WGA's 2011 master contract could not have been more different from the previous go-round. On Sunday, March 20, 2011, as a heavy rain pounded Los Angeles, the guild's negotiating committee reached an agreement with the AMPTP on a three-year successor to the contract forged by the one-hundred-day war. In 2011 there was no battle, not even a skirmish. The deal came together after three weeks of quiet negotiations, six weeks before the May 1 expiration of the 2008 contract. It marked the first time in a decade that WGA master-contract talks did not run past the expiration date—as was the case not only in the 2007–8 strike period but in the 2001 and 2004 negotiations as well.

What changed? Plenty. First and foremost, there was no groundswell among members to fight for economic gains this time around. Three years after the strike ended, many writers were still recovering from the financial hits absorbed during the work stoppage and the downsizing of production budgets and pay scales that followed. The broader economic turmoil spurred by the 2008 crisis in the financial markets had a humbling effect, as writers faced the same uncertainty about employment prospects and health care benefits as workers in other industries.

The marketplace gyrations were also unnerving to the creative community. Netflix's emergence as a credible alternative to traditional syndication was a welcome development, especially as it pursued a "long-tail" programming philosophy that benefited cult-favorite series and serialized programs that typically do not command top dollar for rerun rights. But most WGA members also were mindful of the previous decade's dot-com bubble. As Netflix's stock soared in the second half of 2010, topping out at $298.63 in July 2011 before sliding precipitously in the ensuing months, WGA members became as cautious as CEOs about their long-term expectations for the company.

The AMPTP was quick to capitalize on the trepidation among WGA members. The focus of the major Hollywood guilds for the 2011 contracts was shoring up health and pension plans that had incurred big losses from declines in the financial markets. The AMPTP steered its separate negotiations with SAG, the DGA, and the WGA to a template deal that offered an increase in the amount of money employers committed to each guild's health and pension plan in exchange for holding the line on base salary levels and virtually every residual and royalty rate—most especially the ones involving new media.

The leadership of the guild also underwent a significant change when John Wells beat Patric Verrone's favored successor in the WGA West's September 2009 election of officers and board members. That vote reflected the conflicting opinions among guild members on whether the strike had been justified. Wells ran on a pragmatist's platform of tempering the militant rhetoric and working more closely with the DGA and SAG on future negotiations. He downplayed the reality-organizing cause in favor of issues with weight to prominent screenwriters and showrunners, such as the studios' practice of insisting on rewrites without compensation and the "bake-off" approach of hiring multiple writers to work separately on the same idea or adaptation for a feature screenplay.

Wells prevailed by a slim margin in the contest for president against the Writers United candidate, Elias Davis. Wells benefited from name recognition—which is always an advantage in Hollywood guild elections—and his past experience as guild president from 2001 to 2003. But writers rejected the other two candidates on Wells's ticket for the vice president and secretary-treasurer officer posts. They also elected or reelected to the WGA West board of directors numerous members who were part of Verrone's Writers United slate or were vocal proponents of the strike—including Verrone.

In keeping with WGA West tradition, Verrone did not seek a third term after serving two consecutive terms. But he handily won his bid for a seat on the board. In fact, Verrone commanded more votes in the election than any other candidate, including Wells, with Verrone drawing 1,364 votes, or more than half of the 2,348 ballots cast, to Wells's 1,191. In the fall of 2009, WGA West members continued to have great respect and admiration for Verrone, but a majority responded to Wells's message.

John Bowman returned to the bargaining table in 2011 as cochairman of the WGA negotiating committee, alongside screenwriter Billy Ray. Ray was among the group of prominent screenwriters who were privately critical of WGA leadership after the DGA reached its contract agreement with the AMPTP in January 2008. But if there were divisions among WGA

negotiators in 2011, they did not surface in public. The prevailing sentiment was that the hard work had been done the last time around.

In the heady days after the end of the strike, Verrone, Young, and other
WGA leaders were hailed by writers for their bravery and determination—even winning kudos from those individuals who pushed the guild
to end the walkout after the DGA reached its agreement. But the Verrone
administration's reputation took a big hit just two months later when the
WGA West board and WGA East council made the decision to release the
names of twenty-eight guild members who opted to give up most of their
membership privileges in the guild in order to continue working during
the strike. At a moment when WGA members were buoyed by solidarity,
members who made that choice were viewed as cowardly turncoats by
many other members. WGA members who elect to change their status to
"financial core," or fi-core, are prevented from voting in WGA elections,
running for guild office, and participating in the annual Writers Guild
Awards competition. Financial-core members are covered by guild contracts and are eligible to participate in the health and pension plans.

During the strike, one established film and TV writer, John Ridley,
announced his decision to go financial core with an op-ed piece in the *Los
Angeles Times* that detailed his grievances with the guild over the strike
and other issues. But the remaining twenty-seven members made no such
move to publicize their status change. Although guild members disparaged those who went fi-core, there was even more outrage spurred by
the WGA leaders' decision to identify them in a message sent to all guild
members. To some it recalled the McCarthy era of "naming names" in the
1950s when Hollywood was governed by the blacklist.

The e-mail message sent to members on April 18, 2008, from Verrone
and Michael Winship decried the actions of the "puny few" who "must be
held at arm's length by the rest of us and judged accountable for what they
are—strikebreakers whose actions placed everything for which we fought
so hard at risk." The strident tone in the mass mailing was off-putting and
puzzling to many WGA members. That sentiment was reflected in a blog
post by screenwriter John August titled "Ugh." "If anything, it's a call to
unsheath the swords once again, this time to fight enemies among us,"

August wrote in the April 20, 2008, post. "Trying to reignite the flames of guild fury over 28 names is ridiculous. It makes the guild look as crazy as the AMPTP tried to portray us."

Another cloud that lingered over the Verrone regime was the disciplinary action brought against Jay Leno by the WGA's Strike Rules Compliance Committee. The committee pursued the charge that Leno had violated two of the WGA's strike rules by writing his monologue after he returned to work on NBC's *Tonight Show* in January 2008. Leno was questioned before a trial committee composed of five WGA members on two occasions in February and June 2009—more than a year after the end of the strike. The length of time that had elapsed made many guild members question the need to pursue the action at all. It also raised the question of why Leno was the only one of the WGA-member late-night hosts who faced charges in connection with resuming their shows in the middle of the strike.

In the end, the WGA West board of directors decided to take disciplinary action for strike-rule violations against two members, and it also permanently barred a nonmember from joining the guild after he was found guilty of submitting scripts to a struck company for a daytime serial. Leno was ultimately cleared of the charges. The trial-committee report concluded that the host "has been done a disservice and his reputation harmed by these proceedings and (we) believe he is owed a public apology by the guild."

The trial-committee report detailed a series of reversals by the WGA, including its decision to strike an interim agreement with David Letterman's Worldwide Pants after telling Leno it would not do so and conflicting instructions on what was permissible for him in regards to his monologue. The report also cited testimony from the AMPTP's Carol Lombardini about Verrone's promise that the guild would not pursue action against Leno. According to the report, Verrone gave the assurance in front of Lombardini, Bob Iger, and Peter Chernin in response to a request from an NBC Universal executive in the waning hours of negotiations before the strike was halted. Verrone later said he never relayed that statement to the Strike Rules Compliance Committee or the WGA West board. The report also acknowledged the "political pressure" on WGA

West leadership to bring charges against Leno because of the remarks in his first monologue back that stirred such ire among hard-core strike supporters. But coming a year after the picket lines came down, the focus on Leno seemed misguided to many members.

The WGA West never offered a mea culpa to Leno. When the details of the trial-committee report surfaced in *Daily Variety*, David Young told the newspaper, "Jay Leno does not owe the guild an apology, nor vice versa."

SAG underwent an even more dramatic leadership transformation in the aftermath of the strike. Forty-eight hours after the writers' strike ended, the AMPTP issued a statement pressuring SAG to immediately begin contract negotiations. That same day, February 14, 2008, four of SAG's most high-profile members took out a full-page ad in *Variety* asking both sides to begin talks as soon as possible for a successor to the contract that would expire on June 30. The ad signed by George Clooney, Robert De Niro, Tom Hanks, and Meryl Streep asserted that "nothing can be solved until both parties agree to sit down together and JUST TALK. Not later, but now. There's too much at stake to wait."

Despite the pressure from the studios and the stars, contract talks between SAG and the AMPTP did not begin for another two months, and SAG would not come to terms on a contract for more than a year, until June 2009. In the intervening months, the strong-willed Doug Allen was fired as SAG's executive director and chief negotiator, and Alan Rosenberg's faction gradually lost their grip on SAG's national board of directors. A new faction of members critical of Allen and Rosenberg's militant approach ran for board seats and officer positions on the platform that actors had suffered while SAG's idealistic leaders pursued quixotic goals. Ken Howard, a veteran actor best known as the star of the 1978–81 CBS drama series *The White Shadow*, easily won the September 2009 election for national president of the guild over Rosenberg ally Anne-Marie Johnson.

In November 2010, SAG was the first of the guilds to reach an agreement with the AMPTP on a successor contract. After the long struggle, the AMPTP insisted that SAG's 2009 contract (which was backdated to 2008 to keep it in sync with the WGA and DGA deals) mandated that SAG agree to six weeks of bargaining in October 2010, in an effort to avoid the pressure of negotiating up against the deadline of the June 2011 contract expiration.

The lack of organized opposition among WGA members to the successor contract reached by the guild in March 2011 spoke volumes about the state of the creative community, three years after the debilitating work stoppage. Nerves were rattled, among writers and executives alike, a few months later when Patric Verrone declared himself a candidate for the presidency of the WGA West. Although his campaigning was minimal and employed none of the fiery rhetoric of the past, there was a consensus among many that electing Verrone would signal to the studios that writers were looking for another fight.

On September 16, six years almost to the day that Verrone's Writers United coalition first swept into elected guild positions on a tide of discontent, John Wells's ally Christopher Keyser defeated Verrone for the presidency. The margin of victory was wide enough to make a statement, with Keyser drawing 60.2 percent of 2,102 ballots cast, compared to 39.8 percent for Verrone. The membership that Verrone galvanized four years before had already moved on.

Notes

Index

Notes

Introduction

1. Information about the November 9, 2007, mass rally outside the Fox Plaza building comes from the author's firsthand reporting.

1. Fear of the Unknown

1. WGA press release, "Writers Guilds Issue Pattern of Demands for Contract 2007 Negotiations," May 18, 2007.

2. News conference, WGA West headquarters, November 2, 2007.

3. AMPTP transcript, "Producers Respond to WGA Proposals," July 18, 2007.

4. Author's interview, December 17, 2008.

5. Aaron Smith, Pew Internet and American Life Project, "Home Broadband 2010," Pew Research Center, Washington, DC.

6. Nielsen, "State of the Media: DVR Use in the U.S.," December 2010.

7. Brian Steinberg, "Advertisers Champing at Bit for Nielsen's First C3 Ratings," *Advertising Age*, October 8, 2007.

8. Disney acquired Pixar Animation Studios for $7.5 billion in 2006.

9. Cynthia Littleton, "On the Download: Dialogue with Anne Sweeney," *Hollywood Reporter*, September 26, 2006.

10. Author's interview, October 16, 2008.

11. Joint Statement from the Writers Guilds of America, East and West; Directors Guild of America; and Screen Actors Guild on CBS Internet Television Program Streaming, WGA/DGA/SAG press release, August 17, 2006.

12. 2004 Writers Guild of America–Alliance of Motion Picture and Television Producers Theatrical and Television Minimum Basic Agreement.

13. The first in the wave of self-dealing lawsuits was filed by Wind Dancer Productions, the company behind the hit ABC sitcom *Home Improvement*, against Disney in February 2007. Joe Flint, "Disney *Home* Invasion," *Daily Variety*, February 25, 1997. Among the high-profile suits that followed included David Duchovny's claim against 20th Century Fox

for profits on *The X-Files,* Steven Bochco against 20th Century Fox for *NYPD Blue,* and Alan Alda against 20th Century Fox for *MASH.* Like the Wind Dancer case, all were eventually settled out of court. Jenny Hontz, "Disney, Wind Dancer Settle," *Daily Variety,* April 8, 1999.

14. Author's interview, February 12, 2008.

15. Author's interview, May 2008.

2. Path to the Picket Line

1. Unless otherwise noted, information on the November 4, 2007, WGA-AMPTP negotiating session at the Sofitel hotel came from interviews with more than ten people with firsthand knowledge of the negotiating sessions and other events that transpired that day.

2. Author's interview, October 16, 2008.

3. Author's interview, March 16, 2009.

4. Richard Verrier and Claudia Eller, "Countdown to a Walkout," *Los Angeles Times,* November 6, 2007.

5. Author's interview, December 12, 2008.

6. "SEIU Members: Settlement Is the 'Write' Thing," SEIU press release, February 13, 2008.

7. The Screen Writers Guild also faced internal dissent that weakened its ability to present a united front in demanding recognition from the studios.

8. Information about the first day of picketing is based on author's firsthand reporting and other media accounts.

9. Author's interview, March 23, 2009.

10. Dave McNary, "Teamsters Support WGA Picket Lines," *Daily Variety,* October 29.

11. Author's interview, December 16, 2008.

12. *United Hollywood, The Office Is Closed,* November 6, 2007.

13. Sandra Oh, Ellen Pompeo, and Katherine Heigl comments from *United Hollywood* video *Sandra Oh: "How Greedy Can They Get??"*

14. Author's interview, March 16, 2009.

3. Sowing the Seeds

1. Biographical information for Patric Verrone comes from WGA West materials, media reports, and author's interviews.

2. Author's interview, August 2008.

3. Olivier Knox, "Sculptor in Chief: *Futurama* Writer Saves Lives of Tiny Presidents," *Wired,* October 19, 2009.

4. *WGAW President Patric Verrone Speaking on Media Ownership,* WGA West video, October 3, 2006.

5. Tanja Barnes, Verrone interview, *Writers Strike Chronicles* podcast, February 28, 2008.

6. Verrone interview, *Sunday Morning Shootout,* AMC, November 30, 2006.

7. *Writers Strike Chronicles* podcast.

8. Numerous sources have corroborated this account, including the author's interview with Mike Scully, December 16, 2008, and Nick Madigan, "WGAW, Fox in on Toon Pact," *Daily Variety*, August 17, 2008.

9. Dave McNary, "Scribe Tribe Screed," *Daily Variety*, August 31, 2005; Jesse Hiestand, "Verrone's Writers United Sweeps WGA West Vote," *Hollywood Reporter*, September 21, 2005; Patric Verrone, letter to WGA West Members, October 5, 2005.

10. Biographical information for David Young comes from WGA West materials, media reports, and author's interviews.

11. Peter Sanders, Sam Schechner, and Merissa Marr, "Guild's Blue-Collar Guy Gets a Starring Role," *Wall Street Journal*, December 4, 2007.

12. *WGA West Member News*, May 2007.

13. *WGA West Member News*, September 2006.

14. *WGA West Member News*, September 2007.

15. Claudia Eller and Richard Verrier, "Negotiator Cast as Hero—or Hindrance," *Los Angeles Times*, November 12, 2007.

16. Information on the WGA West leadership turmoil in this period comes from media reports, the author's interviews, and the WGA West–commissioned report on the contested 2003 election by William B. Gould, "In the Matter of 2003 WGAW Election Protest: Report and Recommendations," January 5, 2004.

17. Dave McNary, "Scribes Backing New Prez," *Daily Variety*, January 7, 2004.

18. Dave McNary, "Prez Written Out," *Daily Variety*, March 19, 2004.

19. The first Writers United slate of candidates comprised Verrone, David N. Weiss, Elias Davis, Phil Alden Robinson, Tom Schulman, Howard Rodman, Dan Wilcox, Robert King, Nick Kazan, Peter Lefcourt, Joan Meyerson, and Scott Frank. Roger Wolfson, "How the WGA Won: A Behind the Scenes Look at the WGA Strike," *Huffington Post*, February 12, 2008.

20. Dave McNary, "WGA Puts Up Pair for Prexy Post," *Daily Variety*, June 24, 2005.

21. WGA press release, "WGAW Officer and Board Election Results," September 20, 2005.

22. Wolfson, "How the WGA Won."

23. Dave McNary, "WGA Chief Gets Axed in Rewrite," *Daily Variety*, September 28, 2005.

24. Verrone, letter to WGA West members, October 5, 2005.

25. David Young, "David (Us) & Goliath (Them): History of the Reality Campaign," undated essay, WGA.org.

26. Robert Battista, Wilma Liebman, Dennis Walsh, Writers Guild of America West, Inc., Universal Network Television, LLC, and NBC Studios, Inc., National Labor Relations Board decision and order, July 31, 2007.

27. WGA press release, "Writers Reach Ground-Breaking Mobile Content Agreement on ABC's TV Series *Lost*," April 26, 2006.

28. Dave McNary, "TV Trio Tackles Trouble on TCA Panel," *Daily Variety*, July 14, 2007.

29. Dave McNary, "WGA Reality Check," *Daily Variety*, June 21, 2005.

30. Daniel J. Blau, "The WGA Already Lost Round 1," *Los Angeles Times*, November 20, 2007.

31. Dave McNary, "Tensions Fan *Model* Flame," *Daily Variety*, July 28, 2006.

32. *WGA West Member News*, September 2006.

33. Carl DiOrio, "WGAW Members Rally for Reality Show Writers," *Hollywood Reporter*, September 21, 2006.

34. Dave McNary, "*Model* Writers Threaten Walkout," *Daily Variety*, July 21, 2006.

35. Dave McNary, "WGA, IATSE Take Off Gloves," *Daily Variety*, December 6, 2006.

36. Carl DiOrio, "Counter: Set Up WGA Talks," *Hollywood Reporter*, November 28, 2006.

37. Author's interview, May 23, 2008.

38. Verrone interview, *Sunday Morning Shootout*, AMC, November 30, 2006.

4. Brinksmanship Across the Table

1. Information about the Chair Incident comes from author's interviews and media reports.

2. T. L. Stanley, "Writers Guild Protests TV Product Placements," *Advertising Age*, September 27, 2005.

3. Marc Graser and T. L. Stanley, "Actors, Writers Unions Protest at Madison and Vine," *Advertising Age*, February 13, 2006.

4. Author's interview, July 2008.

5. Producers' Comprehensive Proposal to the Writers Guild of America, West, Inc., and Writers Guild of America, East, Inc., July 16, 2007; Producers' Proposals to the WGA—Limited Issues Package, July 16, 2007.

6. Jim Benson, "Producers Make Dramatic Call for Residuals Revamp," *Broadcasting and Cable*, July 11, 2007.

7. Greg Hernandez, "Writers Rallying in Fight for Benefits," *Los Angeles Daily News*, September 21, 2006.

8. WGA video, *Writers Guild Contract 2007 Negotiations Press Briefing*, July 18, 2007.

9. "Contract 2007 Opening Remarks from Negotiating Committee Chairman John F. Bowman," WGA press release, July 18, 2007.

10. Author's interview, July 2008.

11. AMPTP press release, July 16, 2007.

12. WGA press release, July 16, 2007.

13. Information drawn from author's interviews with firsthand witnesses to the negotiating session.

14. WGA video, July 18, 2007.

15. Ibid.

16. Ibid.

17. Michael Schneider, "Networks Commit Through '08," *Variety*, August 12, 2007.

18. Author's interview, February 2008.

19. WGA press release, September 18, 2007.

20. Author's interview, December 12, 2008.

21. Author's interview, October 16, 2008.

22. AMPTP press release, October 5, 2007.

23. Dave McNary, "Directors Want Final Cut on WGA's Rules," *Daily Variety*, October 29, 2007; Writers Guild of America, West, 2007 Strike Rules.

24. Dave McNary, "Biz Bunkers Down," *Daily Variety*, October 16, 2007.

25. Dave McNary, "Short's Temper," *Daily Variety*, October 12, 2007.

26. Dave McNary, "A Break in the Fever?," *Daily Variety*, October 17, 2007.

27. "Writers Guild Strike Authorization Vote Passes by Resounding Majority, Vote Draws Record High Turnout," WGA press release, October 19, 2007.

28. WGA press release, October 25, 2007.

29. Dave McNary, "Vid Bid Hits Wall," *Daily Variety*, November 1, 2007.

30. Information on the WGA's November 1 Los Angeles Convention Center meeting comes from author's interviews, WGA video, and media reports on the event.

31. Author's interview, December 16, 2008.

32. *Writer Speaks Out*, WGA video, November 1, 2007.

33. Information on the November 2 news conference at WGA West headquarters comes from author's firsthand reporting.

5. United Showrunners

1. Information about the November 3, 2007, meeting of showrunners at the Sheraton Universal comes from author's interviews with participants.

2. Author's interview, December 11, 2008.

3. Author's interview, December 2008.

4. Author's interview, December 11, 2008.

5. "Pencils Down Means Pencils Down" advertisement, *Daily Variety*, November 1, 2007, 9.

6. Author's interview, December 19, 2008.

7. Ibid.

8. *American Broadcasting Cos. v. Writers Guild*, 437 US 411 (1978).

9. "WGA Issues Pattern of Demands for Contract 2007 Negotiations," WGA press release, May 18, 2007.

10. Author's interview, December 11, 2008.

11. Information about the WGA's internal dissent in the 1985 and 1988 strikes comes from author's interviews and numerous media sources, including John Horn, "Shootout at the WGA Corral," *Los Angeles Times*, September 1, 1985; Michael Cieply and Lee Margulies, "Writers Rejection of Pact May Further Slow Industry," *Los Angeles Times*, June 24, 1988;

Aljean Harmetz, "Some Striking Writers Give Ultimatum to Guild," *New York Times,* July 16, 1988; Lionel Chetwynd, Michael Russnow, Brenda Lilly, at the table, Patric M. Verrone, Larry Gelbart, Lynn Roth, and Peter Lefcourt, "Seven Letters to the Editor: A Roundtable Discussion on Politics in the Writers Guild of America," *Written By,* April 2005.

12. Author's interview, December 11, 2008.

13. Author's interview, December 16, 2008.

14. Author's interview, October 16, 2008.

15. Author's interview, December 2008.

16. Information on the November 7, 2007, showrunners' picket and lunch meeting comes from author's interviews with participants and media reports.

17. Josh Friedman, *I Find Your Lack of Faith Disturbing* blog, posted January 10, 2006.

18. Author's interview, December 2008.

19. Ibid.

20. Author's interview, December 19, 2008.

21. "A Portrait of Generation Next," Pew Research Center for the People and the Press, January 9, 2007.

22. Laeta Kalogridis, "Nikki Finke Is Clairvoyant—or Maybe the Playbook Is Too Obvious," *United Hollywood,* December 7, 2007.

23. Michael Schur, "A Modest Proposal: CEOs Go First," *United Hollywood,* November 11, 2007.

24. Joss Whedon, "Do Not Adjust Your Mindset," *United Hollywood,* February 6, 2008.

25. Author's interview, December 19, 2008.

26. Author's interview, March 23, 2009.

6. Angst in the Executive Suite

1. Author's interview, December 2008.

2. The difference stems from the fact that residuals for broadcast TV reruns of a program are based on a percentage of the applicable WGA minimum payment a writer would receive for that kind of program. Residuals for basic-cable reruns are based on a percentage of the revenue generated by the sale of the program.

3. Author's interview, December 17, 2008.

4. Dave McNary and Elizabeth Guider, "Sabers Rattle in Labor Fray," *Daily Variety,* July 12, 2007, 1.

5. WGA West video of July 18, 2007, news conference, WGA.org.

6. Author's interview, December 2008.

7. The Association of Talent Agents' last franchise agreement with SAG expired in 2002, after more than a year of negotiations to revamp the terms to allow agencies more flexibility in their ownership structures and to enhance their ability to help finance productions featuring their clients—which SAG views as a conflict of interest. SAG and ATA

have not come to terms on a new pact, but the sides have generally abided by the terms of the expired agreement.

8. Information about the meeting of top talent agents and Bryan Lourd's and outreach to the WGA comes from author's extensive interviews with firsthand participants and media reports. Nikki Finke, "Talks Restarted at Bryan Lourd's Home after Weeks of Quiet Backchannel," *Deadline Hollywood,* November 17, 2007.

9. According to the no-strike clause in SAG's master film and TV contract with the AMPTP, actors who were under contract to AMPTP signatory companies were barred from withholding their services in sympathy with the WGA strike, even if it meant crossing a picket line.

10. *Actors in Support of Writers—Universal Studios, United Hollywood* video, November 13, 2007.

11. *Picketing with the Stars,* WGA West video, November 13, 2007.

12. Information and quotations from the WGA's Hollywood Boulevard march come from videos of the event posted on YouTube and media reports. Dave McNary, "The Rally Before the Rematch," *Daily Variety,* November 21, 2007, 1; "Hollywood Rally for Hollywood Writers: WGA Stages Solidarity Rally and March Through the Heart of Hollywood," WGA press release, November 20, 2007.

13. Harold Meyerson and Kate Sheppard, "Hollywood on Strike: Union Leaders Talk," *American Prospect,* November 16, 2007.

14. Author's interview, May 1, 2009.

7. Rallies, Retrenchment, and Late-Night Returns

1. Information about the bargaining sessions at the Renaissance Hotel comes from author's interviews with firsthand participants.

2. "According to the WGA, the AMPTP's $130 Million Looks a Lot Like $32 million," *Variety*'s *Scribe Vibe* blog, December 4, 2007.

3. AMPTP statement, November 29, 2007.

4. Patric Verrone and Michael Winship, letter to WGA members, November 29, 2007.

5. Author's interview, March 23, 2009.

6. Information about the November 30, 2007, Hollywood Homecoming rally comes from the author's firsthand reporting.

7. Cynthia Littleton, "Poll: WGA Wins Hearts; Studios Retain Muscle," *Daily Variety,* November 26, 2007, 1.

8. Author's interview, December 12, 2008.

9. Peter Bart, "'They' Shoot Writers, Don't They," *Variety,* December 24, 2007, 1.

10. Dave McNary, "Sides Talking in Sequel Terms," *Daily Variety,* November 29, 2007, 1.

11. Nielsen Media Research ratings data for Persons 2-Plus, January 1–March 31, 2007, compared to January 1–March 31, 2008.

12. Cynthia Littleton and Michael Schneider, "Conan Foots Staff Bill," *Daily Variety*, November 30, 2009, 1.

13. Information on the discussions among late-night hosts comes from interviews with firsthand participants and media reports.

14. Michael Winship, letter to WGA East members, December 10, 2007.

15. Dave McNary, "Direct Action," *Daily Variety*, December 6, 2007, 1.

16. WGA statement, December 5, 2007.

17. AMPTP statement, December 5, 2007.

18. Patric Verrone and Michael Winship, letter to WGA members, December 7, 2007.

19. Information and quotations from the December 7, 2007, Fremantle rally come from the author's firsthand reporting.

20. AMPTP statement, December 7, 2007.

21. Information on the December 7 bargaining session at the InterContinental Hotel comes from interviews with firsthand participants, WGA and AMPTP statements, and media reports.

22. AMPTP transcript of Carol Lombardini statement, December 7, 2007.

8. Cue the Directors

1. Information about the DGA's preparations for contract negotiations comes from interviews with firsthand participants and media reports.

2. Michael Apted, letter to DGA members, December 13, 2007.

3. AMPTP statement, December 7, 2007.

4. Author's interview, October 16, 2008.

5. Statement from IATSE president Thomas Short, December 7, 2007.

6. Author's interview, March 23, 2009.

7. "AMPTP Breaks Off Talks," WGA press release, December 7, 2007.

8. AMPTP Fact Sheet, December 7, 2007.

9. Michael Winship letter, December 10, 2007.

10. Author's interview, March 23, 2009.

11. Author's interview, December 19, 2008.

12. Information on the Jami Gertz Hanukkah dinner comes from interviews with participants.

13. Josef Adalian, "Strike Beards Fever: Catch It!," *Variety*'s *Scribe Vibe* blog, December 11, 2007.

14. Josef Adalian, "A Late Shift Comeback?," *Daily Variety*, November 16, 2007, 1.

15. NBC press release, December 17, 2007.

16. "Notice to All WGA Members Writing for Comedy/Variety Shows," WGA message to members, December 17, 2007.

17. "Writers Guild Reaches Agreement with Worldwide Pants," WGA press release, December 28, 2007.

18. Author's interview, December 12, 2008.

19. "Legal Eagle," *DGA Quarterly* (Spring 2008).

20. "DGA and AMPTP Reach Tentative Agreement on Terms of New Contract," DGA press release, January 17, 2008.

21. "Writers Guild Decides on Golden Globes and Academy Awards Show Waivers," WGA press release, December 17, 2007.

22. Information about the December 19 Los Angeles City Council hearing comes from the author's firsthand reporting.

9. Deal or No Deal?

1. Information about Alan Wertheimer's hiring by the WGA comes from interviews with firsthand participants and media reports. Cynthia Littleton, "Dealmaker Worked to End Strike," *Variety*, February 17, 2008, 3.

2. AMPTP statement, January 17, 2008.

3. DGA press release, January 17, 2008.

4. AMPTP signatory companies fund DGA, WGA, and SAG pension and health funds through payments that are based on a fixed percentage of guild members' earnings—on top of the total compensation employers pay guild members. In contrast to other private employer-provided health plans, guild members are not required to make a matching contribution. But guild members have to meet certain earning thresholds to be eligible for health coverage.

5. DGA press release, January 17, 2008.

6. Information about the January 19 meeting of the WGA negotiating committee at John Bowman's house comes from interviews with several firsthand participants.

7. Marc Graser and Tatiana Siegel, "Power Outage," *Daily Variety*, January 10, 2008, 1; Josef Adalian and Michael Schneider, "Black Monday Brings Blitz of Pinkslips," *Daily Variety*, January 15, 1.

8. Cynthia Littleton, "Guilds Flatten the Globes," *Daily Variety*, January 8, 2008, 1.

9. Gina Serpe and Marc Malkin, "NBC Can't Spin New-Look Globes," *E! Online*, January 7, 2008.

10. "Dear Ben Silverman: Prom Is Not Canceled," *United Hollywood*, January 8, 2008.

11. Information on the discussions between WGA officials and Jay Leno regarding his *Tonight Show* monologue comes from interviews with firsthand participants, media reports, and the final report from the WGA West's five-member trial committee following hearings on Leno charges in 2009. "WGA vs. Jay Leno Trial Committee Report," August 2009.

12. *The Tonight Show with Jay Leno*, January 2, 2008.

13. Larry Mantle (host), *AirTalk*, KPCC-FM (Pasadena, Calif.), January 3, 2008.

14. Cynthia Littleton, "WGA West Board Member David Weiss: 'It's about Walking in the Rain,'" *Variety*'s *Scribe Vibe* blog, January 4, 2008.

15. Information about the January 10 meeting comes from interviews with firsthand participants and media reports, including Richard Verrier and Claudia Eller, "Private Overtures Led to Strike Breakthroughs," *Los Angeles Times*, February 12, 2008.

16. In May 2009, Endeavor orchestrated a takeover of its larger rival, the William Morris Agency. The tightening of the poststrike job market for writers was a major factor in Endeavor's pursuit of the merger.

17. John Aboud, "Breaking: Ben Silverman Prom Postponed Due to DGA Negotiations," *United Hollywood*, January 14, 2008.

18. Letter from Patric Verrone and Michael Winship to WGA members, January 22, 2008.

10. The Finish Line

1. Information on the Paul Attanasio dinner comes from interviews with participants and media reports, including Richard Verrier and Claudia Eller, "Private Overtures Led to Strike Breakthrough," *Los Angeles Times*, February 12, 2008, 1.

2. John Wells letter posted on *The Artful Writer* blog, January 18, 2008.

3. Author's interviews on picket line at NBC, January 18, 2008.

4. Craig Mazin, "Howard Gould on Unity, Demonology, and the Legend of the Dirty Thirty," *The Artful Writer*, February 15, 2008.

5. Author's interview, March 23, 2009.

6. Information about the January 22 Luxe Hotel meeting comes from interviews with firsthand participants and media reports.

7. Author's interview, March 16, 2009.

8. Author's interview, May 1, 2009.

9. Josef Adalian, "Moonves, Verrone, and Young: Let's Do Dinner," *Variety*'s *Scribe Vibe* blog, January 27, 2008.

10. Dave McNary, "Gotham Gathering Comes . . . Then Goes," *Daily Variety*, January 31, 2008, 1.

11. Dave McNary, "SAG Stirs Things Up," *Daily Variety*, January 30, 1.

12. Author's interview, December 12, 2008.

13. Information about the Magic Castle party comes from interviews with firsthand participants.

14. Verrier and Eller, "Private Overtures Led to Strike Breakthrough," 1.

15. Author's interview, February 4, 2008.

16. Message from Patric Verrone and Michael Winship to WGA members, February 5, 2008.

17. Timothy M. Gray, "Oscar Seeks Good Vibes from Scribes," *Daily Variety*, February 7, 2008, 1.

18. Information and quotations come from the author's firsthand coverage of the February 7 picket.

19. Message from Patric Verrone and Michael Winship to WGA members, February 8, 2008.

20. Dade Hayes, "NY Meeting Comes to an End," *Variety*'s *Scribe Vibe* blog, February 9, 2008.

21. Information and quotations from attendees of the February 9 Shrine Auditorium meeting come from the author's interviews outside the Shrine.

22. Information and quotations from the WGA's February 12 press conference come from the author's firsthand coverage.

11. The Bloodletting

1. Writers Guild of America, West, Inc., Annual Financial Report, June 29, 2010.

2. Author's interview, December 12, 2008.

3. Author's interview, May 1, 2009.

4. William Triplett and Cynthia Littleton, "TV Biz Told to Prep for Major Makeover," *Daily Variety*, January 30, 2008, 7.

5. WGA West 2009 annual report; Darnell M. Hunt, PhD, Writers Guild of America, West, "Rewriting an All-Too-Familiar Story?," 2009 Hollywood Writers Report, May 2009.

6. 2007 WGAW Annual Report, June 10, 2007.

7. Writers Guild of America, West, Inc., Annual Financial Report, May 29, 2009.

8. WGA West 2009 Annual Report.

9. Ibid.

10. 2009 Hollywood Writers Report.

11. Author's interview, May 23, 2008.

12. Author's interview, March 23, 2009.

13. Author's interview, December 11, 2008.

14. Author's interview, July 22, 2008.

15. Author's interview, December 17, 2008.

16. Author's interview, March 23, 2009.

17. Author's interview, December 17, 2008.

18. Author's interview, May 1, 2009.

19. Author's interview, December 17, 2008.

20. Author's interview, March 23, 2009.

21. Author's interview, May 1, 2009.

22. Video of February 10, 2008, news conference, WGA.org.

23. Author's interview, July 22, 2008.

24. Author's interview, December 16, 2008.

25. Author's interview, March 16, 2009.

26. Author's interview, December 12, 2008.

27. Author's interview, March 23, 2009.

28. Author's interview, May 1, 2009.

29. WGA West video of February 10, 2008, news conference, WGA.org.

30. Author's interview, December 11, 2008.

Index

ABC, 114, 135; Academy Awards, 184, 201, 216, 225–26; iTunes and, 6, 10–15, 54–55. *See also specific show*

ABC.com, 6, 14, 54–55

Aboud, John, 93, 94–95, 109, 112, 174

Academy Awards, 184, 201, 216, 225–26

Academy of Motion Picture Arts and Sciences (AMPAS), 184, 226

actors, 35–36, 37. *See also* Screen Actors Guild (SAG); *specific actor*

Advertising Age, 65

advertising and marketing: AMPTP's recoupment proposal and, 70; audience funneling function of, 8–9; DVRs and ad skipping, 8–10; Internet as promotional activity, 14–15, 116–17, 192–93, 222; poststrike, 234; product placement, 8, 17; profits, 2–3, 7, 168, 209; protests against, 65; showrunners "Pencils Down" ad, 92; social media and, 256; Web streaming and, 6, 11, 14–15. *See also* market share and ratings; viewership

Albers, Chris, 189

Alda, Alan, 269n13

Alexander, Jason, 129

Alias, 14

Allen, Doug, 119, 138–39, 220, 264

Allen, Woody, 148

Alliance of Motion Picture and Television Producers (AMPTP), xiv, 2; charter, 113; leadership of, 113–14, 115, 134–36, 150, 169; New Economic Partnership, 140–44, 155–58; as picketing site, 185; public relations, 134, 148–51, 156, 160, 170, 173; recoupment proposal, 65–72, 80–81, 83, 118, 120–22, 156; strategy of, 27–28, 65, 118–19, 134–36, 138, 165, 169–71, 240–43; study proposal, 63, 65–72, 120. *See also specific executive or member*

Amazon, 257, 259

American Federation of Television and Radio Artists (AFTRA), 59, 205, 206

American Gladiators, 152

American Idol, xiv, 135, 152, 156, 159

America's Most Wanted, 102

America's Next Top Model, xix, 50–51, 55–56; walkout, 57–62, 65, 69

Anderson, Brooke, 203

animation, 79, 115, 163, 170–74, 198; New Economic Partnership (AMPTP) and, 142, 156

Anisa Productions, 58–59

antitrust investigations, 114, 115

Apatow, Judd, xiv–xv

Apple, Inc., 1–2, 10–14, 252. *See also specific product*

Apted, Michael, 167, 168, 169

arbitration and mediation, 82–83, 101

Army Wives, 105

Artful Writer, The (blog), 146, 216

Association of Talent Agents (ATA), 122–25, 274n7

Attanasio, Paul, 212

audience. *See* viewership

August, John, 146, 262–63

Avenue of the Stars, xi, xii, xiv, xv, xvii, xxii

award shows, 184, 201–4, 216, 219, 225–26

Baby Borrowers, 152

Baer, Neal, 85, 98, 121–22, 160, 162, 164, 241

Banks, Tyra, 58

Bart, Peter, 149

Bass, Ron, 197–98

benefits. *See* health and medical benefits; pensions

"Ben Silverman High Winter Prom," 204, 210

Berg, Jeff, 123

Berkus, Jim, 123

Berman, Jeff, 93

Bewkes, Jeffrey, 258

Big Brother, 151

Big Love, 153

BitTorrent.com, 11

Black, Jack, 158, 161

blacklisting, 31, 262–63

Black Wednesday, 200

Blau, Daniel, 58, 60

blogs, 93–95, 109–11, 146–47, 156, 213

Bocho, Steven, 269n13

Bodow, Steve, 189

Bones, 105

Bowe, Kai, 161

Bowman, John, xvii, 4, 23–24, 39, 71, 191, 261; on AMPTP's recoupment proposal, 69–70; attends LA City Council meeting, 185–87; Chair Incident, 64–65, 82; on importance of Internet in organizing, 249–50; leadership role and style, xvii, 98–99, 216, 248–49; Levitan and, 125–26; on sense of community among writers, 112

Braff, Zach, 129

brand name placement, 8, 17

broadcast and network television, 1, 102; competition, 117; contingency strike plans, 36–39, 72–74; development season, 38; fin-syn rule, 18–20; golden era of, 20–21; poststrike, 234–37, 258–59; retransmission-consent rights, 258–59. *See also* prime-time television; *specific network or show*

Brogliatti, Barbara, 150

Brolin, Josh, 148

By Ken Levine (blog), 146

cable television, xx, 1, 98, 117; authentication, 258; Internet vs., 4; poststrike, 234, 238–39, 246, 257–58; programming, 153; residuals and, 69, 80–81, 238–39, 274n2; scripted shows, 238

Cagney, James, 30

Caliendo, Frank, 98

Camera, Jorge, 201–2

Cantor, Eddie, 30

Capital Cities/ABC, Inc., 18

Carell, Steve, 35

Carson, Johnny, 154, 177–78

Carvell, Tim, 189

Cates, Gilbert, 166–67, 168, 169, 191, 194; Academy Awards and, 226; defining distributor's gross, 182; DGA agreement, 191, 192, 195, 196

CBS.com, 2

CBS Corporation, xii, 15, 130; consolidations and mergers, 18, 58; Grammy Awards, 219; memo to employees, 133; as picketing site, 33, 60, 146; poststrike, 236, 241–42; programming and scheduling, 73, 151–52, 236–37; stock price of, 219–20. *See also specific show*

CBS Radford, 146

Celebrity Apprentice, 152

Century City, xi, xii

Chair Incident, 63–65, 82

Chase, David, 69–70

Chernin, Peter, xiv, 42, 113–14, 116–17, 149, 242; on consumer/viewer behavior, 244, 246–47; on impact of technology, 246–47; leadership role and style, 27, 115, 131, 136, 190, 191, 217, 220; meeting at home of, 207–10

Cherry, Marc, 69–70, 85, 98, 121–22; Chair Incident, 64–65; organizes "Picketing with the Stars," 128–29; *Top Model* walkout, 69

Chetwynd, Lionel, 101

Clooney, George, 264

Coca-Cola Company, xvii

Colbert, Stephen, 37, 176, 178, 207

Colbert Report, The, 37, 176, 178, 180, 189

Colick, Lewis, 35

Colton, Michael, 109

Columbia Pictures, xvii

Comcast Corporation, 257, 258

Comedy Central, 180

Commander in Chief, 14

commercials. *See* advertising and marketing

compensation. *See* income (writers); residual payment system

Condon, Bill, 69, 85, 160, 162

Connelly, John, 59

consolidation and mergers, xviii, 18–20, 27, 149–50, 249, 269n8; FCC ownership policy, 41, 110; "self-dealing," 19, 269n13

consumer behavior, 1, 168; cable television and, 252; effects of recession on, 233; effects on music industry, 11; poststrike, 233, 235, 244, 247, 250, 256, 257–58; reports and studies, 6–7. *See also* viewership

contract captains, 46, 75

contracts: force-majeure provisions, 198–201, 214; interim agreements, 177, 187; master, 2, 5–6, 119, 123, 260–63, 275n9 (ch. 6); Minimum Basic Agreement (MBA), 6, 52–53, 112, 206; in 1980s and 90s, 17–20; overall deals, xxii, 90, 199, 200, 223; "separated rights," 51–52. *See also* fees and licensing

Cops, 102

copyright and piracy, 1–2, 4, 11–12, 257

Counter, J. Nicholas (Nick), xiv, 22, 33, 217; AMPTP's recoupment proposal, 65–72, 80–81, 83, 118, 120–21; Chair Incident, 64–65; leadership style, 155; on NLRB's webisodes ruling, 55; structural proposals for negotiations, 65–72; study proposal, 63, 65–72, 120

Creative Artists Agency (CCA), xi, xiv, 122–25, 128, 137, 139

Critic, The, 42

Crossing Jordan, 51

Cryer, Jon, 129

CSI, 92, 105, 116, 130, 237

CSI: Crime Scene Investigation, 185

CSI: Miami, 237

Cuse, Carlton, 55, 85, 98, 103, 121–22

CW Network, 58–59, 60, 80

Daily Show with Jon Stewart, The, 37, 176, 178, 180, 189

Daily Variety, 43, 74, 92, 226, 264

Daly, Carson, 37, 153–54

Daniels, Greg, 35, 51–52, 53, 54, 89–90, 93, 125

Darnell, Mike, 73

Dauman, Philippe, 218

David, Marjorie, 46

Davis, Elias, 261, 271n19

DeadlineHollywoodDaily.com, 148

Deitchman, Ian, 93

de la Rocha, Zack, xvi

Dempsey, Patrick, 35

De Niro, Robert, 264

derivative programming, 141–42, 193–94

Desperate Housewives, 6, 9, 10–11, 14, 92, 105, 128, 237

Devon, Dayna, 203

Dexter, 152

Dick Clark Productions (DCP), 201–4

digital technology, xii, xviii, 1–7, 27, 28–29; copyright and, 1–2, 4, 11–12, 257; effects on income, 232; jurisdiction of, 190–94, 217; as organizing tactic, 94–95, 147–49. *See also* new media; *specific technology*

Directors Guild of America (DGA), xix, 28–30, 165–89, 190–96, 210–18; formation of, 30–31; late-night television, 176–81; leadership of, 166–67, 213; leverage with studios, 168–69; master contracts, 5; participation of members in WGA strike, 79; poststrike, 261–62; producer's gross and, 101, 182; reports and studies, 167–68, 232; response to SAG memo, 220; strategy of, 231–32; strength of, 28–30, 120; Touchstone Television and, 54–55. *See also specific member or leader*

DirecTV, 257

"Dirty 30," 214–16

Disney Company. *See* Walt Disney Company

distribution platforms, 1, 6–7, 15, 256–57. *See also specific platform*

distributors' gross, 163, 171, 182–83, 191, 208–9, 217, 222

Dougherty, Joseph, 145

downloads: copyright and, 10; as form of home video, 10, 13–14, 66–67, 162, 167; markets share and, 62, 168, 245, 246; profits generated by, 2–3, 17, 116, 168, 209; residuals for, 66–67, 80–81, 83, 111, 133, 141, 157, 162–63, 181, 190–92, 210

DreamWorks Animation, 115

Dr. Horrible's Sing-Along Blog, 259

Duchovny, David, 269n13

DVDs, 2, 26, 168, 214, 232; "80/20" formula and, 13; Netflix, 253, 256, 257, 259, 260; residuals for, 80, 83, 189, 192; sales of, 12, 17, 68, 239, 246

DVRs, 1–2, 7, 8–10, 168

economy: entertainment industry and, 99, 243, 245; global recession, 233–34, 235, 257, 260; media industry and, xviii, 18, 233, 235, 246–47, 254–55, 257, 260; strike impact on Los Angeles, 185–87

"80/20" formula, 13

Eisner, Michael, 12

electronic sell-through (EST), 210–11, 214. *See also* downloads

Emanuel, Ari, 207

Embassy Communications, xvii

Endeavor, 122, 123, 207

entertainment industry, xii, 1, 3–4, 15, 27, 45; economics of, 99, 243, 245; future of, 157, 243, 256–57; poststrike, 259; unions and, 96–97

Entourage, 153

Ephron, Nora, 189

ER, 16, 92, 105

Espensen, Jane, 146

Fabiani, Mark, 150, 156, 160, 170

Facebook, 256

fall TV, startups and, 37–39

Family Guy, 92

Fans4Writers, 147

Farriday, Ann, 173

feature films, 5, 67–68, 79–80, 192, 231, 238, 239, 261

Federal Communications Commission (FCC), 18, 41, 110, 258

Federal Mediation and Conciliation Service, 82

fees and licensing, 8, 19; carriage, 258; international, 3; poststrike, 234; profits and, 28–29, 168; repeats and, 15–16; scripted shows, 151; Walt Disney and iTunes, 6, 10–14

Ferguson, Craig, 37, 177–78, 187, 188

Ferrera, America, 36

Field, Sally, 129

Fillion, Nathan, 259

film and television studios, 113–36, 198–201; antitrust investigations, 114, 115; consolidation and mergers, xviii, 18–20, 19, 27, 149–50, 249, 269n8; contingency strike plans, 37–38, 72, 74, 76–77; internal documents disclosure obligation, 195; labor negotiations in earlier generations, 114–15; post-strike, 232–36; production budgets, 16, 194, 234, 235, 236, 246; relationship between top four CEOs, 113–14;

TV-film divide, 99–100, 101. *See also* broadcast and network television; *specific studio, person, or show*

FilmLA, 186

financial core membership, 102, 262–63

Finke, Nikki, 93

fin-syn (financial interest and syndication rule), 18–20

Fios, 257

Fischer, Sam, 125–27, 174–76, 197

Flockhart, Calista, 129

Fontana, Tom, 73–74

force-majeure provisions, 198–201, 214

Ford, John, 30

Fox Broadcasting Company, 42

Fox Entertainment Group, xiv, 18, 114. *See also specific subsidiary*

Fox TV, 9, 18, 102, 135, 152

Frank, Scott, 271n19

Frank TV, 98, 243

FremantleMedia North America, 156, 158–61, 162, 171

Friedman, Josh, 107–8, 146

Fury, David, 34, 35

FX channel, 98

Gaghan, Stephen, 85, 99

game shows, 56, 73

Ganis, Sid, 226

Garcetti, Eric, 186

Garrett, Brad, 129

Gass, Kyle, 158, 161

gay and lesbian writers, 130

"Gay Gate," 130

Geffen, David, 115

General Electric, 18

George, Terry, 85, 99, 228

Gertz, Jami, 174, 175

Gionfriddo, Gina, 189

Goldberg, Marshall, 49

Golden Globe Awards, 184, 201–4, 226

Goldsman, Akiva, 99, 132–33, 212

Gonzalez, Juan Carlos, 82

Goodman, David A., 98

Google, 116

Gorham, Keith, 53, 162

Gossip Girl, 105

Gould, Howard Michael, 85–86, 215

Gould, William B., 47

Graboff, Marc, 55

Grammy Awards, 219

Grant, Susannah, 85, 99

Grazer, Brian, 73

Green, Seth, 129

Grey's Anatomy, 35, 92, 151, 237

Griffith, Rachel, 129

guilds: poststrike, 260–61; role and
    strength of, 29–30. *See also specific guild*

Gurian, Naomi, 101

Haggis, Paul, 99, 161

Hanks, Tom, 264

Harris, Neil Patrick, 129, 259

Hart, Mary, 203

Hawks, Howard, 30

HBO, 81, 153

health and medical benefits, xx–xxi, 52,
    69, 110–11; earnings and, 277n4; effects
    of recession on, 260–61; guilds as pro-
    viders of, 29; production staffers and,
    56; reality producers and, 171; WGA
    financial core membership status and,
    102, 262–63; Writers Guild-Industry
    Health Fund, 75–76, 86, 101

Heigl, Katherine, 35, 36

Helgenberger, Marg, 129, 185

Hermanson, Jeff, 103–4, 173

Heroes, 9, 51, 53, 105

Herskovitz, Marshall, 152

Hickenlooper, George, 148

Hiestand, Jesse, 150

Holland, Charles, 46, 47, 49

"Hollywood 10," 30–31

"Hollywood accounting," 70, 195

Hollywood Boulevard march, 132–34

Hollywood Foreign Press Association
    (HFPA), 184, 201–4

"Hollywood Homecoming" rally, 144–45

Hollywood Reporter, 74, 92, 149

Hollywood Teamsters (Local 399), 33, 35,
    96, 97, 132, 186

Hollywood Writers Report for 2009 (Hunt),
    239–40

home video, xviii, 3; AMPTP's recoup-
    ment proposal, 65–72, 80–81, 83;
    AMPTP's study proposal, 63, 65–72,
    120; downloads as form of, 10, 13–14,
    66, 210–11; poststrike sales of, 239, 245;
    residuals for, 24–27, 31, 100–101, 141,
    162–64, 190, 192

House, 92, 105

House Un-American Activities Commit-
    tee, 31

Howard, Ken, 264

Huffman, Felicity, 129, 148

Hughes, Eric, 47

Hulu, 246, 257, 258; effects on network
    reruns, 244, 251; formation of, 6, 131,
    251, 256; iTunes and, 251; profits, 253;
    subscription TV's response to, 252–53

Hunt, Darnell, 239–40

hyphenates. *See* showrunners

I Find Your Lack of Faith Disturbing (blog),
    146

Iger, Robert, 12, 27, 113–14, 208, 242; leadership role and style, 27, 131, 169, 190, 191, 217, 220

income (writers), 27, 186; differences among WGA members, 102, 170; "economic justification," 140–41; "80/20" formula, 13; loss of during strikes, 96–97, 214, 231; New Economic Partnership (AMPTP) and, 140–44, 155–58; poststrike, 233–34, 237–40; promotional activities and, 14–15, 116–17, 192–93, 222; reports and studies, 167–68, 232; royalties, 5–6, 29, 246, 261; for showrunners, 90. *See also* contracts; health and medical benefits; pensions; residual payment system

interim agreements, 177, 187

Intermix Media, 116

International Alliance of Theatrical Stage Employees (IATSE), 29, 61, 79, 96–97, 171, 186, 203–4

International Creative Management (ICM), 122, 123

Internet, xx, 3–4, 28, 109–10; as democratizing force, 259; as distribution mechanism, 147–49, 193–94; made-for-Internet productions, 141–42, 192, 193–94, 218, 219; as promotional tool, 14–15, 116–17; as strike organizing tool, 94–95, 147–49

iPad, 252

iPod, 6, 7, 10, 12, 252

Isaacs, Harry, 25, 219

iTunes, 1, 15, 46, 243, 246; agreement with Walt Disney Company, 6, 10–15, 54–55; *Dr. Horrible's Sing-Along Blog*, 259; Hulu vs., 251; licensing initiatives with, 131; *Missing Pieces*, 54–55; *The Office* and, 89; profits, 116

Jackoway, Jim, 188

Jackson, Jesse, xv, xvi–xvii

JaneEspensen.com, 146

Jay Leno Show, The, 236

Jean, Al, 42

Jimmy Kimmel Live, 37, 154, 176, 178

Jobs, Steve, 10, 11–12, 14

JohnAugust.com, 146

Johnson, Anne-Marie, 264

Kaling, Mindy, 93

Kalogridis, Laeta, 93, 110–11

Katsir, Jay, 189

Katzenberg, Jeffrey, 115, 125

Kazan, Nick, 271n19

Keitel, Harvey, 148

Kennedy, Robert F., 114

Kessinger, Rebecca, 173

Kessler, Jason, 51–53

Keyes, Alicia, 132

Keyser, Christopher, 265

"Kids Day," 129–30

Kimmel, Jimmy, 37, 154, 176, 178, 207

King, Robert, 215, 271n19

Korduner, David, 182–83

Krafft, Laura, 189

Kring, Tim, 53, 54

Kudrow, Lisa, 129

Kung Fu Monkey (blog), 146

Kurtzman, Howard, 182–83

Kyser, Jack, 186

Laborers' California Organizing Fund, 44

labor movement, 27, 29, 94

Lachmund, Hank, 162

Last Call with Carson Daly, 37, 153–54

Late Late Show with Craig Ferguson, The, 37, 177–78, 187

late-night television, 37, 153–54, 176–81. *See also specific show or host*

Late Night with Conan O'Brien, 37, 153–54, 176–81, 189

Late Show with David Letterman, The, 37, 147, 154, 176–81, 187–89, 202, 204–5

LateShowWritersOnStrike.com, 147, 148

Latt, David, 93

Laurie, Hugh, 129

Law and Order, 189

Law and Order: Criminal Intent, 189

Law and Order: SVU, 92, 105, 151

laws and legislation: antitrust investigations, 114, 115; FCC policies, 18, 41, 110; fin-syn ruling, 18; media ownership, 41, 110; NBC webisodes, 49–50, 53–54, 55; NLRB rulings, 49–50, 53–54, 55, 58–59, 102; right to change guild membership status, 102; showrunner strike participation, 95–96

Lawson, John Howard, 30

lawsuits, "self-dealing," 19, 269n13

Lear, Norman, xv, xvii–xviii

Lefcourt, Peter, 271n19

Lehane, Chris, 150, 156, 160, 170

Leight, Warren, 189

Leno, Jay, 154, 176–81, 184, 188, 201; covers staff salaries, 153; disciplinary action against, 204–7, 227, 263–64; *The Jay Leno Show*, 236; picketing against, 205, 207

Letterman, David, 154, 176–81, 185, 187–89, 202, 204–5, 263

Levine, Ken, 146

Levinson, Barry, 73–74

Levitan, Steve, 106–8, 125–27, 174–76, 240, 254–55; leadership role and style, 88, 91, 97, 99, 103; participation of in

protesting, 105, 132; "Pencils Down" ad, 92; poststrike work, 254–55

licensing. *See* fees and licensing

Lieberstein, Paul, 93

Lindelof, Damon, 55

Linney, Laura, 148

"Live Plus Same Day," 9

"Live Plus Seven Day," 9

Lloyd, Christopher, 91

Lombardini, Carole, 26, 113, 162–64; Chair Incident, 64–65; on future of television, 4–5; on home video formula, 13, 83; Leno and, 227, 263–64; on WGA picketing, 104

Lorimar Television, 113

Los Angeles City Council, 185–87

Los Angeles County Economic Development Corporation, 186

Los Angeles Police Department (LAPD), xii, 132

Los Angeles Times, 149

Lost, 6, 9, 14, 54–55, 92, 105, 116

Louise-Dreyfus, Julia, 132

Lourd, Bryan, 123–28, 136, 137–40, 142–43, 154–55, 156–58, 164; leadership role and style, 123, 124, 134, 137, 138, 139, 144; meeting at home of, 127–28, 130, 131–32

Lowe, Rob, 129

Lynton, Michael, 135, 174, 218

MacFarlane, Seth, xv

Macy, William H., 148

made-for-Internet productions, 141–42, 192, 193–94, 218, 219

made-for-TV movies, 25

Mad Men, 97

Mangan, Mona, 24, 26

Marion, Frances, 30

marketing. *See* advertising and marketing

market share and ratings, 2–3; decline in prime time, 102, 153; effects of DVRs on, 9–10; late-night television, 153–54, 176; poststrike, 236–37; for repeats, 16. *See also* viewership

MASH, 269n13

master contract agreements, 2, 5–6, 119, 123, 260–63, 275n9 (ch. 6)

Mazin, Craig, 146, 216

MCA/Universal, 114

McLean, John, 23, 43–44, 49

Medeiros, Joe, 97

media industry, xii, 27, 256–57; economics of, xviii, 18, 233, 235, 246–47, 254–55, 257, 260; FCC ownership policy, 41, 110. *See also* broadcast and network television; consolidation and mergers; film and television studios

mediation. *See* arbitration and mediation

medical benefits. *See* health and medical benefits

Mendelsohn, Carol, 71–72, 85, 98, 121–22, 160, 162

mergers. *See* consolidation and mergers

Meyer, Barry, 5, 113–14, 135, 207–10, 241; on AMPTP's recoupment proposal, 68, 120–21; leadership role and style, 27, 68, 131, 169; memo to Warner Bros. employees, 133; on new business models, 118; on programming and scheduling, 244, 245

Meyerson, Gregory Z., 54

Meyerson, Joan, 271n19

MGM, 113

Minimum Basic Agreement (MBA), 6, 52–53, 112, 206

Missing Pieces, 54–55

Modern Humorist, 109

Mok, Ken, 58–59, 61

Monk, 152

Moonves, Leslie, 113–14, 149, 207–10, 218, 242; on AMPTP's recoupment proposal, 68, 120–21; leadership role and style, 27, 68, 115, 130, 135, 169, 219–20; memo to CBS employees, 133

Moore, Michael, 228

Moore, Ron, 146

Morello, Tom, xv–xvi

Moret, Jim, 203

Morgan, Ralph, 30

Motion Picture Association of America (MPAA), 186

movies, made for TV, 25

MTV Networks, 18

Murdoch, Rupert, 18, 42, 114, 149

music industry, 11, 219

My Dad Is Better than Your Dad, 152

MyNetworkTV, 80

MySpace, 116–17

Napster, 11

National Association of Television Program Executives (NATPE), 235

National Labor Relations Board (NLRB), 49–50, 53–54, 55, 58–59, 102, 193

NBC.com, 89

NBC Universal, xii, 18, 113, 135, 225, 241; authentication, 258; Golden Globe Awards, 184, 201–4, 226; Hulu and, 6; as picketing site, 159, 214, 225; poststrike business practices, 235–36; prime time programming, 73, 152–53; webisode production, 49–50, 51–55, 89. *See also specific show*

Nelson, Michael Alan, 146

Netflix, 253, 256, 257, 259, 260

network television. *See* broadcast and network television

New Economic Partnership (AMPTP), 140–44, 155–58

new media, 1–21, 249–50; film-TV divide and, 99–100; growth of, xii, 256–57, 259; new media paradigm of, 1–3, 253–54; reports and studies, 29, 63, 65–72, 120, 128, 167–68, 232; sharing of internal documents about, 195; uncertainty of predicting new markets for, 251–52. *See also* digital technology; *specific media*

News Corporation, xii, xiv, 114, 130, 236, 241; Hulu and, 6; MySpace and, 116–17. *See also specific subsidiary*

New York Times, 149

Nielsen Media Research, 9, 102

Niemöller, Martin, xxii

Novak, B. J., 93

Noxon, Marti, 97

NYPD Blue, 269n13

O'Brien, Conan, 153–54, 176–81, 183–84, 207

Office, The, 9, 35, 51–52, 89, 105, 116; "Pencils Down" campaign, 92; "Picketing with the Stars," 129; poststrike, 237

Office is Closed, The, 35, 93–94

off-network series, 17, 234

Oh, Sandra, 35, 36, 132, 133

on-demand programming: AMPTP's study proposal, 63, 65–72, 120; DVRs and, 1–2, 7, 8–10, 168; effects on repeats and syndication, 15–17; profits and, 17, 168; as promotional activity, 14–15, 116–17, 222. *See also* downloads; Web streaming

1 vs. 100, 152

overall deals, xxii, 90, 199, 200, 223

"over-the-top" outlets, 257

Ovitz, Michael, 123

Paramount Pictures, 18, 33, 35, 57, 115, 130, 185

pay TV, 80–81

Pedowitz, Mark, 182–83

"Pencils Down" campaign, 92, 95, 97, 105, 108

Penn, Sean, 148

pensions, xx–xxi, 29, 52, 86, 101, 110–11; earnings and, 277n4; effects of recession on, 260–61; financial core membership status and, 102; production staffers and, 56; reality producers and, 171

Perry, Matthew, 129

Petrie, Daniel, Jr., 47, 56

Pew Internet and American Life Project, 7

Pew Research Center for People and the Press, 110

Philanthropist, The, 73

picketing, 60, 227; at AMPTP headquarters, 185; at CBS Corporation, 33, 60, 146; Leno and, 205, 207; Lombardini on, 104; at NBC Universal, 159, 214, 225; at Paramount Pictures, 185; "Picketing with the Stars," 128–29; showrunners and, 3, 34–35, 79, 89–90; at Sony Pictures Entertainment, 33, 144–45, 146, 225; at 20th Century Fox, 33, 34, 105, 130, 146, 185, 224, 225, 229; at Universal Pictures, 185; at Walt Disney Company, 33, 105–6, 159, 185, 225, 226–27; at Warner Bros., 33, 130, 140, 159, 225

"Picketing with the Stars," 128–30

pilot television shows, 38, 73, 151–53, 235–36

piracy and copyright, 1–2, 4, 11–12, 257

Pixar Animation Studios, 10

Pompeo, Ellen, 35, 36

Prestwich, Dawn, 91, 97

prime-time television, 69; decline in market share, 102; development, 37–39; poststrike, 233, 234; programming and scheduling, 151–53

Prince, Jonathan, 215

Private Practice, 35, 97

producer's gross, 13, 67, 100–101, 182, 209; New Economic Partnership (AMPTP) and, 141

product placement, 8, 17

profits (studios), 2–4; distributor's gross, 163, 171, 182–83, 191, 208–9, 217, 222; downloads and, 2–3, 12, 17; "80/20" formula, 13; foreign sales, 17; "Hollywood accounting," 70, 195; poststrike, 232–36; producer's gross, 13, 67, 100–101, 141, 182, 209; promotional activities and, 14–15, 116–17, 192–93, 222; reports and studies, 167–68; scripted vs. unscripted shows, 16–17, 20–21; syndication and, 117, 199, 238, 243, 245, 257. *See also* fees and licensing; residual payment system

programming and scheduling, 37–39, 151–53; cable television, 153; derivative, 141–42, 193–94; poststrike, 235. *See also* late-night television; on-demand programming; prime-time television

protest-march symbolism, xiv, xvi–xvii, xxiii

protests and rallies: "Ben Silverman High Winter Prom," 204, 210; Fremantle-Media North America rally, 156, 158–61, 162, 171; Hollywood Boulevard march, 132–34; "Hollywood Homecoming" rally, 144–45; "Kids Day," 129–30; "Scene of the Crime"

rally, 185; *Top Model* walkout, 58–62, 65, 69; unity rally, 60–61. *See also* picketing; *specific strikes*

Psych, 152

Purdy, Kate, 93

Quarterlife, 152–53

quiz shows, 56

Rage Against the Machine, xv–xvi

Raleigh Studios, 36

rallies. *See* protests and rallies

Rancic, Guiliana, 203

ratings. *See* market share and ratings

Ray, Billy, 261

reality TV, xx, 151–52; boom in, 56–57; flexibility of, 73; as low cost programming, 246; New Economic Partnership (AMPTP) and, 142, 156; organizing of, 44, 45, 48, 50–51, 56–62, 159–61, 163, 170–75, 177, 198, 217; poststrike, 20–21, 261; reserves of shows, 36. *See also specific show*

recession, 233–34, 235, 257, 260

recoupment proposal (AMPTP), 65–72, 80–81, 83, 118, 120–22, 156

Reed, Leo, 33, 133–34

Reiss, Mike, 42

repeats and reruns, 3, 15–17, 69, 117–18, 238–39, 260, 274n2

reports and studies: AMPTP's study proposal, 63, 65–72, 120; consumer behavior, 6–7; DGA new media, 167–68, 232; *Hollywood Writers Report for 2009* (Hunt), 239–40; necessity of strike, 145; new media, 29, 63, 65–72, 66, 120, 128, 167–68, 232

residual payment system, 40, 128, 162–64;
AMPTP's recoupment proposal,
65–72, 80–81, 83, 118, 120–22, 156; as
bonus income, 69; cable television and,
69, 80–81, 238–39, 274n2; categories of,
4–6, 66–67, 190–96; importance of, 5,
39, 68–70; poststrike, 238–39; repeats
and reruns, 15–16, 69, 117–18, 238–39,
274n2. *See also* profits (studios); *specific
format or media*
retransmission-consent rights, 258
revenues. *See* profits (studios)
Revue, 114
Rhimes, Shonda, 35, 132
Rhoden, Cheryl, 49
Ridley, John, 262
Rintels, David, 47
Riskin, Robert, 30, 47
Riskin, Victoria, 46–48, 49
Rivers, Joan, 42
Robbins, Tim, 148
Roberts, Brian, 258
Roberts, Vince, 10–11
Robinson, Phil Alden, 60, 271n19
Rodman, Howard, 271n19
Rogers, John, 146
Romano, Ray, 129
Rosen, Rick, 123
Rosenberg, Alan, xviii, 59, 85, 119, 138,
220, 264
Rosenthal, Phil, xv
Ross, Gary, 212
Roth, Jay, 120, 167, 168, 169, 182, 191, 194;
leadership role and style, 166
royalties, 5–6, 29, 246, 261
Rubel, Michael, 137
Ryan, Shawn, 73, 85, 98

Salmons, Melissa, 189

Sarandon, Susan, 148
satellite television, 1, 117, 257, 258
Saturday Night Live, 37, 132
"Scene of the Crime" rally, 185
scheduling. *See* programming and
scheduling
Schiff, Robin, 98
Schmidt, Steve, 150, 156
Schulman, Tom, 271n19
Schur, Michael, 93, 111
Screen Actors Guild (SAG), xviii, xix;
advertising industry protests, 65;
ATA agreement with, 274n7; contract
with AMPTP, 119; formation of, 30–31;
Golden Globe Awards support, 202,
203; leadership of, 264–65; master contracts, 5, 119, 275n9 (ch. 6); memo on
DGA deal, 220; producer's gross and,
101; residuals and, 36, 67; strength
of, 28–30, 29–30, 270n7; support for
WGA, 37, 85, 185; *Top Model* walkout,
59; Touchstone Television and, 54–55;
Wasserman and, 114. *See also specific
member or leader*
screenwriters, 24, 29, 46, 70, 74, 79–80, 85;
TV writers vs., 99
scripted shows: banking of, 37, 80; on
cable television, 238; costs of, 151, 235,
236, 244, 246; fin-syn and, 19; new
production of, 38; niche outlets vs.,
246; poststrike, 236, 242, 244, 246; as
"trade secrets," 79; unions and, 29;
unscripted shows vs., 16–17, 20–21,
72–74, 151–52
Scully, Mike, 34, 84, 104, 229
Segall, Tony, 20
Seinfeld, 129
"self-dealing," 19, 269n13
Selman, Matt, 229
"separated rights," 51–52

sequels, 51–52

Sereboff, Alan, 148

Service Employees International Union (SEIU), 75

Sheen, Martin, 148

Shield, The, 73, 98, 105

Short, Thomas, 61, 79, 171

showrunners, 88–112; banking of scripts, 80; bartering uncompleted episodes, 108; compensation, 90; deadlines and, 99; defined, 24, 78, 95; duties, 39, 95, 96; entertainment industry unions and, 96–97; in modern era, 31; "Pencils Down" campaign, 92, 95, 97, 105, 108; on picket line, 3, 34–35, 79, 89–90; post-strike, 234; Smoke House restaurant meeting, 106–7, 108; Supreme Court decision on strike participation, 95–96; webisodes and, 49–50, 52–55, 72; WGA unity rally, 60. *See also* United Showrunners

Showrunners Training Program, 138

Showtime, 81, 152

Silbermann, Chris, 123

Silverman, Ben, 204, 210

Silverman, Sarah, 129

Simpsons, The, 17; profitability of, 42, 70, 121

Sinese, Gary, 146

Singer, Sarah, 91–92, 96–97, 173

Sloan, Harry, 218

Slocum, Chuck, 221–22

Smoke House, 106–7, 108

social media, as promotional tool, 256

Solomon, Aaron, 161

Solomon, Ed, 160, 162

Sony Corporation, xii, 135

Sony Pictures Entertainment, 2, 113, 233, 241; as picketing site, 33, 144–45, 146, 225

Sopranos, The, 17

Sorkin, Aaron, 111, 212

Speechless, 148

Spencer, Lara, 203

Spielberg, Steven, 115

spin-offs, 51–52

Star Trek, 130

start-ups, 38

Stewart, Jon, 37, 176, 178, 180, 207

Stiller, Ben, 129

St. John, Thania, 91, 97

Streep, Meryl, 264

strike (1973), 96; (1981), 31; (1985), 13

strike (1988), xii, xix, 31, 39, 74, 96–97; outcome, 100–102, 176; Union Blues and, 173

strike (2007): captains, 75, 92–93, 104, 173–74, 227; economic impact, 185–87; first day of bargaining, 70–72; leadership of, 27–28, 32; legacy of, 20–21, 27, 231–36; logistics, 75, 104; media coverage, xxi, 27, 68, 71, 74, 86–87, 92, 93–95, 129, 139; protest-march symbolism, xiv, xvi–xvii, xxiii; rules for, 78–80, 95–96, 263–64; timing of, 76–77; *Variety* subscriber poll on necessity of, 145; vote to authorize, 78–79, 80, 81–87, 103; vote to end, 229–30. *See also* picketing

studies. *See* reports and studies

studios. *See* film and television studios; *specific studio*

study proposal (AMPTP), 63, 65–72, 120

Sunday Morning Shootout, 62

surveys. *See* market share and ratings; reports and studies

Survivor, 56

Sweeney, Anne, 10–13, 68

syndication, 3, 4, 12, 234; alternatives to, 260; effects of on-demand access on,

syndication (*cont.*)
15–17; financial interest and syndication rule (fin-syn), 18; poststrike, 238; profits and, 117, 199, 238, 243, 245, 257

Tabb, Michael, 227
talent agencies, 108–9, 122–25, 127–28, 207–8
talk shows, 37, 153–54, 176–81, 185, 187–89. *See also specific show*
TBS, 98
Teamsters Local 399 (Hollywood), 33, 35, 96, 97, 132, 186
technology. *See* digital technology
telco providers, 256, 257
Telecommunications Act (1996), 18
television studios. *See* film and television studios; *specific studio*
Tenacious D, 158, 159, 161
Terminator: The Sarah Connor Chronicles, 107
Thomas, Betsy, 186
Time Warner, xii, 130, 227, 233, 258. *See also specific subsidiary*
TiVo, 7, 8
Tonight Show with Jay Leno, 37, 97, 105, 153–54, 176–81, 202, 204–7, 227, 263–64
Touchstone Television, 54–55
Towne, Robert, 134
True Blood, 153
20th Century Fox, xi, xii–xiv, 18, 42; as picketing site, 33, 34, 105, 130, 146, 185, 224, 225, 229; "self-dealing" lawsuits, 269n13
Twitter, 256
Two and a Half Men, 92, 105, 130, 151, 237

Ugly Betty, 36, 130
Union Blues, 101, 173, 216

United Hollywood (blog), 93–95, 109–11, 146, 148, 204, 209–10
United Showrunners, 103, 125–26, 132; formation of, 90; "Pencils Down" campaign, 92, 95, 97, 105, 108; Smoke House restaurant meeting, 106–7, 108; strategy of, 100
United Talent Agency, 122, 123
Universal Studios, 18, 114, 128–29
unscripted shows: bias against, 57, 159; boom in, 56–57; costs of, 151, 235, 244; jurisdiction over, 156; scripted shows vs., 16–17, 20–21, 72–74, 151–52; stocking up on, 72–73, 151. *See also* reality TV
UPN, 58
USA Network, 152
U.S. Department of Labor, 47
U.S. Justice Department, 114
U.S. Supreme Court, 95–96

Variety, 145, 149, 264
variety shows, 56
Verizon Fios, 257
Verrone, Patric, xxi–xxiii, 54, 87, 109–10, 127; appointments and offices held, 20, 23, 31–32, 42–43, 48, 56, 57, 72, 261, 265; Chair Incident, 64–65; credibility with younger writers, 111–12; leadership role and style, xii–xiii, xvi, xxii, 27, 40–43, 45–46, 49, 60–61, 99, 111–12, 119, 127, 170–71, 185, 248–49; Leno and, 204–7, 227, 263; participation of in protesting, 65, 160–61; poststrike, 261, 262–64, 265; "the Writers Guild doctrine for the 21st century," 60–61. *See also* Writers United
Viacom, xii, 18, 113, 180, 227, 233, 241
video cassette recorders, 8

Vidor, King, 30

View, The, 189

viewership: DVRs and, 9, 168; poststrike, 102, 236–37, 247; younger, 1, 6–7. *See also* advertising and marketing; consumer behavior; market share and ratings

Vivendi, 18

Waid, Mark, 146

Walt Disney Company, xi–xii, 2, 3, 33, 114, 130, 241; agreement with Apple iTunes, 6, 10–14, 54–55; consolidations and mergers, 18, 269n8; Hulu and, 251; as picketing site, 33, 105–6, 159, 185, 225, 226–27; poststrike, 233, 236, 252. *See also specific subsidiary*

Warner Bros., 5, 57, 68, 113, 114, 135, 241; authentication, 258; memo to employees, 133; as picketing site, 33, 130, 140, 159, 225; UPN/WB Network merger, 58

Wasserman, Lew, 114

WB Network, 58

Web streaming, 1–3, 25, 190–96; advertising and, 6, 11, 14–15; AMPTP's study proposal, 63, 65–72, 120; authentication for, 258; Hulu, 6; income and profits from, 17, 162–64, 221–22; NBC and, 49–50, 51–55; New Economic Partnership (AMPTP) and, 141–44, 155–58; piracy and, 10–11; as promotional activity, 14–15, 116–17, 192–93, 222

Weeds, 105

Weiner, Matthew, 97

Weiss, David, 161, 271n19

Wells, John, 48, 209, 212–14, 261

Wertheimer, Alan, 188, 190, 191, 198, 207, 217, 218, 223

WGA East, 22, 47, 101, 225, 227–28, 229; joint policy statement of, 15; late-night television, 180; leadership of, 24, 76–77, 98–99; picketing, 227; relationship with WGA West, 24; release of names, 262–63; strike authorization voting process, 78; votes to end strike, 229–30; votes to strike, 25, 26, 81, 86–87, 103; Winship's letter to members, 172. *See also specific member or leader*

WGA West, xii–xiii, 43, 47–48, 49, 225–26; *America's Next Top Model* and, 50–51, 57–62; annual earnings of members, 231–32, 237–40; Chair Incident, 63–65, 82; home video formula, 100–101; internal battles, 46–48, 100, 101; joint policy statement of, 15; leadership of, xiii, xviii, 23–24, 42–45, 49, 65, 173, 197–98, 261, 265; Leno trial committee report, 263–64; philanthropic arm of, 94, 210; relationship with WGA East, 24; release of names, 262–63; reports and studies, 239; strike authorization voting process, 78; Union Blues faction, 101, 173, 216; votes to end strike, 229–30; votes to strike, 25, 26, 86; work waivers, 184. *See also* Writers United; *specific member or leader*

Whedon, Joss, 111, 224, 259

White, Byron, 95

Who Wants to be a Millionaire, 56

Wiatt, Jim, 123

Wilcox, Dan, 271n19

William Morris Agency, xiv, 122, 123

Williams, Maiya, 40, 41

Wilmore, Larry, 72

Wind Dancer Productions, 269n13

Winship, Michael, 24, 26, 76–77, 147, 172, 227–28

Wolf, Dick, 62, 240

Wolfson, Roger, 48–49

Woodard, Alfre, 161

work waivers, 184

Worldwide Pants, 177–81, 187–89, 202, 204–5, 263

Worst Week, 73

Wray, Fay, 47

writers: prospects in 1980s and 90s, 17–20; reinstatement of terminated, 223; sense of community among, xiii, 112; TV vs. film, 99; younger generation, xv, 31, 35, 69–70, 74, 89, 107, 110–12, 239

Writers Coalition, 101–2

Writers Guild Foundation, 94, 210

Writers Guild-Industry Health Fund, 75–76, 86, 101

Writers Guild of America (WGA), xii–xxiii, 231–32; budget, 43, 48; contract captains, 46, 75; film-TV divide among members, 99–100; financial core membership, 102, 262–63; formation of, 30–32; negotiating committee, 98–99, 121–22, 215, 220, 223, 228; strategy of, 42–43, 94, 176–77, 180, 197, 204; strength of, 29–30; strike (1973), 96; strike (1981), 31; strike (1985), 13, 31, 173; strike authorization voting process, 78; Strike Rules Compliance Committee, 263–64; twenty-six-point proposal, 24–27, 66–72, 83; Writers

Coalition faction, 101–2. *See also* health and medical benefits; pensions; strike (1988); strike (2007); WGA East; WGA West; *specific member or leader*

Writers United, 31, 45–46, 57, 60, 212–13, 261; formation of, 43, 48–49, 271n19

Xbox, 257

X-Files, The, 269n13

Yorkin, Nicole, 91, 97

Young, David, 44, 62; background of, xviii–xxii, 23, 44, 57–58, 155; Chair Incident, 64–65; "the Golden Globes scam," 203; leadership role and style, xiii, 23, 31–32, 44, 46, 49, 55, 62, 99, 103, 111–12, 122, 127, 228, 247–49; Leno and, 204–7, 264; letter to Wall Street analysts regarding CBS stock, 219–20; poststrike, 262

Young and the Restless, The, 105

YouTube.com, 46, 93–94, 116, 148, 193–94

Ziffren, Ken, 125, 168, 182–83, 196, 206, 212

Zucker, Jeff, 135, 180, 202, 218, 235–36

Zweibel, Alan, 189

Zwick, Ed, 152